Analyzing Syntax and Semantics

Analyzing Syntax and Semantics

A Self-Instructional Approach for Teachers and Clinicians

Virginia A. Heidinger

with technical assistance from Martin R. Noretsky

Gallaudet University Press
Washington, D.C.

Gallaudet University Press, Washington, DC 20002
© 1984 by Gallaudet University. All rights reserved
Published 1984. Second Printing, 1988. Third Printing, 1993
Printed in the United States of America

Library of Congress Cataloging in Publication Data

Heidinger, Virginia A. 1920-
    Analyzing syntax and semantics.

    Bibliography: p.
    Includes index.
    1. English language—Study and teaching (Higher)
2. English language—Grammer, Generative. 3. Deaf—
Education—English language. 4. Individualized instruction.
I. Title.
PE1066.H45 1984   428'.007'11   84-10296
ISBN 0-913580-91-0 (text)
ISBN 0-913580-94-5 (set)

CONTENTS

PREFACE

Human beings, regardless of race or culture, develop language in order to communicate with one another. Most children develop language by listening, watching, and interacting with the people in their environments. There are some children, though, who are incapable of acquiring language through the normal processes, either because of physical or psychological impairments. These children need special help in order to develop a language system.

Teachers and clinicians who work with language-delayed children must have a basic understanding of syntax (the structure of language) and semantics (the meaning of words in specific syntactical arrangements). This knowledge enables them to instruct their students effectively as well as evaluate and apply recent research findings, new language curriculums, and new procedures for analyzing language.

Analyzing Syntax and Semantics is a self-instructional, objective-based text. It can be used as an introductory course for prospective teachers and clinicians and as a refresher course for classroom teachers. The text, workbook, and accompanying unit tests have been evaluated over a period of three years with three groups of students (45–60 students per group) enrolled in graduate courses in a teacher-preparation program for teachers of the hearing impaired.

In a self-instructional approach, students may pace their accomplishment of the objectives, determine their readiness for testing, and complete the work with or without the help of proctors and the instructor. This approach has proven successful with all but a few of the students who have enrolled in the course. Although the text has been evaluated with graduate students, it should be appropriate for undergraduate students preparing for teaching or clinical work.

ACKNOWLEDGMENTS

I wish to extend my thanks to Martin Noretsky of the Gallaudet College Instructional Development and Evaluation Center for his tireless work in the development of the selected approach, for his help in editing the text and tests, for his direction of the evaluation process, and for his willingness to give of his own time to serve as a proctor during the evaluation period. I also wish to thank the graduate students at Gallaudet College who participated as proctors or students in the evaluation process and all that it entailed. Their comments and suggestions were invaluable.

INTRODUCTION

Language acquisition is a difficult task for children with hearing impairment and learning disorders. These children must be led through the language development process in as natural a way as possible. It is not possible to teach children all the sentences they will ever need to communicate and to acquire knowledge. Nor should they be taught the rules to generate sentences and to use words appropriately. It is the teacher's or clinician's responsibility to provide students with sufficient and, in some instances, controlled language input so that they can generalize the rules for themselves. Thus, the person responsible for developing language in children must have knowledge of normal language acquisition patterns as well as knowledge of the aspects (components) of the language in question.

The Aspects of Language

Most languages have phonological, grammatical (syntactic and morphological), and semantic aspects. The phonology of the language is its sound system. Children learn to recognize and produce the sounds of the language by listening to its spoken form. The syntax of a language is the set of rules for arranging words into sentences. Native speakers of a language internalize syntactic rules without giving them much thought. The internalization process is part of the natural language acquisition process. For example, the child whose native language is English learns

- the rules for arranging words in basic sentences;
- the rules for arranging words in parts of sentences, e.g., noun phrases and verb phrases;
- the rules for making changes in a single sentence to express the same idea in another way or to convey a different meaning;
- the rules for combining a number of simple sentences or for generating complex sentences that will make communication more efficient; and
- the rules for using particular structures across sentences.

The morphology of a language involves its rules for compounding words or applying inflections and derivational suffixes and prefixes to base words to form other words. Children internalize these rules as they are exposed to the language.

The semantics of the language refers to the meanings of words and how to use them appropriately. Children gradually learn the important features of words that govern how words can and cannot be used. The semantic features include the meanings of the stress and intonation patterns, the meanings of idiomatic and figurative expressions in the language, and, above all, the different relationships that can be expressed in sentences.

1

In most instances, native language speakers employ the rules of the language so as to use it in the generally accepted form. For the most part, we learn our native language through hearing it and needing it to communicate. No one taught us the rules of English, yet by the time we entered first grade, and even before that, we could generate the sentences that we needed to communicate our needs, wants, and ideas. We could ask questions, could command or give directions to others, and could make both positive and negative declarative statements. We were using the rules of the language even though we could not specify what they were.

The teacher or clinician must have a thorough understanding of the aspects of language to be able to assess a child's language status, devise a program of language development, and periodically evaluate the child's progress in language in order to prescribe a further program.

New Approaches to Language Development

The prospective teacher or clinician, although a native and proficient user of the language, often has not had courses in linguistics and may or may not have had grammar courses when in elementary and/or high school. Yet teachers and clinicians are expected to read and evaluate the current research and curriculums pertaining to language development. They must also have the skill to specify those syntactic and semantic rules that children need in order to reach their full potential in language.

Most of the approaches to language development proposed for children with delayed language are based on normal language acquisition. In the past we primarily had developmental milestones to follow. The explosion of knowledge in psycholinguistics and linguistics has resulted in far better descriptions of language development in the normally hearing child in all aspects, i.e., pragmatics, semantics, syntax, morphology, and phonology.

New Assessment Techniques

Application of this new knowledge has been or is being extended to language assessment and language programming for learning-disabled children, aphasic children, and hearing-impaired children. Teachers and clinicians wishing to evaluate and/or try out the new approaches and means of assessment must acquire a different orientation to language, one that uses new terminology and new concepts and requires a better understanding of language.

The older means of syntactic assessment centered around a child's use of the different parts of speech and constructions such as compound or complex sentences. The evaluator noted errors such as substitutions, omissions, and additions. Semantic development was assessed by giving the child vocabulary, word association, reading comprehension, and vocabulary tests. Transformational grammar and its application to language development affords us a more definitive description of a child's syntactic functioning.

Some of the newest tests of syntactic ability standardized on hearing and hearing-impaired children require that the teacher and clinician have a good understanding of the structure of the English language. The Test of Syntactic Abilities (Quigley, Steinkamp, Power, & Jones, 1978), the Grammatical Analysis of Elicited Language—Simple Sentence Level (Moog & Geers, 1979), the Grammatical Analysis of Elicited Language—Complex Sentence Level (Moog & Geers, 1980), and the Rhode Island Test of Language Structure (Engen & Engen, 1983) assess syntactic ability in areas such as sentence modalities, auxiliary and verb structures, determiner and noun structures, pronominalizations, conjoinings, relativization, complementation, and nominalization. Some of the procedures and tests that predate those mentioned were aimed at children with delayed language not necessarily stemming from hearing impairment. These procedures and tests, which include Developmental Sentence Scoring (Lee, 1974), the Test for Auditory Comprehension of Language (Carrow, 1973), and the Carrow Elicited Language Inventory (Carrow, 1974), were based on modern syntactic theory. This is true of some of the more recent tests, such as the Test of Language Development (Newcomer & Hammill, 1977) and the Clinical Evaluation of Language Functions (Semel & Wiig, 1980).

New information resulting from research in the area of semantics and case grammar has had an impact on the assessment of children's semantic capabilities. Bloom and Lahey's language sample analysis (1978) includes the classification of utterances as to the use of various semantic categories. The focus is first on semantic analysis and then on syntactic analysis. The spontaneous language analysis procedure of Kretschmer and Kretschmer (1978), developed for assessment of hearing-impaired children, also puts stress on describing the restrictions and deviances in syntactic and semantic performance and on assessing communicative competence or the pragmatic aspect.

New Methods of Language Development

Current methods of language development for children with delay due to hearing impairment or other causes call for the newer means of assessment. These methods stress the pragmatic, semantic, and syntactic aspects of language; they are based on modern linguistic theory. Methods devised for hearing-impaired children include the Rhode Island curriculum (Blackwell, Engen, Fischgrund, & Zarcadoolas, 1978) and procedures suggested by Streng, Kretschmer, and Kretschmer (1978) and by Kretschmer and Kretschmer (1978). All of the above stress a developmental approach based on what we know today about normal pragmatic, semantic, and syntactic development. Materials for language development such as McCarr's *Lessons in Syntax* (1976) and those designed for use after assessment with the TSA (Quigley & Power, 1980) are based on transformational theory.

Modern linguistic theory has also had an impact on techniques of reading assessment and on the development of reading materials. Some of the newest reading materials (Quigley & King, 1981, 1982, 1983, 1984, in press) have been designed to more adequately develop reading skills in those with delayed language.

For one to be better able to evaluate and make decisions as to the use of the various means of assessment, language curriculums, and materials, a basic under-standing of normal language development and of the syntax and semantics of the language is mandatory. Thus, it is the purpose of this text to provide teachers and clinicians with basic knowledge in both syntax and semantics. With this knowledge, they will be able to better serve hearing-impaired or other children and youth who are experiencing difficulties or delays either in language acquisition or in developing full competence in the use of the English language.

The approach to grammar in the text is based primarily on transformational grammar in that it uses the terminology and some of the concepts from this area of linguistics. The writer has endeavored to use the terminology that one will meet in recent or current research, recent texts, and curriculums for language development.

The focus of the instruction in the text is on the basic syntactic and semantic aspects of English. The first five chapters present what are considered to be the building blocks for later chapters—information on the constituents of noun and verb phrases and basic sentences. Chapters 7 through 12 consider modality changes and operations on a single sentence. The next sets of chapters present the more complex syntactic operations used in sentences that represent a number of propositions or bits of information. In all chapters, the semantic aspects related to the syntax of the structures are given. The review chapters after each block of information provide the basics for semantic and syntactic analyses of language development in addition to a review of the chapters. The order, however, is not representative of how language develops in children nor of how one would intervene to promote language development in children.

The pragmatic dimension of language (i.e., the functions of language) and the means of evaluating competence in this area have not been included in the text. How-ever, some references are made to the ways in which different syntactic forms are used to serve varying communication functions. It must be understood, though, that linguistic competence can only be demonstrated within the context of communication and the functions for which language is used.

CHAPTER 1

Nouns and Noun Phrases

The child learns the syntax of language by internalizing the rules for generating sentences rather than by acquiring individual words and building sentences out of this vocabulary. An effective language development program, one that follows the normal pattern of development, will focus on sentences (the important units of the syntax of our language) and on the combining of sentences in discourse.

The **noun phrase** (NP) is a basic sentence constituent. It consists of a head word, the **noun** (N), and a **determiner** (Det) that precedes and signals the noun. The noun carries the primary meaning, and the determiner adds some specific dimension of meaning. Although many nouns indicate persons, places, or things, not all nouns can be defined in this way. Some nouns indicate abstract concepts. We shall say, then, that nouns are words like *Tony, Chicago, shirt,* and *truth.*

Unit 1: Noun Phrases

Objectives
- Specify the features of selected nouns presented in sentences
- List determiners in each determiner category
- Categorize determiners as definite or nondefinite
- Identify noun phrases in given sentences
- Specify the types of determiners used in given noun phrases (including the null determiners)
- Write the symbols used for *determiner, noun phrase, feature,* and *consists of*
- Write the phrase structure rules for given noun phrases
- Write English noun phrases for given phrase structure rules

Features of Nouns
In communication, the individual decides on the message to be conveyed and then selects the type of sentence to use. The type of sentence governs in part the lexical items or range of items that may be used.

5

The lexical items, the words of a language known to a user of that language, make up one's **lexicon**. A large part of the lexicon consists of nouns. Each lexical item, whether a noun, verb, or adverb, has **features** that impose constraints upon its use. For example, these features govern the types of determiners and modifiers used with nouns and govern the other words that can co-occur or be used appropriately with nouns in sentences.

The following is a listing of some of the features that nouns carry.

human	nonhuman	[±human]
animate	inanimate	[±animate]
concrete	abstract	[±concrete]
count	noncount	[±count]
common	proper	[±common]
singular	plural	[±singular]

The word *boxes* has the features [+count], [−animate], [+concrete], and [−singular]. The plus symbol indicates the presence of a feature, and the minus symbol, the absence. As *boxes* is [−animate], it is termed inanimate. As a function of being inanimate, there are restrictions upon the verbs that can be used with *boxes*. *Lay* may be used, but not *walk* or *sleep* because they are verbs requiring animate subjects.

Animateness, humanness, and gender are inherent features of some nouns. The words *boy, woman,* and *butcher* are [+human] nouns. Since they carry the feature of humanness, these words are also animate, which need not be given as a separate feature in the lexical entry when a noun is [+human]. Certain verbs, such as *think* or *remember,* can co-occur with human nouns but not with those that are only animate. As was mentioned in the case of the word *boxes,* there are restrictions on the words that can be used with inanimate or nonhuman nouns. However, when using language figuratively or in children's stories (e.g., *The tugboat smiled as she safely guided the ocean liner through the channel*), human characteristics may be assigned to an inanimate noun as denoted by the use of *smiled* and *she.* Human nouns also carry the feature of gender, being either masculine or feminine.

The feature [+animate] of nouns such as *dog, ladybug,* and *shark* indicates living but nonhuman. Some confusion can result when referring to animate nouns as living things since not all living things are animate. Plants and trees are living things, but they are inanimate [−animate]. Verbs such as *grow* and *die* can co-occur with words that refer to inanimate living things, but not with inanimate nonliving things, such as *tables* or *boxes.* Thus, one must take into account the additional features of living and nonliving for inanimate nouns.

Another feature of nouns is [±count]. Count nouns are those that name things that can be counted. Words such as *girl, bug,* and *box* are [+count]. Noncount nouns designate masses that cannot be counted. For example, *sand, sugar,* and *milk* are [−count]. All human and animate nouns are count nouns. Some inanimate nouns may be count or noncount. One may use a word such as *stone* as either [−count]—*Much stone is used for building in Pennsylvania*—or as [+count]—*Jack picked up six large stones.* Mass or [−count] nouns are always singular, and count nouns usually have both a singular and plural form (boy-boys; mouse-mice). Whether a noun is count or noncount imposes restrictions on the determiners that can be used. The determiner *much* can occur with noncount nouns but not with count nouns. The converse is true with determiners like *a* or *many,* which are only appropriate with count nouns.

The features of singularity [+singular] and plurality [−singular] impose restrictions on the verbs, pronouns, and determiners that may be used with the noun when these categories of words have both singular and plural forms. One is constrained to use plural determiners such as *many, these,* and *five* with plural nouns. A singular subject requires a singular verb form and determiner, as in *That boy is happy.*

Nouns may also be classified as concrete [+concrete] or as abstract [−concrete]. Concrete nouns such as *table, sand,* and *boy* indicate things that can be seen or touched. *Happiness, loyalty,* and *idea* are examples of abstract nouns. All concrete nouns, except those referring to masses, are [+count]. Abstract nouns, with a few exceptions, are [−count]. *Happiness* is an example of an abstract, noncount noun, whereas *idea* is abstract but [+count].

Nouns are also classified as common [+common] or proper [−common]. This set of features is not critical to the meaning of nouns as is the case with humanness or animateness. Proper nouns name particular people, places, or things—*John, New York,* and *the Mona Lisa*; the correlates *boy, state,* and *masterpiece* are common nouns. Proper nouns are capitalized and common nouns are not, except as the first word in a sentence.

There are other features of nouns that are learned in the process of acquiring and expanding the meanings of words which will ultimately make up one's lexicon. To be able to use nouns both meaningfully and grammatically, the individual must adhere to the constraints imposed by the important features of the word: features inherent in the word such as humanness, the grammatical category of the word, and selectional features such as plurality.

Examples of features that one would adhere to in using selected nouns follow. The selected features are based on the noun within the context of a sentence.

> One pig's house was made of *brick*.
> > brick: [−count]
> > [−animate]
> > [+concrete]
> > [+common]
> > [+singular]

Her *humor* does not amuse everyone.

humor: [−count]
[−concrete]
[+common]
[+singular]

Jack threw many *stones* at the squirrels.

stones: [+count]
[−animate]
[+concrete]
[+common]
[−singular]

Determiners

Although hearing-impaired children and language-delayed children may exhibit little difficulty in acquiring a vocabulary of nouns, they experience great difficulty in the development of semantically and syntactically appropriate noun phrases. This is due in part to the syntactic complexity of the determiner system and in part to the semantic complexities of determiner use.

Many of the words that are called **determiners** were called adjectives in traditional grammar. Words such as *two, every,* and *many* were traditionally designated as **adjectives** (i.e., modifiers of nouns). Determiners, as was mentioned before, signal or determine that nouns will follow. Determiners also serve to qualify nouns as being definite, nondefinite, a certain number, a particular order, a degree of proximity, etc.

Articles

Articles comprise an important group of determiners. An article (art) may be definite [+definite] or nondefinite [−definite]. Definite articles are words such as *the, each, every, neither,* and *either.* The nondefinite articles include words such as *a, an, some, any, another, no,* and *enough.* To use articles correctly one must observe the features of nouns such as [±count] and [±singular]. For example, all of the articles may be used with count nouns; noncount nouns may not be preceded by articles such as *a(n), each, either,* or *neither.*

The most often used articles are *a(n), the,* and *some.* These determiners may account for a large number of the errors made by severely hearing-impaired children, and the errors may often persist into adulthood. When the speaker or writer uses *the,* a specific person or thing is referred to, one that has already been identified to the listener or reader. The nondefinite article *a(n)* is used to refer to one of a possible number, and *some* refers to an unidentified number of a group or part of a mass.

a boy	unspecified boy
the boy	specified boy
some boys	unspecified number of boys
some sand	unspecified amount of a mass

An important distinction in the use of *a* or *some* vs. the use of *the* is that *a* or *some* is used to code new information and *the* indicates old information. Proper use of *a* or *some* and *the* depends upon their use in discourse rather than in only a noun phrase or a single sentence. Note the use of these determiners in the following pair of sentences.

Mother bought *a* dress yesterday.
She wore *the* dress to work today.

The use of *a(n)* poses particular difficulty for children who cannot hear. Appropriate use is determined by the initial **phoneme** (sound) in the noun: *a* is used before consonants—*a* boat, *a* fish, *a* spoon—and *an* is used before vowels or **diphthongs**—*an* apple, *an* elf, *an* owl.

The **null (∅) article**, which is nondefinite, is used before plural count nouns when making a general statement about people or things, before a mass noun used in a general sense, and before names. The italicized words in the following sentences carry the null determiner.

Marta likes *boys*.
Helium is a gas.

Streng (1972), in commenting on the difficulty of the null article for hearing-impaired children, stated that both proper and plural nouns are regarded as having a nondefinite article in the **deep structure**, but that it often does not appear in the **surface structure** (the form we hear spoken or see written). A proper noun, such as *Tim* in the sentence *Tim is happy*, carries the null article, as do *children* and *games* in the sentence *Children like games*.

The presence or absence of *the* before nouns is difficult for individuals who have language difficulties or who are learning English as a second language. Consider the following:

Virginia is a state in *the United States*.
Brooklyn and *The Bronx* are boroughs of New York.

I went to *class*; Jack went to *the library.*

I play *tennis.* He plays *the piano.*

Oatmeal is a cereal. *The oatmeal* was hot.

When examining a language sample and writing the rules a child is using, one can indicate the syntactic rules of noun phrases as follows:

Daddy (or Jack) is big.	NP → $\emptyset$ art + N
The doggie barked.	NP → +def art + N
I want *a cookie.*	NP → −def art + N
I like *nursery school.*	NP → $\emptyset$ art + Noun adjunct + N

The → means *consists of,* and N is used for *noun.* A child who says *I want cookie,* with omission of the nondefinite article, is using a child's or nonadult grammar rule so that it could be noted as NP → N.

Demonstratives

The **demonstrative determiners** are *this, that, these,* and *those.* An important feature of demonstratives is that of proximity. *This* and *these* carry the [+near] or nearness feature, and *that* and *those* carry the [−near] or distance feature. The reference point may be from the speaker or from the person spoken to. A child in the early stages of language and cognitive development uses *this* or *that* as a designator to point out a particular thing or person prior to reaching the conceptual level at which he or she can specify the nearness or remoteness feature.

The demonstratives also carry the [+definite] feature because they are used to refer to specific people or things. *This* and *that* are used with singular count nouns and with mass or noncount nouns (e.g., this *boy,* that *milk*), and *these* and *those* are used with plural count nouns. In analyzing the noun phrases in a language sample, the syntactic rule for *that dog* is NP → dem + N, but one should also note its semantic use as designative or indicative of the feature of nearness or remoteness from the child or the person to whom the communication is addressed.

Cardinals

The term *cardinal,* as used in mathematics, refers to the number of items in a set. The **cardinal determiners** are *one, two, three,* etc., as far as one can count. Also included in this group of determiners are *many, few,* and *several.* Cardinals carry the [−definite] feature, and are indicated in the syntactic rule as *card.* Some of the articles and the demonstratives may occur before the cardinals in a noun phrase. The rules for NPs with one or more determiners, one of which is a cardinal, would be written as follows:

fifty children	NP → card + N
those two boys	NP → dem + card + N
the three coins	NP → +def art + card + N

As one might expect, the use of cardinal determiners by young children is dependent upon their development of number concepts. Although preschoolers may use *many, five,* or *one hundred,* their meanings for the words may be different from those of adults.

Ordinals

The **ordinals** include words such as *first, second, third,* etc., as well as other words indicating rank or order in a series, such as *last, final, other, middle,* and *next.* The ordinals are preceded by other determiners, such as articles or demonstratives, that will designate the noun phrase as definite or nondefinite.

When the ordinals are used in NPs with cardinals, the ordinals precede the cardinals and follow another determiner that is [+definite], such as *the* or a demonstrative.

the last two days	NP → +def art + ord + card + N
those first few days	NP → dem + ord + card + N

The use of ordinals by children is also dependent upon their conceptual development. Appropriate semantic use should not be expected of children in their preschool years.

Comparatives

Words such as *more, most, less, least, fewer,* and *fewest* denote a comparison. These comparatives will be considered later with transformations. Although these words serve as determiners, they are used only when the speaker or writer has referred to a particular number or quantity and when the speaker or writer has indicated a recurrence, as in *more milk.*

Bobbie wants some *more* milk.
Blondes have the *most* fun.
Mary has *fewer* freckles (than Jay).

As can be noted in the above sentences, the comparatives in noun phrases occur after articles such as *some, the,* and ∅.

Prearticles

The **prearticles** include *just, only,* and *even,* and two- or three-word determiners with *of,* such as *all of, two of, a quarter of, both of,* and *lots of.* They add the meaning of number or quantity to the noun phrase. In some instances, *of* will be deleted—*both those boys, all the boxes.* Any of the cardinal and ordinal numbers combined with *of* are prearticles, as are nouns indicating quantity plus *of*—*cup of, gram of,* and *carton of.* These words serve to qualify the meaning of the NP in a restrictive sense rather than to add a general or specific meaning of number or quantity.

The prearticles occur as the first element in an NP preceding the article. Examples of noun phrases with prearticles include

several of these books	NP → preart + dem + N
only the last record	NP → preart + def art + ord + N

Genitives

The **genitive determiners** add the meaning of possession to the sentence. Genitive (a term you may recognize if you studied Latin) is sometimes called **possessive**. The words used as genitive determiners are *my, your, his, her, its, our,* and *their.* Some of the genitives have the same form as the personal pronouns, which you will study in another chapter.

Some authors refer to the genitives as **possessive pronouns**; however, they occur in determiner positions in an NP. A genitive determiner cannot substitute for an NP in a sentence. [The * indicates a sentence that is not standard English.]

Kay brought *our* books.
*Kay brought *our.* (must use the pronoun *ours*)

Although a young child will use *my,* as in *my doggie,* in an early stage of language development, use of the other genitives occurs later. In order to use these determiners appropriately, one must observe the features of gender, person, and number of the noun referent.

his dogs	(John's dogs—referent John is masculine, singular, and third person)
their leashes	(the dogs' leashes—referent is third person and plural)
our dogs	(John's and my dogs—referent is first person and plural)

The genitives carry the [+definite] feature when they occur as the first determiner and may only be preceded by a prearticle.

her last two cars	NP → gen + ord + card + N
our first few courses	NP → gen + ord + card + N
both of their cars	NP → preart + gen + N

Mention was made earlier of the complexity of the determiner system in English. We do not always communicate using all of the determiners possible in an NP, yet we often use multiple determiners with no thought to the set order in which they must occur or to the features we must observe to use grammatically and semantically appropriate noun phrases.

In summary, the syntactic rule for determiners can be expressed as follows:

$$Det \rightarrow (preart) + \begin{matrix} art & ord \\ dem & card \\ gen & comp \end{matrix}$$

The rule shows the order in which determiners may occur and the groupings of determiners as predeterminers, determiners, and postdeterminers. The rule does not indicate the complexities, especially in the last grouping (the ordinals, cardinals, and comparatives), as to with which of the other determiners they may pattern.

Turn to Exercise 1 in the workbook for practice in identifying noun features and determiners.

Unit 2: Noun Inflections and Derivations

Objectives
- Identify definitions of *affix, prefix, suffix*, and *morpheme*
- Specify the regular inflectional morphemes for nouns
- Identify the meaning of the inflection as plurality or possession for given inflected nouns
- Identify the derivational affix(es) and the base word from which given nouns were derived

Inflections

A **morpheme** is the smallest unit of meaning in our language. All base words, regardless of the class (noun, verb, etc.), are morphemes. Base words, which may stand alone, are called **free morphemes**. The **affixes** that are added to the base words are called **bound morphemes** because they must be attached to a base word. These affixes may be at the beginning of the word (**prefixes**) or at the end of the word (**suffixes**). The noun *girls* is composed of two morphemes—*girl* and -s—as is the noun *development*—*develop* and *-ment*.

A regular inflection is a suffix that carries grammatical meaning. Reference has been made to the [±singular] feature of count nouns. The majority of the nouns that we use are regular in that they are inflected for the plural in the same way—*boys, books, watches,* and *glasses.* A child does not have to learn the plurals of all regular nouns, but rather, generalizes a rule and applies it to new nouns without having seen or heard the plural forms. Although you may never have seen the nonsense words *flid* and *nutch,* you could readily supply the correct plural in speech or in writing by following **morphophonemic** or spelling rules.

The plurals of nouns that are not regularly inflected must be learned as separate words (e.g., louse-lice, man-men). Some nouns, such as *deer* or *fish,* do not change in form. Instead, the ∅ morpheme is used for the plural inflection. The other regular noun inflectional morpheme, the possessive (e.g., Mary's son, the tree's branches, the boy's bravery), indicates relationship to the noun of another person, a thing, or a characteristic.

The plural and possessive morphemes have allomorphic variations that are dependent upon the phonemic environment in which they occur. The **allomorphs**, (variants of the morpheme) depend upon the final phoneme of the inflected word. All words ending in vowel sounds (e.g., *boy, shoe, pea*) and words ending in voiced consonants (e.g., *girl, bed, ham*) have the /-z/ allomorph for the morpheme. Words ending in voiceless consonants (e.g., *hat, cup, Nick*) have the allomorph /-s/. Words ending in /-s/, /-z/, /-sh/, /-zh/, /-ch/, and /-dj/ have the allomorph /-əz/, which is written as -es in the plural. The following examples illustrate the occurrence of the /-əz/ allomorph. All of the plural forms listed are pronounced as two syllables although the base word is a monosyllable.

kiss	kisses
fez	fezzes
bush	bushes
rouge	rouges
church	churches
judge	judges

The singular possessive has the same three allomorphs as the plural.

Pam + 's = Pam + /-z/
cat + 's   = cat + /-s/
Mitch + 's = Mitch + /-əz/

Since a word can have only one inflectional suffix, the plural form of the possessive has the /∅/ allomorph, meaning that nothing is added in the pronunciation of the word to indicate that it is possessive. In writing, the plural possessive is shown by a change in punctuation: the apostrophe follows the plural -s or -es as in *the students' books.* The word *students',* then, would be student $+ /$-s$/$ (plural) $+ /\emptyset/$ (possessive).

Through hearing inflected nouns and generalizing rules about them, children apply the regular plural and possessive morphemes before they learn the spelling or punctuation of the words. Prior to acquiring the rules and being able to extend them to new words or unknown forms, children may overextend the rule to irregular words and thus produce plurals such as *sheeps* or *fishes.*

Derivations

Derivational affixes are used to derive words from base words of the same or different class and thereby serve to increase our vocabularies. The rules for derivational affixes, which are suffixes for **nominalizations** (noun formations), are not as regular as are the inflectional rules. Examples of some of the commonly used noun-forming affixes are shown in Table 1. The derivational affixes *-ment, -er,* and *-ion* are added to verbs to form nouns. Other nouns are derived from adjectives with affixes such as *-ness, -y, -ty,* or *-ance.* Still other nouns are derived from nouns with affixes such as *-ship, -hood,* or *-ry.*

Table 1
Common Derivational Affixes

Base Word	+	Derivational Affix	=	Noun
develop (verb)		-ment		development
teach (verb)		-er		teacher
estimate (verb)		-ion		estimation
happy (adjective)		-ness		happiness
royal (adjective)		-ty		royalty
relation (noun)		-ship		relationship
chemist (noun)		-ry		chemistry
child (noun)		-hood		childhood

Turn to Exercise 2 for practice using noun inflections and derivations.

CHAPTER 2

Verb Phrase Constituents

A sentence must consist of a noun phrase (NP) and a verb phrase (VP). This chapter concentrates on adverbials that are obligatory or optional in verb phrases and on adjectives that are obligatory constituents in one type of sentence or that elaborate noun phrases. **Obligatory** indicates that the word or phrase is necessary to complete the meaning of the verb phrase. **Optional** indicates that the word or phrase may be used to expand the information or meaning in the sentence but that the sentence would be syntactically complete without it. The following examples illustrate both obligatory and optional adverbials and adjectives.

Obligatory Adverbials:	The meeting will be *at ten o'clock*.
	(*The meeting will be.)
	The boys are *outside*.
	(*The boys are.)
Optional Adverbials:	Mary hit Tom *with a bat*.
	Jack sleeps *all morning*.
Obligatory Adjectives:	Sue is *intelligent*.
	George became *upset*.
Optional Adjectives:	Dad bought a *new* car.
	A *small* child should drink milk.

Unit 1: Adverbials

Objectives

- List the major types of adverbials
- Write question words associated with one-word adverbials
- Identify one-word adverbials in sentences and specify the type of each as denoting time, manner, place, frequency, or duration
- Write the symbols used for adverbial, preposition, and prepositional phrases
- Identify noun phrase and prepositional phrase adverbials in sentences and specify each as denoting time, manner, place, frequency, and duration

- Identify the form of adverbials in sentences as one word, noun phrase, or prepositional phrase
- State the order used by Fitzgerald for adverbials denoting time, manner, place
- Identify the derivational affix(es) of derived adverbs and the base word from which the adverb was derived

Associated Question Words

In her book, *Straight Language for the Deaf*, Fitzgerald (1926) displayed in the Key the different kinds of **adverbials** and their usual order when they pattern together. She used words such as *where, how long,* and *when* to designate the adverbials. These are the question words one would use for asking about time, location, etc. Figure 1 gives some of the Fitzgerald Key headings showing the order for the subject, verb, object, and various kinds of adverbials (Fitzgerald, 1926, Plate A). An illustrative sentence using four different kinds of adverbials demonstrates the ordering of adverbials according to Fitzgerald. This sentence has the **locative** or adverbial of place (*at the club*) first; an adverbial indicating with whom (*with his sister*) next; then an adverbial of frequency (*every morning*); and last, the adverbial of time (*this week*).

Who: Whose: What:	= ⊏	What: Whom: Whose: Whom: What:	Where:	For . . . : With . . . : How: Why:	How far: How often: How long: How much:	When:
Tom played		tennis	at the club	with his sister	every morning	this week.

Figure 1
Word Order in Sentences

The question words that can be associated with different kinds of adverbials are as follows:

adverbial of manner:	How? (carefully, with a knife)
adverbial of reason:	For what or whom? Why? (for exercise)
adverbial of frequency:	How often? (daily, every Sunday)

adverbial of duration:	How long? (three days, for a day)
adverbial of place:	Where? (outside, under the table)
adverbial of time:	When? (later, at three o'clock)

The Fitzgerald Key, however, does not account for other positions in which adverbials may occur; nor does it account for adverbs that are sentence modifiers that may shift. The Key appears to limit the positions in which adverbials do occur. It could lead one to think that all adverbials are complements of the verb phrase that must follow the verb. In practice, this was not Fitzgerald's intent. In her language development program, children were presented with adverbs that were **preposed** (shifted) to another position in the sentence. In the beginning, however, when children were dealing with basic sentences, adverbials were placed after the verb with time adverbials following the locatives.

Types and Forms of Adverbials

The major syntactic groupings given in English grammars are adverbials of place, time, manner, and frequency. Some adverbials indicate duration—*for three hours*. Others indicate reason—*for exercise*. Adverbials can take the form of one-word adverbials (adverbs), noun phrases, or prepositional phrases.

One-Word Adverbials

Examples of one-word adverbials in each of the major groupings are found in the following list.

adverbial of time:	now, tomorrow, today, later, Saturday
adverbial of place:	here, there, outside, indoors
adverbial of frequency:	weekly, occasionally, often, never
adverbial of manner:	hard, fast, slowly, gracefully, calmly

Many of the one-word adverbials may be preposed (shifted) to several different positions.

Henry *never* has been in New York.
Henry has *never* been in New York.
Tomorrow the team leaves for Chicago.
The team leaves *tomorrow* for Chicago.
Joyce walked *slowly* down the stairs.
Joyce *slowly* walked down the stairs.

Noun Phrase Adverbials

Examples of adverbials that have the form of noun phrases include the following:

adverbial of time:	this week, next Sunday, tomorrow morning
adverbial of frequency:	each week, every day, every Saturday
adverbial of duration:	an hour, three hours, all day

Prepositional Phrase Adverbials

A large number of adverbials are in the form of prepositional phrases. A prepositional phrase (PP) consists of a preposition (Prep) plus an NP (PP → Prep + NP). Streng (1972) states that there are about 60 simple prepositions (one-word) and about 25 compound [two (+) words] prepositions among the structure or function words in English. Examples of some of the simple, most often used prepositions are given below.

across	from	over
after	in	round
among	into	since
at	like	through
before	near	to
between	off	under
by	on	until
during	out	up
for	opposite	with

Examples of compound prepositions include *in back of, by means of, in front of, instead of, on account of,* and *on top of.*

Examples of prepositional phrases that could be used as adverbials include the following:

adverbial of time:	in the morning, at sundown, after the game, on Tuesday
adverbial of place:	to the drugstore, in the basement, at school, near the door, on a corner
adverbial of manner:	in a hurry, with a knife, like a dog, by machine
adverbial of duration:	for three hours, throughout the night, until midnight, about two days

Semantic Cases of Adverbials

From a developmental standpoint in language, the semantic content of each utterance is more important than the syntactic, especially in the beginning stages. The preceding discussion presented the syntactic forms and types of adverbials. In analyzing the language competence of children and charting their development, a semantic description that will indicate the different meanings the child expresses should be included. The terms used for adverbial cases in a semantic description are *location, time, manner, reason*. Time may be further specified as *duration* or *frequency*. These adverbial cases will be further described in the units on sentences.

A child in the early stages of language development may use adverbial cases similar to the following italicized words or phrases.

location: Kitty *table*. (The kitty is on the table.)
time: Daddy come *now*. (Daddy is coming now.)
manner: Doggie run *fast*. (The doggie is running fast.)
reason: I making cake *for party*. (I'm making a cake for the party.)

Adverb Derivations

Many one-word adverbials, or adverbs, are derived from other words by adding the commonly used derivational affix *-ly*. These adverbs, which are adverbials of manner, make up a large group of derived words in our language.

Some adverbs of manner are derived from adjectives, such as *calmly, slowly, vividly,* and *sadly*. Others are derived from adjectives that were derived from nouns, such as *emotionally* (emotion + *-al* + *-ly*) and *sleepily* (sleep + *-y* + *-ly*), or from adjectives derived from verbs, such as *agreeably* (agree + *-able* + *-ly*) and *seductively* (seduce + *-tive* + *-ly*).

A small number of adjectives form adverbs with the ∅ affix, so that the words *fast, straight,* and *hard* have the same form when used as an adjective (Adj) or an adverbial (Adv).

Jane stands *straight*.   (Adv)
Ryan's hair is *straight*.   (Adj)
Dad works *hard*.   (Adv)
The ice cream is *hard*.   (Adj)

This differentiation will be more easily understood after study of later units on adjectives and sentence patterns. Further information on adverbials and their movability and patterning with verbs also is presented in later units.

Turn to Exercise 3 for practice in recognizing and using adverbials.

Unit 2: Adjectives

Objectives

- Write the symbol for adjective
- State the test for determining if a word is an adjective
- Identify adjectives from among nonadjectives
- Identify adjectives in sentences
- Define noun adjunct
- Differentiate adjectives from noun adjuncts in noun phrases
- Write the inflectional suffixes used for the comparative and superlative forms of regularly inflected adjectives
- Write the comparative and superlative forms of given adjectives
- Differentiate adjectives that are regularly and irregularly inflected
- Identify the derivational affix and the base word for derived adjectives

Adjectives are words we use to comment on the characteristics of, or assign attributes to, the persons or things about which we speak and write. We also use adjectives to describe ourselves, especially our feelings. It is important, then, that children acquire a variety of adjectives so they not only may be better able to describe other things but also may better express their feelings. An adjective (Adj) may state the condition, quality, size, shape, age, or color of a noun.

Streng, Kretschmer, and Kretschmer (1978) comment on the difficulty of acquiring the meanings of adjectives due to the degree of abstractness inherent in them. There can be degrees of roundness, wideness, or redness depending upon what the referents are, as well as upon what one's perceptions are regarding the referents. The word *tall*, when used to describe people, denotes a different size than when used to describe buildings. A small or medium-sized dog, such as a cocker spaniel, that knocks down a child may be *big* to that child but small to a child with a pet dalmatian.

Syntactic Aspects

Adjectives are used in sentences as a constituent in a verb phrase in a sentence (The kitten is *tiny*) or as a modifier of a noun in an NP (The *tiny* kitten). The sentences in the left column show adjectives used as verb phrase constituents; those in the right column show adjectives used as **prenominal modifiers** (modifiers preceding a noun).

The lecture was *boring*.	Jane baked a *delicious* cake.
His work is *tedious*.	His *tragic* death saddened everyone.
Mother seems *irritable*.	Jimmy is an *angelic* child.

Streng (1972) suggested a test to determine the adjectival quality of a word. If a word fits into the blanks in *"The very _____ (noun) is very _____"* (p. 175), the word may be considered an adjective. Using this test, we would find that *long* is an adjective but *toy* is not in the sentences *The very long trip is very long* and **The very toy dog is very toy.*

Use this test on the following NPs and determine if the italicized words are adjectives or not.

a *rain* forest   a *nylon* dress
a *wild* ride   a *large* horse
a *sturdy* chair   a *baby* carriage
a *circus* animal

You should have identified the words *wild, sturdy,* and *large* as adjectives. The other modifiers—*rain, circus, nylon,* and *baby*—are nouns. When nouns are used before the head noun in an NP, they are called **noun adjuncts.**

The embedding of adjectives used as noun modifiers and of noun adjuncts are **noun phrase elaborations.** These should be noted in the syntactic description of a child's language.

Semantic Aspects

In the introduction, reference was made to the meanings that can be expressed with adjectives and to the importance of the child's acquisition of a variety of adjectives. The semantic description of a language analysis should provide information on the presence of the different adjective or modifier cases that the child expresses.

Kretschmer and Kretschmer (1978) give the following as modifier cases: cardinal, ordinal, size, shape, color, quality, condition, and age. These meanings are expressed by adjectives used either as sentence constituents or as noun modifiers. Examples of some of the modifier cases that are adjectives include

I have a *huge* dog. (size)
Joan's hair is *clean.* (condition)
Terriers are *hardy* dogs. (quality)

When adjectives and noun adjuncts are embedded in sentences as elaborations of noun phrases, one is able to include another bit of information, or **proposition.** In a semantic description of a child's language, we are interested in the number of propositions expressed in comparison to the total number of utterances. A child may express two or more propositions in a single utterance by embedding adjectives and noun adjuncts. Propositions can also be added by using possessive nouns and genitive determiners. The following sentences illustrate this.

Faye has a big dog.

    Proposition 1: Faye has a dog

    Proposition 2: the dog is big

Fred made a paper airplane.

    Proposition 1: Fred made an air-
                  plane

    Proposition 2: the airplane is paper

Faye's dog is big.

    Proposition 1: dog is big

    Proposition 2: Faye has a dog

His airplane can fly.

    Proposition 1: airplane can fly

    Proposition 2: Fred has an air-
                  plane

Adjective Inflections

Adjectives may be inflected with -er and -est when they are used to indicate comparison. The adjectives that take these suffixes are referred to as regular adjectives. The regular adjectives are either monosyllables or words of two syllables, the second of which is -y.

Examples of the two forms of regular adjectives that are inflected with -er and -est include *cool, wild, fast, deep, new, crazy, shaggy, mighty, snappy,* and *airy.*

As in the case of nouns, when children generalize the rules that -er and -est are added to adjectives to indicate degree when comparing things, they may apply the rules to new adjectives and need not learn the comparative and superlative forms as discrete lexical items.

There are three degrees of adjectives: the base form, which is said to be the positive degree; the -er form, the comparative; and the -est form, the superlative.

The comparative is used for comparing two people or things, and the superlative is used for comparing more than two people or things, as illustrated in the sentences *Mary is prettier than Jane* and *Tom is the tallest boy in the class.*

Some examples of the comparison forms of regular adjectives are listed below. Note that with *mighty* and *airy* an English spelling rule causes the -y to become an -i before the inflectional suffixes can be added.

Positive	Comparative	Superlative
cool	cooler	coolest
new	newer	newest
mighty	mightier	mightiest
airy	airier	airiest

Irregular adjectives include a large group of two-syllable adjectives (not ending in -y) and adjectives with three or more syllables. The comparison forms of these adjectives are produced by using *more* and *most* with the base form. Some examples follow.

Positive	*Comparative*	*Superlative*
important	more important	most important
nervous	more nervous	most nervous
powerful	more powerful	most powerful

Other irregular adjectives may have different forms for each of the degrees, internal changes, or affixes other than -er and -est, with only two forms generally used. The appropriate use of the comparative and superlative forms of such adjectives is much more difficult for the language learner.

Positive	*Comparative*	*Superlative*
good	better	best
little	less	least
far	farther	farthest
eastern		easternmost

Adjective Derivations

Adjectives may be derived from nouns and verbs. Table 2 lists some derived adjectives, the base noun or verb from which each was derived, and the derivational suffix for each. The listed suffixes represent commonly used adjective-forming affixes.

Table 2
Adjective Derivations

Noun	or	Verb	+	Suffix	=	Adjective
		touch		-able		touchable
		digest		-ible		digestible
tide				-al		tidal
element				-ary		elementary
flax				-en		flaxen
sorrow				-ful		sorrowful
hero				-ic		heroic
fiend				-ish		fiendish
		invent		-ive		inventive
power				-less		powerless
man				-ly		manly
knob				-y		knobby

Turn to Exercise 4 for practice in recognizing and using adjectives.

CHAPTER 3

Verbs and Verb Phrases

In this chapter, as in the preceding ones, the discussion of the sentence constit-uent is, much of the time, out of the context of sentences, and, for the most part, will be concerned with the grammatical aspects of verbs and their auxiliaries. The verb, however, and the predication it expresses are central to the meaning of the sentence, so that the semantic aspects are of prime importance. As the semantic and other features of verbs cannot be presented outside the context of sentences, such aspects have been deferred to the following chapters on sentences.

Unit 1: Verb Forms

Objectives
- List two tenses in English
- Write the verb phrase structure rules for present or past tense verbs in sentences
- Identify the form of given regular and irregular verbs as the $\emptyset$, -ed, -ing, -s or -en form
- Write all verb forms for given verbs, labeling each
- Label verb forms as finite or nonfinite in given sentences
- Identify verbs as regular or irregular past or present tense

Principal Parts of Verbs

All the verbs of English, except for *be*, have three, four, or five different forms. Each verb has a **base,** or uninflected form. This form can be designated *V-$\emptyset$*. Verbs also have a third singular present form, which can be termed *V-s* or third singular; a past form, which is designated by *V-ed*; a progressive participle, the *V-ing* form, and a second participle form, termed the *V-en* form. Some verbs (e.g., hit) use the same spelling for as many as three of the principal parts. Table 3 indicates the principal parts of a number of verbs.

Table 3
Principal Parts of Verbs

Finite Nonfinite Base V-∅	Finite 3rd Singular V-s	Finite Past V-ed	Nonfinite Progressive Participle V-ing	Perfect Participle V-en
kick	kicks	kicked	kicking	kicked
cry	cries	cried	crying	cried
push	pushes	pushed	pushing	pushed
run	runs	ran	running	run
go	goes	went	going	gone
eat	eats	ate	eating	eaten
hit	hits	hit	hitting	hit

The first three verbs in Table 3 are regular verbs in that the past form ends in *-ed* and the *-en* form has the same ending as the past form.

V-*ed*: The dog barked.
V-*en*: The dog has barked for hours.

Children must learn the base forms of regular verbs as discrete units. They will generalize rules for the regular inflectional suffixes—*-ed, -s,* and *-ing*—and need not learn the verb forms with these endings as discrete lexical units. Irregular past forms, such as *ate, broke,* and *hit,* and the irregular *-en* forms *gone* and *eaten* must be learned individually.

The V-*ing* form is extremely regular since the *-ing* is applied to the base form of all but a few verbs. The V-*s* is also a very regular form since the *-s* morpheme is applied to the base of all verbs except *do (does), have (has),* and *be (is).*

In Table 3, the forms of the verb are grouped **finite** and/or **nonfinite.** Finite indicates that the verb form must stand alone. The base form of the verb is used as a finite verb when it is the simple present. It is nonfinite when used with an auxiliary, as in *can swim* or *do play.* Nonfinite indicates that the verb form cannot be used without an auxiliary when appearing as the main verb in a sentence. In the following sentences the complete verb is enclosed in parentheses; the verb in each sentence is italicized.

Finite: Some babies (*cry*) a lot.
            Mary often (*cries*).
            Mother (*cried*) at the wedding.

Nonfinite: Babies (*do cry*).
             The baby (is *crying*).
             The baby (has *cried*) all morning.
             The baby (must have *cried*) all night.

Tense

The term **tense** as applied to verbs is an obligatory element in verb phrases. All verb phrases will be either **present** or **past** tense. Tense is a grammatical term and does not refer to clock or calendar time. As tense is not equivalent to time, a verb phrase (VP) which is marked for the present (pres) or past tense does not necessarily refer to the time of action, state, or process. English has other ways of expressing time relationships. For example, in the sentence *Our team plays (is playing) in Baltimore next week*, the verb phrases, *plays* and *is playing* (both of which are appropriate in the sentence), are present tense, but the time of the action is future, as designated by *next week*. In the sentence *That child should play in her yard*, the tense of the VP is past. The time is not designated; the important meaning in the VP is that it is necessary that the child play in the yard, possibly because where she is playing, or may play, is unsafe.

Simple Present and Past Tense

Verbs in English, except for *be*, have two forms for the simple, or habitual, present tense: the base verb and the *V-s* form. The simple present tense is finite [+finite], i.e., it appears alone as the main verb in a sentence.

The verbs in the following sentences are present tense:

Fish *swim*.
Rosa *leaves* for work at 7:00 a.m.
The teams *play* in Baltimore next week.

The simple present may imply a generalization, as it does in the first sentence, or a habitually or frequently recurring activity, as in the second sentence. In the third sentence, the verb together with the adverbial implies an activity that will occur in the future. In this case the verb alone does not indicate time; time is designated by the adverbial.

Examples of some specific adverbials that pattern with the simple present tense are *every day, often, always, never,* and other adverbials of frequency; adverbials of duration, such as *all morning*; and adverbials of time, indicating a future time such as *next week*.

The present tense form that ends in *-s* is used with third person singular nouns and pronouns (the boy, the girl, the dog, he, she, it). Third person designates the person or thing referred to as opposed to first and second person, which respectively indicate the speaker and the person spoken to.

The uninflected form, which you will note is the same as the base form of the verb, is used with plural noun phrases and with the pronouns *I, you, we,* and *they.*

The phrase structure rule for verbs such as *swim* and *leaves* would be written as VP → pres + V (VP → pres + swim and VP → pres + leave, for the specific verbs given).

The simple past tense is marked by *-ed* in regular verbs. This rule of marking verbs for past tense with *-ed* is generalizable to a large number of verbs so that the child need not learn the past form of each individually. Other verbs, often referred to as *strong* verbs, have irregularly inflected or formed past tense forms. The following list shows the past tense forms of selected regular and strong verbs.

Regular Verbs	Strong Verbs
played	ran
offered	came
kicked	saw
tasted	hit
laughed	went

The simple past tense verb form is finite. An auxiliary (was, can, do) cannot be used in the verb phrase. Thus, the sentence, *Tom was kicked the ball*, would be ungrammatical.

The past tense ordinarily implies past time. It is often used with adverbials of time to express a definite time in the past.

The bus left at 10:00 a.m.
The girls baked a cake yesterday.
Mary received her degree in 1973.

In other cases, a definite time will not be indicated, but the activity will have gone on or occurred in the past.

Mr. Thompson taught in a residential school.
The carpenters worked for a long time.
The cook dropped the eggs.

The phrase structure rule for verbs in the past tense is VP → past + V; and for specific verbs would be

played: VP → past + play
came: VP → past + come
went: VP → past + go

When writing a phrase structure rule, *past* indicates the inflection, and the base form of the verb is used.

Turn to Exercise 5 for practice in identifying verb tenses.

Unit 2: Verb Phrases with Auxiliary Verbs

Objectives
- Label modal auxiliaries as present or past
- Write verb phrases from structure rules for t + modal + v
- Write verb phrase structure rules for verb phrases containing modals
- State possible meanings of modal auxiliaries in sentences
- Label forms of the *be* auxiliary as present or past
- Write verb phrase structure rules for verb phrases containing the *be* auxiliary
- Write verb phrases from structure rules for t + be + -ing + v
- Label forms of the *have* auxiliary as present or past
- Write the verb phrase structure rules for verb phrases containing the *have* auxiliary
- Write verb phrases from structure rules for t + have + -en + v

Verb phrases that are other than the simple present or past tense have one or more helping words, or **auxiliaries**. Thus, verb forms in such verb phrases are nonfinite and could be the base form, the *-ing* form, or the *-en* form.

When there is one auxiliary word in the verb phrase, it carries the tense, present or past. In the case of more than one auxiliary (*could have* gone) the first auxiliary denotes the tense. The auxiliaries that will be discussed in this unit are the modals (can, will, etc.) and the *be* and *have* auxiliaries. The *do* auxiliary (do, does, did) is presented in a later unit.

Modal Auxiliaries

The **modals** are an important group of auxiliaries. The base forms of these auxiliaries are the same as the present forms. These are listed below with the past forms.

Present	Past
can	could (past + can)
will	would
shall	should
may	might
must	(no past form)

When a modal (M) is the only auxiliary in a VP, it is used with the base form of the verb: *can see*, *should* arrive, *may* go. In this case, the verb will be nonfinite as there is an auxiliary. Modals may not be used alone as the verb in a sentence. In a sentence such as *Mary can (swim)*, the verb may be deleted when it has already been identified, and the listener understands what action or process is being discussed.

The phrase structure rule for verb phrases made up of a modal auxiliary and the base form of the verb is VP → t + M + V. Rules for the following verb phrases would be:

should arrive:	VP → past + shall + arrive
may go:	VP → pres + may + go
could see:	VP → past + can + see

Modal auxiliaries are also used with other auxiliaries before the verb. Verb phrases with more than one auxiliary are presented in a later part of the chapter.

The modals add a number of different meanings to verbs. They may be used to indicate permission, possibility, capability, necessity, obligation, expectation, doubt, intention, reaffirmation, or willingness. One of the meanings of *will* and *shall* is future time; however, these are the only modals that imply time as an important meaning. Except for the meaning of future time, the modals convey meanings that may be difficult for one who is learning the English language. In some cases, the use of a modal is subtle, as when the intent of the speaker may be to direct another person to do something—*I would like a drink, please, Would you (Can you, Will you) get me a drink?*

The speaker may expect, as a result of the statement or questions, that the listener will get the drink. The speaker uses what is considered a more polite way of asking *Get me a drink (please)*.

Examples of some of the many possible meanings that the modals may indicate are listed in Table 4.

Be Auxiliary

The *be* auxiliary has a number of forms: *am, is, are, was, were, be, being,* and *been*. The present and past tense forms are:

Present	*Past*
am (first person singular)	was (singular)
is (third person singular)	were (plural)
are (plural)	

When the *be* auxiliary is used to carry the tense in a verb phrase, the verb must have the affix *-ing* or *-en*—*is coming, was pushed*.

Table 4
Meanings Conveyed by Modals

Modal	Sentence	Meaning
can	Bobby *can* learn to swim.	capability
	You *can* go outside now.	permission
could	The teenagers *could* wash their own clothes.	capability
	You *could* get to New York before midnight.	possibility
shall	We *shall* see you at the conference.	future time (formal use)
should	Betty *should* arrive soon.	possibility expectation
	You *should* pay your parking fines.	obligation
will	Our class *will* see a movie next week.	future time
	Our class *will* see a movie.	promise
	My car *will* go 120 mph.	capability
would	I *would* like to go.	strong desire
	Jerry *would* help you.	willingness
may	You *may* have some dessert.	permission
might	The train *might* be late.	possibility
must	Carla *must* leave now.	necessity
	The boys *must* have arrived.	possibility

The -*ing* affix of verbs denotes **progressive aspect**, [+progressive], a verb feature. The progressive aspect conveys various meanings and relationships, such as the following:

   a. an activity or process going on in the present and continuing—*Dad is working in the yard (now)*.
   b. future time (with adverbial denoting future)—*Mary is arriving tomorrow*.
   c. an activity or process going on in the past and not necessarily concluded at the present time—*Joan is knitting a sweater for her father, The boys were playing in the park (an hour ago)*.

Not all verbs have the feature [+progressive], and such verbs cannot be used in verb phrases with *be*. Some of these verbs—*like, need, want, interest,* and *seem*—if used with *be*, would result in ungrammatical sentences (e.g., **John is liking potatoes,* and **Mother was seeming tired*).

The rule for verb phrases with *be* as the auxiliary used with *V-ing* is t + be + -ing + V. Note that the suffix *-ing* attached to the verb is given prior to the verb in the rule.

is working   VP → pres + be + -ing + work
was arriving   VP → past + be + -ing + arrive

Since the *-ing* participle is a nonfinite verb form, it cannot be used alone as the verb in a sentence (e.g., *My daddy working now). However, the use of the *V-ing* as a VP, as in the example, is a child's rule of grammar and is to be expected before the development of the *be* auxiliary of adult grammar.

The *be* auxiliary is also used in verb phrases with *V-en*, a nonfinite verb form—*was* removed, *were* seen. The rule for the verb phrase is t + be + -en + V. This is a rule for passive voice verb phrases, and it will be discussed in chapter 12 on the passive transformation.

Have Auxiliary

The *have* auxiliary requires the affix *-en* in the verb phrase. When *have* is the auxiliary carrying the tense, the *-en* inflection is an obligatory element in the verb phrase. The forms of the *have* auxiliary are the base *have*, which is also the present tense form used with I, you, or plural noun phrases; *has*, the present form used with he, she, it, or singular noun phrases; and *had*, the past form. Sample VPs would be as follows:

has, have left   VP → pres + have + -en + leave
had completed   VP → past + have + -en + complete

Verb phrases with the rule t + have + -en + V have the feature [+perfect]. The **perfect aspect** denotes various meanings. Although this aspect may indicate an activity completed in the past, it may not co-occur with adverbials denoting a specific past time, such as *last Saturday* or *yesterday*. Adverbials of frequency or duration, however, can be used with the perfect aspect, as in *John has lived in New York for three years*, and *The girls have worked every night this week*.

In sentences with perfect aspect verb phrases, the activity may have been completed or may still be going on.

Mother has left for New York.   (activity completed)
The two boys have watched TV for   (activity going on in the past and
two hours.   continuing)

Multiple Auxiliaries

More than one auxiliary verb may be used in verb phrases. Because of the set patterns for the order of the words in verb phrases and the combinations of meanings that may be expressed, the semantic and syntactic rules for these complex verb phrases are difficult to acquire.

Thus far we have had these phrase structure rules:

pres + V:	play, plays
past + V:	played
t + M + V:	may, might (etc.) play
t + be + -ing + V:	is, was, (etc.) playing
t + be + -en + V:	is, was, (etc.) played
t + have + -en + V:	have, has, had played

The nonfinite participle -ing combines with more than one auxiliary in the verb phrase rule t + M + be + -ing + V—can, could, (etc.) be playing.

Rules for complex verb phrases in which the verb has the -en affix include

t + have + -en + be + -en + V:	have, has, had been played
t + M + have + -en + be + -en + V:	may, might, (etc.) have been played

Turn to Exercise 6 for practice in identifying auxiliaries.

Unit 3: Tense and Aspect

Objectives

- Specify the tense and aspect of verb phrases with *have* or *be* auxiliaries
- Specify given VPs as present or past tense and identify the auxiliary(ies) as *be, have,* or modal
- Write the phrase structure rules for verb phrases with more than one auxiliary
- Identify the type of inflectional morpheme affixed to given verbs as the third singular, the progressive, or the past morpheme.

The aspect features [+progressive] and [+perfect] were mentioned in earlier units of the chapter. Verb phrases may have both perfect and progressive aspect. Progressive aspect requires a *be* auxiliary and an *-ing* affix in the VP; perfect aspect requires the *have* auxiliary and an *-en* affix. The first auxiliary in the verb phrase carries the tense. Some examples of verb phrases with progressive, perfect, or perfect progressive aspects are listed below.

Verb Phrase	Tense	Aspect
have completed	pres	perfect
had gone	past	perfect
was working	past	progressive
may be coming	pres	progressive
has been playing	pres	perfect progressive
could have been playing	past	perfect progressive

Regular Inflections of Verbs

The regular verbs in English are inflected with -ed for the past tense. All verbs except *do, have,* and *be* are regularly inflected with the -s morpheme for the third singular present tense, and the majority of verbs, except for those which do not have the feature [+progressive], may be inflected with the morpheme -ing.

The past tense morpheme has three allomorphs: /-t/, /-d/, and /-əd/. Verbs ending in unvoiced consonants, except for /-t/, have the /-t/ allomorph.

kick (kik) + -ed	=	kick + /-t/
rush + -ed	=	rush + /-t/
pass + -ed	=	pass + /-t/
laugh (laf) + -ed	=	laugh + /-t/
hop + -ed	=	hop + /-t/

Verbs ending in vowels or diphthongs and in voiced consonants, except for /-d/, have the /-d/ allomorph.

rob + -ed	=	rob + /-d/
tag + -ed	=	tag + /-d/
judge (juj) + -ed	=	judge + /-d/
bail + -ed	=	bail + /-d/
ram + -ed	=	ram + /-d/
play + -ed	=	play + /-d/
combine + -ed	=	combine + /-d/

Verbs that end in /-t/ and /-d/ have the allomorph /-əd/, which adds a syllable to the word.

bat + -ed   =   bat + /-əd/
bond + -ed   =   bond + /-əd/

The verb morpheme -s has the same allomorphs as the noun plural and singular possessive: /-s/, /-z/, and /-əz/. Examples of verbs that have these allomorphs for the third singular are

hits, kicks, hops, laughs: /-s/
plans, rubs, loves, rams: /-z/
pushes, kisses, buzzes, watches: /-əs/

The -ing morpheme has no variants and is applied to all verbs with the progressive aspect feature. The -en affix of regular verbs that forms the past with -ed is the same form as for the past and thus has the same allomorphic variations.

Children begin to mark verbs with the -ing morpheme early, usually at the two-word level. As with some of the other morphemes, children are selective in the verbs to which they apply the -ing morpheme. Studies of the acquisition of the inflections indicate that the order of acquisition of verb inflections is -ing, irregular past, regular past, and third singular -s (de Villiers & de Villiers, 1978). Children who use the past of irregular verbs, or strong verbs (went, ran, saw), before marking verbs with -ed, may then overextend the rule to irregular verbs and use runned and breaked. The -s morpheme, although it may occur during the preschool years, is late in the order of acquisition, and the rules for its use are ordinarily not established prior to age six or seven. Semantic and grammatical complexity, frequency of use, and perceptibility in speech are all considered possible determinants of the order of acquisition of inflectional morphemes.

Turn to Exercise 7 for practice in recognizing and analyzing verb phrases.

CHAPTER 4

Sentence Patterns 1 and 2

Children learn a language through hearing or, in the case of deaf children, through hearing and/or seeing connected language. In comprehending a message they get meaning not only from the individual words in the sentence, but also from the important constituents and the semantic roles of these constituents in sentences. Although in early utterances (the two-word stage) children may have some idea of word order and do adhere to some word orders, they are primarily expressing meaning and functional relationships. This continues into the later stages when they are acquiring more complex syntactic rules.

A main characteristic of the English language is word order. The arrangement of words in sentences (i.e., syntax) is important because our language has very few inflections and, thus, does not mark the important words or constituents in sentences to indicate their syntactic roles. If given a sentence with nonsense words, such as *The flids drebbed a mab*, you would easily locate the verb by the *-ed* and by its position in the sentence. You would identify *The flids* as the subject by its appearance at the beginning of the sentence and because of the determiner signal. To gain knowledge of the structure of the English language one must study the arrangement of words in sentences and the rules governing the various possible arrangements of the constituents to express meaning.

The concept of **kernel sentences** was postulated in early generative-transformational theory (N. Chomsky, 1957). Kernel sentences were seen as simple sentences generated by phrase structure rules. **Transformations**—grammatical operations on the kernel sentences, such as addition, substitution, omission, or rearrangement of the word order—resulted in complex sentences. An individual, in learning a language, learned the phrase structure and transformational rules and, thus, was capable of generating an infinite number of sentences.

On the basis of Chomsky's concept of kernel sentences, Hamel (1971) and Streng (1972) proposed that there were five basic kernel sentence patterns in English.

The acquisition of the rules, both syntactic and semantic, for the basic sentence patterns is suggested by both Streng, Kretschmer, and Kretschmer (1978) and Blackwell, Engen, Fischgrund, and Zarcadoolas (1978) as important for deaf or other language-delayed children experiencing difficulties in acquiring language competence in English.

The term *basic*, or kernel, sentences, when used in language curriculums such as that of the Rhode Island School for the Deaf (Blackwell et al., 1978) or *The Appletree*

Curriculum (Anderson, Boren, Caniglia, Howard, & Krohn, 1980) generally refers to simple, active, positive, declarative sentences. Kernel sentences would not be questions or commands and would not contain negatives such as *not*, pronouns, or other complexities. They are also single proposition sentences. Such sentences convey one idea or one piece of information.

Noun phrases, to begin with, would not be elaborated with adjective or noun adjunct modifiers; nor would NPs be expanded with clauses. Adverbials would be phrases (one-word, noun phrase, or prepositional phrase as to form) rather than adverbial clauses.

Unit 1: Pattern 1 Sentences

Objectives

- State the meaning of the arrow in a formula
- Write two formulas for a sentence
- Write the formula for a Pattern 1 sentence
- State the meaning of the parentheses in (Adv)
- Divide Pattern 1 sentences into their constituents
- Divide Pattern 1 sentences having verbs with particles into their constituents
- Identify the semantic relationships of nouns and verbs in given single proposition Pattern 1 sentences

A sentence grammatically consists of an NP and a VP, so that the rule for a sentence would be $S \rightarrow NP + VP$. Traditional grammar used the terminology **subject** and **predicate** for NP and VP, respectively. Thus, another rule for a sentence could be $S \rightarrow$ subject + predicate.

In some curriculums, such as that of Rhode Island (Blackwell et al., 1978), Sentence Pattern 1 is the first pattern introduced in formal language work. Through formal language work on this pattern the child is expected to grasp the noun-verb or subject-verb relationship.

Syntax

The formula for a Pattern 1 sentence is $NP + V_i + (Adv)$. The verb in this pattern is **intransitive** [−transitive], as indicated by V_i. An intransitive verb does not require that an NP or Adv be used as a **complement** (i.e., to complete its meaning). A Pattern 1 sentence may consist only of an NP and a verb. The only other constituent that may be used is an adverbial, or more than one adverbial. The use of an adverbial in the

pattern is optional, which is indicated by the parentheses around adverbial (Adv).
Examples of Pattern 1 sentences would be

    NP V_i
    Fish / can swim.
    NP V_i Adv
    Nancy / slept / all day
      NP V_i Adv   Adv
    The boys / played / in the park / this morning.
        NP V_i Adv
    Grandfather / is walking / slowly.

Adverbials of time, location, manner, frequency, and duration may be used in Pattern 1
sentences. As stated before, the adverbials will be simple phrases.

Intransitive verbs may consist of a verb plus a **particle** (prt). The particle is a
complement of the verb that completes its meaning. Particles include the words
down, up, around, out, and *in.* The meaning of the verb plus the particle is usually
different from the individual meanings of the two words. Note the meaning of the
italicized verb plus particle in each of the following sentences and the difference in the
meanings of the words when used separately.

    The furnace *blew up.*   Fred *blew* his nose.
    The Smiths *checked out* at noon.   Tim *checked* his schedule.

Other examples of verbs plus particles that appear as intransitive verbs in Pattern 1
sentences are given in the following sentences. The sentences are divided into their
constituents: NP and V_i in the first three and NP, V_j, and Adv in the last four.

    Our lawn / dried up.
    The teacher / passed out.
    The first three batters / struck out.
    Jim / turned in / at 10:00 p.m.
    Mary / works out / in the gym.
    Mother / calls up / every day.
    The children / sat down / quickly.

A great many of the verbs plus particles are idioms in English and may cause
problems for those learning the language. Also we add new ones to the language,
whether for formal use or as slang (e.g., *freak out*).

Semantics

In analyzing a language sample, the occurrences of the syntactic rule for a Pattern 1 sentence and the NP and VP rules could be indicated. A syntactic description does not, however, tell us the meanings and relationships that the child is capable of expressing. Thus, we must give a description of the semantic relationships expressed in the child's utterances when analyzing the language sample. In Pattern 1 sentences we have a number of possible relationships that can be expressed.

Mover—action:	Jason ran.
Patient—action:	The trees swayed.
Experiencer—process:	Our turtle died.
Instrument—action:	This knife cuts.
Patient—process:	The sugar dissolved.
Entity—stative:	Cathy remained (at the party).

Mover designates a person or animate creature that performs an action. The action affects the mover and does not have an effect on another person or thing. This means a mover acts under its own power and is not moved by some other force or agent. The syntactic form for movers would be as the subject of a verb that does not have an object. Thus movers would appear in a linear position before an intransitive verb in English. Semantically, movers occur with action verbs.

Patient, as used in the second sentence, denotes a person or object on whom an action is performed or who receives the effect of an action or a process. Some other examples of patients expressed syntactically in a linear position before the verb are *The engine* started, *The paint* oxidized, and *The cup* fell on the floor. In these three sentences and in the first set of examples, the nouns that are patients denoted something that is not moving under its own force, but rather for which some other agent is responsible. Possibly it is the wind that caused the trees to sway, a combination of agents that caused the paint to oxidize, and someone or something that caused the cup to drop.

The term **experiencer** designates a person or animate being that undergoes or experiences a change. Experiencers perform or are affected by processes and syntactically are expressed as subjects of process verbs. The process may be a mental process (learn, see, think) or a change in condition or bodily process (weaken, perspire, die).

The **instrument** is occasionally expressed syntactically as a subject of an action or process verb. In the fourth sentence, *knife* indicates the instrument that cuts, but it must be held and manipulated by some person.

Entity is the term used for a person or thing that is in a particular state or condition. Entity is used as the subject of a stative verb.

Verbs are classified in general into three types: **action, process**, and **stative**. Action verbs denote movements or activities that can be seen or heard. This does not mean, however, that because we can see someone doing something that the person is performing an action. A person who is studying can be observed, but what the person is doing—reading, making judgments, committing facts to memory, or whatever—is a process that cannot be seen. Processes refer to other activities that occur internally such as seeing and hearing or to changes in condition of persons or things that would be experiencers or patients. Again, one can observe an icicle melting, but as it is undergoing a change in condition, *melt* denotes a process, not an action. Stative verbs denote that persons or things are in a particular state or condition. Verbs that occur in sentence patterns other than Patterns 1 and 2 are stative verbs the majority of the time. However, verbs such as *stay* and *remain*, which may be stative verbs, are commonly intransitive.

One cannot always designate particular verbs as being of one type only because the meaning of the verb may vary. If a boy sits at a window all day, he is in a particular state; however, if he sits down quickly, he performs an action. The meaning of the verb in relationship to the nouns, adverbials, and adjectives with which it occurs may be action in one instance, and process or stative in other instances.

According to Kretschmer and Kretschmer (1978) intermediate types of verbs are common. Examples of some intermediate types are stative-process and action-process. Actions and processes may be designated also as affective or causative, and statives as ambient, static, or dynamic. For the explanations of the semantic relationships in the text, however, the general types of verb (action, process, stative) will be used.

Examples of some action and process verbs that could be used to express the semantic relationships in a Pattern 1 syntactic form are in the following list.

Action	Process
talk	learn
eat	think
kick	study
climb	digest
cry	faint
sing	perspire
play	rust

The addition of adverbial elements in sentences adds to the case relationships that can be expressed. The adverbial cases include time, location, manner, reason, and instrument. Other cases that pertain to time are specified as duration and frequency, as shown in the following sentences. In these sentences, the case relationship expressed by the first noun phrase and the verb is that of a mover performing an action. The adverbials are varied to show different adverbial cases.

Mover	Action	Adverbial	Case
The boys	walked	home.	Location
The boys	walked	slowly.	Manner
The boys	walked	this morning.	Time
The boys	walked	every morning.	Frequency
The boys	walked	all night.	Duration
The boys	walked	for exercise.	Reason
The boys	walked	with crutches.	Instrument

Note that with the semantic cases of adverbials much of the same terminology is used as in the syntactic description. The difference is in the specification of **instrument**. Although syntactically *with crutches* is an adverbial of manner, *crutches* refers to an instrument and is thus designated.

Turn to Exercise 8 for practice in analyzing and using Pattern 1 sentences.

Unit 2: Pattern 2 Sentences

Objectives

- Write the formula for a Pattern 2 sentence
- Divide Pattern 2 sentences into their constituents
- State the term used for the NP^2 in traditional grammar
- State the two features that nouns must have to be used as indirect objects
- List two prepositions that introduce phrases containing indirect objects
- Identify and label NPs in Pattern 2 sentences as the subject, the direct object, or the indirect object, differentiating indirect objects from adverbials of place or reason
- Divide Pattern 1 and 2 sentences into their constituents
- Divide verb phrases into their constituents differentiating particles from prepositions
- Identify the semantic relationships of given Pattern 2 sentences

The second of the sentence patterns is the most frequently used of the five patterns. This pattern expresses the subject-verb-object syntactic relationship, which linguists have found is important in most languages. In approximately 400 samples of spontaneous language of young children collected by graduate students at Gallaudet University over an eight-year period, it was found that roughly 50 percent of the children's utterances, both simple and complex sentences, were of this pattern. The other four patterns together made up the remaining 50 percent. A broad range of semantic relationships can be expressed in Pattern 2 sentences, which makes this pattern particularly functional for purposes of communication.

Syntax

The formula for a Pattern 2 sentence is $NP^1 + V + NP^2 + (Adv)$. The subject, the first NP, is marked with ^{1}. The NP^2 indicates the **direct object,** an NP with a different referent from that of the NP^1. In traditional grammar, the pattern could be designated as subject + verb + direct object. As in Pattern 1 sentences, the adverbials are optional.

The majority of verbs in this pattern have the feature [+transitive]. Verbs carrying this feature are followed by noun phrases and may be changed to passive voice (e.g., *A cat scratched the dog* could be changed to *The dog was scratched by a cat.* A number of verbs, however, that can be used in this pattern and that do take direct objects (NP s) are not transitive because they may not be changed to the passive. Examples are *have, cost,* and *weigh—The dress cost twenty dollars* cannot be changed to * *Twenty dollars was cost by the dress.* The subscript *t* (denoting transitive) has not been used in the pattern in this unit or in the following chapters on the basic patterns; however, you will be dealing only with transitive verbs in Pattern 2 sentences.

The following examples of Pattern 2 sentences have the constituents marked off and labeled.

$$NP^1 \qquad V \qquad NP^2 \qquad Adv$$
The team / played / football / all afternoon.
$$NP^1 \qquad V \qquad NP^2 \qquad Adv$$
John / cleaned / the house / thoroughly.
$$NP^1 \qquad V \qquad NP^2 \qquad Adv$$
The trees / lost / their leaves / early.
$$NP^1 \qquad V \qquad NP^2 \qquad Adv$$
The teacher / read / a story / to the children.
$$NP^1 \qquad V \qquad NP^2 \qquad Adv$$
Jan / brought / some bones / for the dog.

In all of the sentences, the NP^2 is the direct object. In the last two sentences, the phrase that is labeled an adverbial contains a human or animate NP that is a recipient.

These noun phrases are called **indirect objects**. A small group of transitive verbs may have both direct and indirect objects. These include, but are not limited to,

ask	give	read	teach
bring	make	sell	tell
buy	offer	send	throw
find	pay	show	toss

In a basic Pattern 2, the linear positions are subject → verb → direct object → indirect object. The indirect object, syntactically, is the NP in a prepositional phrase introduced by *to* or *for*. A test that one can apply to determine if an NP is an indirect object is to change the sentence by deleting the preposition and preposing the indirect object so that it immediately follows the verb and comes before the direct object (NP^2).

The teacher read a story to *the children*. Jan brought some bones for *the dog*.

The teacher read *the children* a story. Jan brought *the dog* some bones.

The second sentence in each pair contains an indirect object transformation, or indirect object preposing. This will be discussed in chapter 8.

Sentences in which a human or animate noun that is a beneficiary follows *for* may be confusing if one does not know all the verbs taking both direct and indirect objects. In this case, as shown in the following sentences, the beneficiary noun cannot be preposed to a position before the direct object and, thus, is not an indirect object.

Ken washed the car for *Dad*.

*Ken washed *Dad* the car.

A large group of verbs that may be used in Pattern 2 sentences have particles as complements. You will find in the literature that verbs such as these are called **double verbs**, or two-word verbs. Particles were introduced in the discussion of Pattern 1 sentences, where they were used to complete intransitive verbs. Verbs with particles are found much more often as transitive verbs in Pattern 2 sentences. Examples of instances of verbs plus particles in this pattern are given below.

NP^1	V	NP^2	NP^1	V	NP^2
Doris /	*ran off* /	thirty copies.	The teacher /	*turned on* /	the lights.
The boys /	*figured out* /	the puzzle.	Our neighbor /	*brought over* /	some cookies.
Jane /	*took off* /	her hearing aid.	The wind /	*blew away* /	our newspaper.
Mother /	*warmed up* /	the chicken.	Dad /	*turned down* /	the offer.
			The students /	*handed in* /	their papers.

The particles *off, out, up, on, over, away, down,* and *in* may be combined with verbs other than those used in the sentences, so that a list of all possible double verbs would be relatively extensive.

The words used as particles are also used as prepositions. In determining the syntactic pattern of sentences, one must take into consideration the meaning relationships rather than the structure alone. Consider the following paired sentences:

	NP^1	V	NP^2
Pattern 2	Jim / turned off / the lights.		

	NP	V_i	Adv
Pattern 1	Jim / turned / off the main highway.		

	NP^1	V	NP^2
Pattern 2	The teachers / talked over / their problems.		

	NP	V_i	Adv
Pattern 1	The teachers / talked / over our heads.		

The VP in the first sentence in each pair has a verb plus particle (an action verb) plus an NP^2 which is the patient, the receiver of the action. The VP in the second sentence in each pair consists of a verb plus adverbial, with a locative meaning in *off the main highway,* and indicating manner in *over our heads.*

Semantics

Some of the possible semantic relationships of nouns and verbs that may be expressed syntactically in Pattern 2 sentences are listed below.

Agent—action—patient:	That man kicked the horse.
Agent—action—complement:	Allison sang a song.
Agent—action—patient—beneficiary (recipient):	The teller handed the money to the thief.
Experiencer—process—patient:	Larry loves dogs.
Experiencer—process—complement:	The boys outlined a plan.
Instrument—action—patient:	That knife cuts paper.
Agent—process—complement:	A virus causes measles.
Beneficiary—action—patient:	My boss received an award.
Possessor—process—patient:	Lou has a parrot.
Entity—stative—part:	Owls have wings.

An **agent,** as in the first three sentences, is the performer of an action that affects another being. Agents are usually animate (*woman, dog*), but may be inanimate if they have their own motivating force (*wind*). When agents appear in the surface structure, they are grammatically expressed as subjects of verbs, as are experiencers.

A **patient** is the receiver of the effect of an action or process. Patients are expressed as direct objects of verbs in sentences, as are the receivers of the action or process in five of the previous sentences.

Instrument denotes something that has a part in bringing about an action or process, but it is not the instigator. In a sentence such as *Tom cut the paper with his knife*, the agent that performs the action uses a knife as the instrument. In the sentence *That knife cuts paper*, it must be inferred that there is an agent performing the action since the knife has no force of its own and must be used by an agent.

A **complement** comes into being as the result of an action or process—sing a *song*, make a *pie*, paint a *portrait*. Complements usually denote things that are not animate or human and, in some instances, are not tangible. Complements, however, do not receive the effect of an action. Note the contrasts in the pairs of phrases using the same nouns.

build a *bookcase*:	action—complement
dust the *bookcase*:	action—patient
play *football*:	action—complement
play with the *football*:	action—patient
tear the *dress*:	action—patient
see the *dress*:	process—complement

In the first pair, the *bookcase* comes into existence in the first phrase. In the second pair, *football* denotes a game that comes into existence and is not a tangible thing. This same semantic relationship is also the case when one says something such as *play Monopoly* or *do some things*. Examples of complements with process verbs are have *a party*, hear *a song*, see *a movie*, learn *a lesson*.

Beneficiary may be defined as someone or something animate that profits or benefits from an action or process. One syntactic means of denoting the beneficiary is as the indirect object in a Pattern 2 sentence or in a sentence with a preposed indirect object. However, in a sentence such as *Jim washed the dishes for Mother*, *Mother*, although not an indirect object (**Jim washed Mother the dishes*), would be the beneficiary of the action. Verbs such as *receive*, *accept*, and *get* are used with beneficiaries. The term **recipient** is used by some linguists in place of beneficiary to designate one that gets the benefit of an action.

Possessor denotes someone or something that owns or possesses something. Genitive noun or determiner elaborations in NPs syntactically designate possessors. As was mentioned in chapter 1 on nouns, *Jim's dog* or *his (Jim's) dog* conveys the underlying meaning that *Jim has a dog*. *Jim* is in the role of possessor in any of these three syntactic forms since the meaning conveyed by the three is the same. In the sentence *Lou has a parrot*, *have* is a process verb and *parrot* is the patient. *Lou* came into possession of the parrot by some means or other. Note the difference in the meaning of *have* in this sentence and in *Owls have wings*, where *have* is a stative verb.

All the above noun cases are cited by Kretschmer and Kretschmer (1978), who compiled a list of noun cases that have been identified in language development research. These authors have added the noun case, **part**, which denotes things that are parts of entities. In *Owls have wings, wings* designates **parts** of the owl rather than something owned or possessed by the owl. The addition of this semantic role more accurately specifies the semantic relationship of the verb and noun when the verb is *have*. As stated earlier, the case, **entity**, designates persons or things that are in a state of being and occur with stative verbs. The **vocative** case is used for the person called on, or named, by a speaker—*Mary, the dog should go out.*

The semantic relationships expressed in Pattern 2 sentences are expanded with the addition of any of the adverbial cases mentioned previously.

One can readily see the importance of giving a semantic description of a child's language. A syntactic description can specify the patterns of simple sentences, but this would merely describe a large number of sentences as $NP^1 + V + NP^2$, or subject + verb + object. A child may be using a number of three-word $N + V + N$ utterances, but these may carry a variety of different meanings although they have the same syntactic form. A semantic description, then, gives us much more information about the child's language competence because it specifies the different meanings that can be expressed in a single syntactic form.

Turn to Exercise 9 for practice in analyzing and using Pattern 2 sentences.

CHAPTER 5
Sentence Patterns 3, 4, and 5

The last three of the five basic sentence patterns contain linking verbs that are stative. The most often used of the linking verbs is the copula *be*. Sentences of these patterns may be used to express feelings about ourselves or others and to designate states, conditions, or equivalents of persons or things.

Unit 1: Pattern 3 Sentences

Objectives
- Write the formula for a Pattern 3 sentence
- Identify the tense of given VPs with *be*
- Differentiate finite and nonfinite forms of *be* in given sentences
- Write verb phrases containing the *be* verb for given phrase structure rules
- Divide Pattern 1, 2, and 3 sentences into their constituents
- Differentiate Pattern 1, 2, and 3 sentences having the same verb
- Identify the semantic relationships in given Pattern 3 sentences

Syntax
The adjective is the central word in a Pattern 3 sentence, the formula for which is $NP + V_L + Adj + (Adv)$. The verb, designated as *L*, is a **linking verb**; it links an attribute (the adjective) to the NP, the subject of the sentence. Blackwell, Engen, Fischgrund, and Zarcadoolas (1978) commented that the teachers at the Rhode Island School for the Deaf found this to be the most difficult of the patterns for hearing-impaired children. The authors stated that both the syntactic and the semantic features of the pattern could be responsible for its difficulty.

The copula *be* is the most frequently used of the verbs in Pattern 3. This verb develops relatively late in both normal and language-delayed children. Possible reasons are that the verb contributes no meaning to the sentence; it is usually unstressed in a sentence and often is in the contracted form (*John's, she's, that's*). In addition, the message can be communicated without the verb, as in *Bobby sick* or *I tired*.

There are eight forms of the copula *be*, making this the most irregular of the verbs in English.

Table 5
The Forms of *Be*

	Finite Forms	
Person	*Singular*	*Plural*
1st	(I) am	(we) are
2nd	(you) are	(you) are
3rd	(he, she, it) is	(they) are

Nonfinite Forms	
V-ø	*V-en*
be	been
t + modal + be	t + have + -en + be
(may, might be)	(have, has, had been)
	t + modal + have + -en + be
	(may, might have been)

The five finite forms of *be* are shown in Table 5. There are three nonfinite forms: *be, being,* and *been.* With the exception of *be* when used in an imperative (e.g., *be good*), the nonfinite forms are combined with an auxiliary or auxiliaries when *be* is the verb (*could be, may have been*). The parts of the *be* copula are the same forms as those of the *be* auxiliary used with other verbs.

The following sentences are examples of Pattern 3 sentences with the *be* verb.

    NP   V$_L$ Adj
    John / is / handsome.

         NP   V$_L$ Adj   Adv
    The chairman / was / nervous / this morning.

     NP   V$_L$ Adj   Adv
    Mary / has been / sick / for three weeks.

Other verbs that may serve as linking verbs in Pattern 3 are *taste, feel, smell, look, sound, turn, grow, seem, become, remain, stay, appear.* These linking verbs refer to states or to stative processes. Some of them have another meaning and thus may also occur in Patterns 1 and 2.

                              NP^1 V   NP^2
    Pattern 2 ⎫   Mother / tasted / the coffee.
              ⎬   NP   V$_L$ Adj
    Pattern 3 ⎭   The coffee / tasted / bitter.

Pattern 2 / Pattern 3

$$\text{NP}^1 \quad \text{V} \quad \text{NP}^2$$
Mother / felt / Tommy's forehead.

$$\text{NP} \quad \text{V}_\text{L} \quad \text{Adj}$$
His forehead / felt / warm.

Pattern 1 / Pattern 3

$$\text{NP} \quad \text{V}_\text{i} \quad \text{Adv} \quad \text{Adv}$$
The teachers / remained / at school / until 4:00 p.m.

$$\text{NP} \quad \text{V}_\text{L} \quad \text{Adj} \quad \text{Adv}$$
The teachers / remained / upset / about the decision.

Pattern 1 / Pattern 3

$$\text{NP} \quad \text{V}_\text{i} \quad \text{Adv}$$
A shadow / appeared / at the window.

$$\text{NP} \quad \text{V}_\text{L} \quad \text{Adj} \quad \text{Adv}$$
The children / appeared / upset / this morning.

The first two sets of sentences illustrate instances of the use of *taste* and *feel* as either an action or a stative verb. Because of the relationships expressed, the syntactic form is different. In the first sentence in each set, the verb is an action verb and is followed by an NP^2, the direct object. In the second sentence, the verb is a linking verb and is followed by an adjective.

The second two sets of sentences also illustrate the use of the same verb in different syntactic form because of a difference in the relationships expressed. Syntactically, the differentiation of the patterns is not difficult because of the difference in the constituents following the verb. In Pattern 3 basic sentences, the linking verb is always followed immediately by an adjective, which is a sentence constituent.

Competence in the use of Pattern 3 sentences depends upon the acquisition of a vocabulary of adjectives and knowledge of the different linking verbs that may be used. Undue emphasis in structured language lessons on the verb *be* to the exclusion of the other linking verbs, as is the case in some available curriculums, could tend to limit a child's competence with this pattern.

Expansion with optional adverbials is possible in Pattern 3 sentences, as in the other patterns presented. Adverbials of manner, however, may not occur with the verbs *be*, *remain*, and *seem*. Adverbials of time, place, duration, and frequency may be used with all of the linking verbs.

Semantics

The general semantic relationship that is expressed in Pattern 3 sentences is Entity—stative—attribute. The attribute may denote color, age, size, shape, quality, or condition. As previously mentioned, stative verbs indicate that objects are in a particular state or condition. The object, which may be human, animate, or inanimate, in the particular state or condition is the **entity**.

The following sentences are used to illustrate some of the specific semantic relationships of Entity—stative—attribute that may be expressed in Pattern 3 sentences.

Entity—stative—size:	The table is large.
Entity—stative—age:	Mr. Smith is young.
Entity—stative—condition:	The coffee will be bitter.
Entity—stative—shape:	All the pillows should be round.
Entity—stative—quality:	The boards are rough.
Entity—stative—color:	The water turned blue.
Entity—stative—condition:	The supervisor became mean.
Entity—stative—age:	Mother looks young.

Note that quality refers to an inherent characteristic (*pretty* girl), and condition refers to a state that is not inherent and/or subject to change. In giving the semantic relationships expressed in various sentences, we shall always specify the attributes.

In Chapter 2, it was indicated that adjectives add a second proposition to sentences when they are modifiers of nouns. In the sentence *The big cat is mean*, the noun phrase is elaborated with an adjective modifier. This sentence contains the following propositions and semantic relationships:

the cat is mean:	Entity—stative—condition
the cat is big:	Entity—stative—size

Turn to Exercise 10 for practice in analyzing Pattern 3 sentences.

Unit 2: Pattern 4 Sentences

Objectives
- Write the formula for a Pattern 4 sentence
- Divide Pattern 4 sentences into their constituents
- Identify and label NPs in Pattern 2 and Pattern 4 sentences that are direct objects, indirect objects, and predicate nominatives
- Identify sentences as Pattern 1, 2, 3, and 4 and divide them into their constituents
- Identify semantic relationships in Pattern 4 sentences

Syntax
The formula for Pattern 4 sentences is $NP^1 + V_L + NP^1 + (Adv)$. The NP following the linking verb is marked with a ^{1} because it is an equivalent of the NP that is the subject and because it refers to the same person or thing. In traditional grammar the noun in the

predicate is called a **predicate nominative**. You will find this term or **predicate noun** in some of the older texts dealing with the teaching of language.

The verb most frequently used in the pattern is the copula verb *be*. Other linking verbs, which one rarely finds used by young children, are *become, remain, stay,* and *seem*. There are some additional linking verbs, however, that are useful, especially in fairy tales. These verbs have particle complements and describe a changing state (e.g., *turn into, turn to, change to, change into*).

Examples of Pattern 4 sentences are

$\quad$ NP^1 $\quad$ V$_L$ $\quad$ NP^1
Mary / is / a nurse.
$\qquad$ NP$_1$ $\qquad\qquad$ V$_L$ $\qquad\qquad$ NP^1
The prowler / might have been / a thief.
$\qquad$ NP^1 $\qquad\qquad$ V$_L$ $\qquad$ NP^1
The pumpkin / turned into / a chariot.
$\quad$ NP^1 $\quad$ V$_L$ $\qquad$ NP^1 $\qquad$ Adv
John / became / a fire fighter / last year.

Semantics

The most often used verb in Pattern 4 sentences is *be*, which is stative. Other stative verbs are *seem, remain,* and *appear*. The verb *become* might be more accurately termed a stative-process or stative-dynamic verb as might the other verbs that have similar meanings—*turn to, change into,* etc.

As discussed previously, the noun that has the syntactic role of subject is termed **entity**, and the verb is **stative**. The noun that has the syntactic role of predicate noun is termed **equivalent**. The nouns used as entity and equivalent have some basic equivalence. In the sentences *Mary is a nurse* and *John became a fire fighter,* John and Mary basically remain the same people although they have acquired new knowledge and skills. One could designate the verb *become* as a stative-process and *nurse* as a complement. In that case, however, *Mary* would be more appropriately called an experiencer. Although we shall not use these designations, it is important to be aware of the difference in verbs such as *be, remain,* and *stay* as opposed to *become, change into,* or *turn to*.

The following sentences illustrate the relationships expressed in Pattern 4 sentences.

Entity—stative—equivalent: $\quad$ Ms. Allen should have been a pilot.

$\qquad\qquad\qquad\qquad\qquad\qquad$ Tom will become a dentist.

$\qquad\qquad\qquad\qquad\qquad\qquad$ The apple turned to gold.

$\qquad\qquad\qquad\qquad\qquad\qquad$ The girls stayed friends.

$\qquad\qquad\qquad\qquad\qquad\qquad$ Mrs. Beck remained a teacher.

In a previous chapter, mention was made of the use of nouns to elaborate noun phrases and, consequently, to add another proposition to the sentence. It was indicated that such nouns are called **noun adjuncts** rather than adjectives.

When we find nouns used as elaborations in noun phrases, the propositions and the semantic relationships expressed will be as follows:

The paper hat became a crown.

      the hat became a crown: Entity—stative—equivalent:
      the hat is paper: Entity—stative—equivalent

Muriel has a doll carriage.

      Muriel has a carriage: Possessor—process—patient
      the carriage is for a doll: Entity—stative—reason

Tim likes toy soldiers.

      Tim likes soldiers: Experiencer—process—patient
      the soldiers are toys: Entity—stative—equivalent

Turn to Exercise 11 for practice in analyzing Pattern 4 sentences.

Unit 3: Pattern 5 Sentences

Objectives

- Write the formula for a Pattern 5 sentence
- Divide Pattern 5 sentences into their constituents
- Identify sentences as Pattern 1, 2, 3, 4, or 5 and divide them into their constituents
- Identify semantic relationships in Pattern 5 sentences
- Identify semantic relationships in Pattern 1, 2, 3, 4, or 5 sentences

Syntax

The last of the five basic patterns consists of an NP, the verb *be*, and an obligatory adverbial. A second adverbial is optional. The formula for a Pattern 5 sentence is $NP + V_{be} + Adv + (Adv)$. The most commonly used of the obligatory adverbials are adverbials of place and time. Examples of sentences of this pattern are

       NP V_{be} Adv
The coach / must be / in the gym.

       NP V_{be} Adv
The game / was / on Tuesday.

         NP V_{be} Adv   Adv
The tournament / will be / in Chicago / this year.

Semantics

The semantic relationships in the pattern can be illustrated as follows:

Entity—stative—location:	The girls are outside.
Entity—stative—time:	The meeting is in the morning.
Entity—stative—reason:	The award was for sportsmanship.
Entity—stative—beneficiary:	The trophy is for the team.

This unit concludes the presentation of the five basic sentence patterns. The patterns are representative of simple active declarative positive sentences in the English language. Some of the more recent curriculums, developed for hearing-impaired children or for other children displaying difficulties in the acquisition of language, stress the development of a simple sentence grammar as the basis for future language development. Gradually, the emphasis has been shifting to the development of semantic competence, i.e., the ability to comprehend and express the meanings that dictate the syntactic structures to be used. The chapters up to this point have presented syntactic and introductory semantic information on basic sentences in the language and on the constituents of sentences. Later chapters will deal with the more complex aspects of the language.

Turn to Exercise 12 for practice in analyzing Pattern 5 sentences.

CHAPTER 6

Language Analysis I and Review

Objectives

- Give a syntactic description of basic sentences of the five different patterns, identifying the constituents of each sentence
- Identify the following noun phrase modulations and elaborations in sentences:
  - a. Regular plurals
  - b. Irregular plurals
  - c. Determiner types
  - d. Possessive determiners, including possessive nouns
  - e. Noun adjunct modifiers
  - f. Adjective modifiers
- Identify the following verb phrase modulations in basic sentences:
  - a. Regular and irregular past
  - b. Regular and irregular 3rd person
  - c. Auxiliary type (be, have, modal)
  - d. Uncontracted copula
  - e. Verb aspect (progressive or perfect)
  - f. Particles
  - g. Prepositions
- Determine the frequency of occurrence of the basic sentence types, noun and verb phrase modulations, and NP elaborations in a given sample
- Give a semantic description of basic sentences in a sample
- Give a semantic description of sentences containing more than a single proposition because of embedded noun adjuncts, possessives, or adjectives
- Determine the frequency of occurrence of the following semantic cases in a given sample:
  - a. Noun cases
  - b. Verb cases
  - c. Modifier cases
  - d. Adverbial cases

Review: Units 1-5

- Identify listed words as nouns, adjectives, adverbs, or prepositions
- Identify the regular inflectional morphemes of English
- Identify the semantic features of nouns in given sentences
- Identify, by type, determiners in given noun phrases
- Identify specific modal, *be*, and *have* auxiliaries and/or list designated auxiliaries
- Write verb phrases for given phrase structure rules
- Identify the types of verbs in verb phrases as intransitive, transitive, or linking
- Identify direct objects, indirect objects, and predicate nominatives in sentences
- Analyze and identify the pattern of basic sentences
- Complete a syntactic description of basic sentences
- Write descriptions of the semantic relationships expressed in given sentences

The first five chapters concentrated on constituents in sentences and basic sentences in the language. Basic sentences are sentences without the complexities of negatives, questions, imperatives, personal or other pronouns, contractions, shifted elements, etc., and without clauses that would serve to conjoin or embed one sentence into another. This means that basic sentences are simple active declarative positive sentences. It also means that they are single proposition sentences, conveying one unit of information.

The pattern of normal language development is such that children do not learn all the basic phrase structure rules for noun phrases, verb phrases, or the basic sentences prior to using more complex language. They do, however, learn the semantic relationships that are found in the basic sentences, as well as the syntax for expressing such meanings in communication with others.

The learning of the complexities in the language begins relatively early and it continues throughout the elementary-school years. Even after this, the individual continues to develop language competence so as to communicate more effectively with others.

A child who is delayed in language development or who experiences difficulty with language will need a special language program. First, however, the level of development and the specific difficulties the individual is experiencing must be determined. Therefore, teachers and clinicians who work with language-delayed children and youth must be able to assess language and develop individualized programs to further language development.

One of the most effective ways to assess language is to obtain a language sample and then analyze it syntactically, semantically, and pragmatically.

A **syntactic analysis**, or description of the language, will specify information on the noun phrases, the verb phrases, and the kinds of sentences that the individual uses. It will specify the complexity of the noun or verb phrase as to the determiners or auxiliaries used, as well as the regular and irregular inflections. Additional complexities, including the transformations used, will also be specified.

A **semantic analysis** will describe the relationships expressed in sentences, specifying occurrences of the varying noun, verb, modifier, and adverbial cases.

A **pragmatic analysis**, or analysis of communicative competence, will describe the various functions for which language is used (requesting, commanding, getting or giving information, etc.) as well as how the individual performs in conversation (initiating, pursuing, or terminating it), including the devices used in conversation.

Following is an example of some sentences that could be found in a language sample from a young child. This is a purely hypothetical sample; it is not representative of all of the kinds of utterances that would be found in a sample of language when a child is at a simple sentence level. The sample was contrived so as to present only instances of syntactic and semantic relationships that have been presented thus far in the text. This sample would not be large enough for evaluative purposes. The syntactic description is presented first. At this point we shall be looking for the following:

1. Syntactic patterns of sentences
2. Verb phrase modulations
   a. regular past (jumped)
   b. irregular past (ran)
   c. progressive (walking)
   d. regular third person (jumps)
   e. irregular third person (has)
   f. modal auxiliary (can)
   g. *be* auxiliary
   h. *have* auxiliary
   i. perfect aspect (-*en* form)
   j. uncontracted copula *be* (is)
   k. preposition (on)
   l. particle (put *on*)

3. noun phrase modulations
   a. regular plural (cups, glasses)
   b. irregular plural (men, geese)
   c. articles
   d. other determiners
4. noun phrase elaborations
   a. possessive noun modifier (*Bobby's* hat)
   b. possessive determiner (*his* hat)
   c. noun adjunct modifier (*paper* hat)
   d. adjective modifier (*big* hat)

The noun and verb phrase modulations listed above are the syntactic and morphological additions to what constitutes the major underlying proposition of an utterance. The four elaborations each add a second proposition. In a sentence such as *Two big dogs were playing in the street*, the underlying major proposition is *play dog street*, or to keep it parallel with the form used in the text, *dog play street*. The second proposition is *dog (be) big*. In determining the noun phrase modulations, use the following procedure. After determining the major proposition and the elaborations, put a check over each modulation.

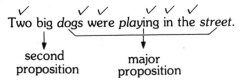

Thus the NP modulations are cardinal, regular plural, and definite article; the VP modulations are *be* aux, progressive (*-ing*), and preposition; the elaboration is an adjective modifier in a noun phrase.

Language Sample
Subject: Tina

1. The kitty likes milk.
2. My daddy is working now.
3. Bob has washed Daddy's car.
4. The big lamp fell on the floor.
5. Mommy / reads / in bed.
6. Two boys can swim fast.
7. That dog is Fido.
8. Fido is shaggy.
9. Fido chewed up Mommy's straw hat.
10. Daddy loves the kitty.
11. Daddy brought some toys for the kitty.
12. The kitty was in the shed.

Syntactic Description

Sentence	*Pattern*
1. The kitty / likes / milk.	$NP^1 + V + NP^2$
VP modulation: regular third person	
NP modulation: +def article, Ø art (*milk*)	
2. My daddy / is working / now.	$NP + V_i + Adv$
VP modulation: progressive	
be auxiliary	
NP elaboration: possessive (gen) det (*my*)	

3. Bob / has washed / Daddy's car. $NP^1 + V + NP^2$
   VP modulation: *have* aux, perfect aspect
   NP modulation: Ø art (2)
   NP elaboration: possessive noun modifier

4. The big lamp / fell / on the floor. $NP + V_i + Adv$
   VP modulation: irregular past
                     preposition (*on*)
   NP modulation: +def article (2)
   NP elaboration: adjective modifier

5. Mommy / reads / in bed. $NP + V_i + Adv$
   VP modulation: regular third person
                     preposition (*in*)
   NP modulation: Ø art (2)

6. Two boys / can swim / fast. $NP + V_i + Adv$
   VP modulation: modal auxiliary
   NP modulation: cardinal
                     regular plural

7. That dog / is / Fido. $NP^1 + V_L + NP^1$
   VP modulation: uncontracted copula
   NP modulation: dem
                     Ø art

8. Fido / is / shaggy. $NP + V_L + Adj$
   VP modulation: uncontracted copula
   NP modulation: Ø art

9. Fido / chewed up / Mommy's straw hat. $NP^1 + V + NP^2$
   VP modulation: regular past
                     particle (*up*)
   NP modulation: Ø art (2)
   NP elaboration: possessive noun
                     noun adjunct

10. Daddy / loves / the kitty. $NP^1 + V + NP^2$
    VP modulation: regular third person
    NP modulation: Ø art
                      +def art

11. Daddy / brought / some toys / for the kitty. $NP^1 + V + NP^2 + Adv$
    VP modulation: irregular past
                      preposition (*for*)
    NP modulation: Ø art, reg plural
                      -def art (*some*)
                      +def art (*the*)

12. The kitty / was / in the shed. $NP + V_{be} + Adv$
   VP modulation: uncontracted copula
                     preposition (*in*)
   NP modulation: +def art (2)

Syntactic Summary

Sentences	Frequency of Occurrence	Comments
Pattern 1	4	adverbials (4)
Pattern 2	5	adverbial (1)
Pattern 3	1	
Pattern 4	1	
Pattern 5	1	

Verb Phrase Modulations		
regular past	2	
irregular past	2	
progressive	1	
perfect aspect	1	
regular third person	3	
irregular third person	0	
modal auxiliary	1	can
be auxiliary	1	is (*is working*)
have auxiliary	1	has
uncontracted copula	3	is, was
prepositions	4	in, on, for
particles	1	

Noun Phrase Modulations		
articles	19	the, Ø (11), some
other determiners	2	that, two
regular plural	2	

Noun Phrase Elaborations		
possessive noun	2	
possessive (gen) determiner	1	
noun adjunct	1	
adjective	1	

Semantic Description

Sentence	Description
Sentence	*Description*
1. The kitty likes milk.	Experiencer—process—patient
2. My daddy is working now.	
Daddy is working now	Mover—action—time
Tina has a Daddy	Possessor—process—patient
3. Bob washed Daddy's car.	
Bob washed a car	Agent—action—patient
Daddy has a car	Possessor—process—patient
4. The big lamp fell on the floor.	
the lamp fell on the floor	Patient—action—location
the lamp is big	Entity—stative—size
5. Mommy reads in bed.	Experiencer—process—location
6. Two boys can swim fast.	Mover—action—manner
7. That dog is Fido.	Entity—stative—equivalent
8. Fido is shaggy.	Entity—stative—condition
9. Fido chewed up Mommy's straw hat.	
Fido chewed up a hat	Agent—action—patient
Mommy has a hat	Possessor—process—patient
the hat is straw	Entity—stative—equivalent
10. Daddy loves the kitty.	Experiencer—process—patient
11. Daddy brought some toys for the kitty.	Agent—action—patient—beneficiary
12. The kitty was in the shed.	Entity—stative—location

Semantic Summary

Noun cases	Frequency of Occurrence
Mover	2
Agent	3
Patient	9
Experiencer	3
Possessor	3
Entity	5
Equivalent	2
Beneficiary	1
Verb cases	
Action	6
Process	6
Stative	5

| | Frequency of |
Modifier cases	Occurrence
Condition	1
Size	1
Adverbial cases	
Time	1
Location	3
Manner	1

The syntactic analysis is presented in full for each of the utterances so that the summary is clear. All that would be needed for a child's file would be the summary and a narrative report summarizing the syntactic and semantic descriptions. The summary lists the noun and verb phrase modulations the child used, the frequency (f) of occurrence of each, and a section for comments. The comments can indicate, for a child in the early developing stages, the specific determiners and the specific auxiliaries that occurred. In the sample, the null article was used appropriately in 11 noun phrases, before proper nouns, possessive noun modifiers, and plural nouns. The definite article occurred in seven noun phrases. There were two occurrences of auxiliaries with a verb (is, can) and the copula forms, is and was, were used. Pattern 2 sentences were the most frequently used, 5 out of 12. The intransitive verb pattern was the second most frequently used. Five of the 12 sentences were expanded with optional adverbials.

The semantic analysis gives the relationships in the sentences first and then the frequency of occurrence of the various noun, verb modifier, and adverbial cases. Had this been a real sample, we could say that the child had a good representation of the various noun cases and that she used all three major kinds of verb cases.

An additional analysis that could be done for a sample at this level, especially if this were a sample from a language-delayed child in the early developing stages, would be to note the features of the noun, verbs, etc., in the child's lexicon. In the sample, the nouns used are largely human or animate. Only one inanimate noun was used as a subject. A pragmatic analysis, an analysis of the child's use of language for communication, would be necessary in a real situation, and we would also note any restrictions and/or deviations in the syntactic or semantic aspects.

Turn to Language Analysis I for practice analyzing a language sample.

CHAPTER 7

Pronominalization

The units in this chapter deal with complexities in sentences, such as questions, imperatives, negatives, passives, and pronominalizations. In generating sentences with such complexities, rules are required in addition to those for the formulation of noun and verb phrases in the basic sentences.

Early syntactic theory held that kernel (basic) sentences were generated with phrase structure rules. The **kernel sentences** were grammatical strings of NP + VP, as presented in the basic sentence patterns. These kernel sentences represented what Noam Chomsky (1965) referred to as deep structures. Grammatical operations upon single kernel sentences that result in more complex constructions in the sentences were called single-base transformations. These operations, or transformations, could be performed by the following methods.

a. the rearrangement of words or constituents in sentences:

kernel sentence:　The baby is crying.
transformation:　Is the baby crying?

b. deletions:

kernel sentence:　You close the door.
transformation:　Close the door.

c. substitutions:

kernel sentence:　John came home.
transformation:　*He* came home.

d. additions:

kernel sentence:　The boys are coming.
transformation:　The boys are *not* coming.

e. or combinations of a, b, c, and d:

kernel sentence:　A girl hit John.
transformation:　John was hit by a girl.

The second sentence in each of these pairs would be a transformed sentence derived from the first one in the pair. The speaker was thought to first generate a kernel sentence and then to alter it with a transformational rule prior to uttering the sentence, which in its spoken form constituted the surface structure.

Current theory explains single transformations from deep structure (underlying meaning and relationships) to surface structure differently. It is thought that the speaker encodes the sentence in its entirety, that is, a fully formed complex sentence is encoded from nodes in deep structures that specify modality changes. Kernel sentences, according to Kretschmer and Kretschmer, could now be defined as "the various predicate-argument propositions underlying the sentence" (1978, p. 31). **Predicate**, used in this sense, refers to the state or action in a sentence, and **argument** refers to the noun or nouns involved in the action or state. A sentence used by a speaker may entail one or more propositions, or single bits of information.

The basic sentences presented in the preceding chapters were single proposition sentences, except in those instances where possessives, adjectives, or noun adjuncts were used as noun modifiers. The following chapters deal with complexities in sentences. These complexities require additional rules and conventions that one must learn in order to master the language. Also, in assessing the language of children, we must look at how they use these rules and conventions so as to more adequately evaluate their performance and chart their growth.

Unit 1: Personal Pronouns

Objectives
- Identify personal pronouns in sentences
- Specify the person, number, case, and gender of given personal pronouns
- Identify and distinguish between nominative, accusative, and dative pronouns in sentences
- Specify the appropriate personal pronouns when given the person, number, gender, and case
- Change noun phrases in sentences to personal pronouns
- Differentiate backward pronominalization from forward pronominalization in sentences

A more apt term for pronouns, defined in traditional grammar as words that take the place of nouns, might be **pronominals**, since pronouns represent full noun phrases, and, in some instances, sentences or ideas. Pronominalization, then, is a transformational operation that involves a substitution.

Pronouns are words such as *she, everyone, himself,* and *this,* which are used to streamline discourse. They refer to old or known information and are used to eliminate the necessity of repeating a noun phrase, a sentence, or even sentences, except for clarity. Speakers and writers use pronouns when they have already identified what or whom they are speaking or writing about.

Personal pronouns occur with high frequency both in oral communication and in writing. For appropriate use of the personal pronouns, the features of **person, number, gender,** and **case** must be observed. In addition, personal pronouns have the feature [+definite], which negates their use with the expletive *there* in the *there* transformation. The sentence *They are in the class* cannot be transformed to **There are they in the class.* The pronouns *he, she,* and *it* are masculine, feminine, and neuter, respectively. Table 6 shows the number and person of the personal pronouns.

Table 6
Personal Pronouns: Person and Number

Person	Number	
	[+Singular]	[−Singular]
First	I	we
Second	(you)	you
Third	he, she, it	they

The pronoun *I*, used to refer to oneself, is said to be **first person. Second person** (*you*) is used by a speaker to refer to the person(s) being spoken to, and **third person** designates the person(s) other than the speaker or listener. The pronoun *we* includes the speaker and at least one other person. Although *you* may refer to one person, and in a sense be singular, it carries the feature [−singular] and is used with plural verb forms.

> You (John) *play* the piano well.
> You *are* an expert.

Word order in English is used to designate subjects and objects. Nouns do not have different forms for the cases **nominative, accusative,** and **dative.** The word *boy* has the same form when it is used as the subject of a sentence (nominative case), the direct object of a verb or the object of a preposition (accusative case), or the indirect object (dative case). The genitive (possessive) case is denoted with the singular inflection *'s* (e.g., *boy's*).

The personal pronouns, however, have different forms for the various cases (see Table 7). The dative case (for the indirect object) is included with the accusative (for NP^2 or the object of a preposition), as the same forms are used for both cases.

Table 7
Case Forms of Personal Pronouns

| | | Case | |
| | | | |
Person	Nominative	Accusative Dative	Genitive
First	I, we	me, us	mine, ours
Second	you	you	yours
Third	he, she, it, they	him, her, it, them	his, hers, its, theirs

Examples of the different cases as they would appear in sentences are:

He is happy.	nominative
Jack saw *me (us, him)*.	accusative
Jane gave the book to *him (her, them)*.	dative
That book is *mine (yours, his)*.	genitive

The genitive forms denoting possession may appear as subject or object (NP^1 or NP^2). The nominative form is used for NP^1. In informal communication, the accusative is sometimes used as the NP^1 after the verb *be*—*It was me*—however, formally, the nominative form would be used—*It was I*.

Personal pronouns are difficult in that the features of number, gender, and case must be appropriate for the referent and for the role the referent plays in the sentence. In addition, pronouns often change referents in discourse. Note the changing referents for the personal pronouns in the following statements in which we can assume that one child is speaking to another.

> I was outside playing when Mother came home. *She* said, "Why didn't *you* walk the dog? That was all *I* asked *you* to do." *I* felt ashamed because *I* knew *she* was right.

The pronoun *I* in the first sentence refers to the speaker. *She* in the second sentence refers to the mother. Then in the second and third sentences, the roles change as the mother is the speaker using *I*, and the child is referred to as *you*. Unless children have good control of pronoun reference, they will have difficulty in following a communication like the sample, whether it is communicated orally or in writing.

The personal pronouns *it* and *they* may have noun referents that are [−animate]. The other personal pronouns usually have [+human] nouns as referents. Exceptions to this, outside of children's stories in which animals or inanimate objects take on human characteristics and talk, think, etc., would include the use of *he* and *she* to refer to a pet, a ship, a car, an airplane, etc. Many people always refer to their dogs, cats, birds, or other pets as *he* or *she*. A ship to its officers and crew is usually *she*, and cars may be referred to by their owners as *she*.

The neuter pronoun, *it*, poses special problems because the referent is not always clear. Note the differences in the use of *it* in the following sentences:

Dad bought *a new car*, but he doesn't like *it*.
It's snowing (raining, very warm).
It's late, so we should leave.

The referent is clear in the first sentence, but in the other sentences there is really no referent for *it*. Streng (1972) states that *it* acts as a place holder in some sentences and is used so that another part of the sentence may be emphasized.

The genitive determiners, some of which have the same forms as the personal pronouns, involve the same kinds of rules as to gender, number, person, and reference as do the personal pronouns. Genitive determiners must be followed by a noun; they cannot be used alone as a noun phrase.

Genitive Determiner	*Pronoun*
My dress is blue.	Mine is blue.
Your turtle goes too fast.	Yours goes fast.
I saw her car.	I saw her.

The last set of sentences contains a genitive determiner in one sentence and a genitive pronoun in the other, both the same form (*her*). This is an important difference. In the noun phrase *her car*, *her* adds the meaning of possession, so there are two propositions in the sentence: *I saw a car* and *she has a car*. In the second sentence, which contains a single proposition, *her* is a pronoun replacement for a noun phrase.

Russell, Quigley, and Power (1976) reported that the patterns of difficulty of the personal pronouns and genitive determiners were similar for hearing and hearing-impaired children. The nominative and accusative forms were easier than the genitive determiners and the genitive pronouns, and singular pronouns were easier than plural. The order of difficulty for person was first, second, and third for hearing children between 8 and 10 years, and first, third, and second for deaf children.

Pronominalization occurs both across sentences and within sentences. Across sentences, the pronominalization is in a forward direction with the referent coming before the pronoun—***Jack*** ran home, ***He*** was hungry.

Within sentences, forward or backward pronominalization may occur.

forward: When *Dad* was a boy, *he* lived in Austria.
backward: When *he* was a boy, *Dad* lived in Austria.

There are, however, more restrictions on the use of backward than forward pronominalization.

Dad lived in Austria when *he* was a boy.
*He (Dad) lived in Austria when *Dad* was a boy.

The second sentence is ungrammatical when *he* refers to *Dad*. If, however, the *he* refers to a person other than *Dad*, possibly *Grandfather*, the sentence will be grammatical.

As sentences become more complex, we can find instances when both forward and backward pronominalization are used.

After *he* chopped the *wood*, *Dad* had to stack *it* behind the shed.
he . . . wood, Dad . . . it

As can be seen, personal pronouns are inherently difficult because of the different forms for gender, number, and person, in addition to the syntactic difficulties associated with case and with referencing.

Turn to Exercise 13 for practice in identifying personal pronouns.

Unit 2: Reflexive Pronouns

Objectives
- Identify reflexive pronouns in sentences
- Specify the person, number, and gender of reflexive pronouns
- Specify the appropriate reflexive pronoun when given the person, number, and gender
- Identify sentences with reflexive pronouns as having reflexive pronoun, reflexive pronoun intensifier, or reflexive pronoun intensifier shift transformation

A second group of pronouns, the reflexives, carry some of the same features as the personal pronouns. In using **reflexive pronouns**, one must observe the features person, number, and gender in the third person singular. Note that case is not a relevant feature for reflexive pronouns because the form does not change according to use in the sentence as the object of a verb or preposition or as an intensifier. Table 8 indicates the features of the reflexive pronouns.

Table 8
Reflexive Pronouns

	Number	
Person	Singular	Plural
First	myself	ourselves
Second	yourself	yourselves
Third	herself - feminine	themselves
	himself - masculine	
	itself - neuter	

Russell, Quigley, and Power (1976) found (a) that the reflexives were more difficult for the hearing impaired than were the personal pronouns and genitive determiners and (b) that the pattern of difficulty was approximately the same as that found for hearing children. The hearing impaired were retarded in the acquisition of reflexives, as well as the other pronouns, but showed no consistent deviancies in pronoun use.

An error that is often found in children other than the hearing impaired is the use of *hisself* and *theirselves* for third person reflexives *himself* and *themselves*. This is a logical error as these two third-person forms are a combination of the accusative case pronouns *him* and *them* plus -self(ves). The other reflexives use the genitive determiner forms, *my-*, *your-*, *her-*, *it-*, and *our-*, as the first morphemes.

As with the reflexive pronouns, there are three third-person singular reflexive forms masculine, feminine, and neuter.

The referent of a reflexive pronoun is the subject of the sentence. A personal pronoun cannot be used in place of a reflexive when the pronoun referent in the sentence is the subject.

Jack hurt *himself*.　　　　　　(Tom)　Jack hurt *him*.

The arrow in the first sentence indicates that *himself* refers to *Jack*. In the second sentence the referent of *him* is someone other than *Jack*. The sentence would be ungrammatical if *him* referred to *Jack* because a reflexive pronoun is required to refer to the subject.

Reflexive pronouns may be used as objects of verbs or of prepositions, so that at times they serve as sentence or phrase constituents.

Direct Object:	The dog saw *itself* in the mirror.
Indirect Object:	Tom bought a suit for *himself*.
Object of Prep:	Jane worked by *herself*.

The reflexive pronouns are used in another way—to serve as **intensifiers**. For emphasis, the reflexive may occur immediately after its referent or at the end of the sentence.

Jane *herself* made that dress. (reflexive intensifier)
Jane made that dress *herself*. (reflexive intensifier movement)

In the first sentence, the reflexive is termed a **reflexive intensifier**. This indicates a different use of the pronoun than when it is used as the object of a verb or preposition. The sentence would be complete without the reflexive, which gives additional emphasis to its referent. The second sentence is said to contain a **reflexive intensifier movement**, as the reflexive intensifier is shifted away from its referent to the end of the sentence. In both the reflexive intensifier and the reflexive movement transformations, a word is added to an already complete sentence. The reflexive intensifier is a more advanced, as well as more formal use of the reflexive pronoun. A child who wanted to emphasize the idea that Jane made the dress herself would possibly use a sentence such as *Jane made the dress (all) by herself*.

The substitution of a reflexive pronoun for a noun (noun phrase) in itself is a transformation—**John hurt John* becomes *John hurt himself*.

The reflexive pronoun intensifier (the addition of a reflexive to an already complete sentence for emphasis) is also a transformation. The reflexive intensifier movement (shifting the added reflexive pronoun to a position away from its referent) adds another operation, and thus, is also specified as a different transformational rule.

Turn to Exercise 14 for practice in identifying reflexive pronouns.

Unit 3: Indefinite and Demonstrative Pronouns

Objectives
- Identify indefinite pronouns in sentences
- Supply indefinite pronouns for noun phrases in sentences
- Identify demonstrative pronouns in sentences
- Identify each demonstrative pronoun as [+near] or [−near]

Indefinite Pronouns

A third group of pronouns is the **indefinite pronouns,** which are compounded words. The determiners *any, every, no,* and *some* are combined with *one, thing,* and *body,* resulting in twelve indefinite pronouns.

anyone	everyone	no one	someone
anything	everything	nothing	something
anybody	everybody	nobody	somebody

Streng (1972) stated that the indefinite pronouns are more like nouns than pronouns because they do not have referents and their use occasionally permits determiners or adjectives to co-occur with them.

On the whole, this group of pronouns has the feature [+singular] so that when an indefinite pronoun is used as the subject of a sentence, the verb will be singular. Also, when used as a referent of a genitive determiner, the form of the determiner will be singular—*Everybody is coming to the picnic* and *Everyone must bring her own lunch.*

The indefinite pronouns may function as subjects, direct objects, indirect objects, or objects of prepositions.

No one was late this morning.
John will eat *anything.*
Mary brought *everybody* cookies.
The teacher gave a gift to *everyone.*
The girls are washing windows for *someone.*

The indefinite pronouns that have *body* or *one* as the second morpheme are [+human] and may be inflected for the possessive with -'s, as is the case with nouns— *That dog must be someone's* and *Somebody's dog is outside.* In the second sentence the possessive or genitive form of the indefinite pronoun functions as a determiner with the noun *dog,* so that the NP in the sentence is *Somebody's dog.* This parallels the use of possessive nouns as determiners, as in *John's dog is huge.*

Streng (1972) discussed the relative difficulty of the various indefinite pronouns. She stated that those with *no* and *every* are easier to understand because they represent the extremes of *none* and *all.* The pronouns with the morphemes *some* and *any* are difficult because of the subtle difference in meaning of these two morphemes. There is a syntactic restriction on the use of the indefinite pronouns with *some* when the verb phrase or some element in the sentence is negative, in which case the corresponding pronoun with *any* is used.

Jean wants *something.*   Jane met *someone.*
Joe doesn't want *anything.*   Judy *never* meets *anyone.*

Streng also alluded to the importance of helping children develop an understanding of the use of *something* because of its frequent occurrence in reading materials, which begins in the preprimers. The implied referent of *something* may vary widely from a specific object to events, series of events, thoughts, or ideas.

Complexities in the use of the indefinite pronouns arise since they may be expanded, as can noun phrases.

Jane likes *anything sweet.*
Bob met *someone that he liked.*
The people had *nothing to eat.*

Deviations in their syntactic functioning, at times due to idiomatic or poetic use, may also pose problems in understanding and using indefinite pronouns. Sometimes determiners, or determiners and adjectives, are used preceding the pronoun. In other instances the indefinite pronouns, although carrying the feature [+singular], may be pluralized.

Mary is *a nobody.*
Bob doesn't date *just anybody.*
You should eat *a little something.*
Those people are *nobodies.*

The word *else* often is used with the indefinite pronouns. The distinction in meaning of the pronouns with and without *else* may be difficult for those experiencing difficulties in language acquisition.

Jane doesn't want *anything.*   *Someone* is coming.
Jane doesn't want *anything else.*   *Someone else* is coming.

Demonstrative Pronouns

The use of a demonstrative (*this, that, these,* or *those*) without a noun can be designated as a pronominalization. It also can be explained as a determiner with a noun deletion when the noun has already been mentioned or is obvious. *This* and *these* have the feature [+near], *that* and *those* [−near].

This book is for you.   Those books belong to George.
This is for you.   Those belong to George.

In the first sentence in each pair, the demonstrative is clearly a determiner. The demonstratives in the second sentences are used as pronouns and can be termed **demonstrative pronouns** or explained as determiners with noun deletions. It is possibly less confusing to accept the term **demonstrative pronoun.** In some instances of use of a demonstrative alone, there is not a particular noun for the determiner to signal. In the following paragraphs, the use of *this* or *that* is more apparent as pronominalization.

> There were guests for dinner on Tuesday. The girls came to dinner with dirty hands and faces. *This* made Mother angry.
>
> Jim was always late when he called for Mary. Then, one night he didn't show up, and he didn't call. *That* was more than Mary could take.

In both examples, there is not an obvious noun that can be used if *this* or *that* is a determiner plus noun deletion. The words are used as pronouns and are examples of rather complex referencing. A whole sentence is the referent of the italicized pronoun in each paragraph. *This* in the first paragraph refers to the girls coming to dinner with dirty hands and faces. The referent of *that* in the second paragraph possibly relates to both the fact that Jim didn't show up and that he didn't call.

At times the referent may be even more lengthy to state if a number of points are made and if a series of sentences serves as the referent of the pronoun.

> John rode his clutch in traffic. Also, when he was on an incline he would let up on the clutch to keep the car from rolling back rather than use the brake. At times he shifted down when he was at too high a speed. *This* could explain why he had to have his clutch replaced at 9,000 miles.

Young children use such sentences as *That's a dog* and *This is a rabbit,* in which *this* and *that* are pronouns. They use the words as designators, calling attention to something or indicating its existence. Much time may elapse before they are able to process the more difficult use of these pronouns in readers, in which the usage is similar to that in the preceding paragraphs.

In addition to the personal reflexive, indefinite, and demonstrative pronouns, two other groups of pronouns will be presented in later sections on questions and relative clauses.

Turn to Exercise 15 for practice in identifying indefinite and demonstrative pronouns.

CHAPTER 8

Sentence Complexities

The preceding chapter on pronominalization introduced complexity of syntax resulting from the use of various kinds of pronouns. The primary operation involved was substitution of a pronoun for a noun phrase, although some pronominalizations involve substitution of a pronoun for a sentence or series of sentences. Pronominalization allows one to streamline communication by not having to repeat already known information.

There are other transformations that make for complexity but serve another purpose, that of allowing for more flexibility in the expression of meaning. In this chapter, three additional transformations are described: adverbial preposing, the intensifier, and the indirect object.

The first of the **modality changes** is also included in this chapter. Modality changes were considered to be transformations in traditional generative transformational grammars. Current theory holds that when one intends to negate, question, or make a request, a transformation of a kernel sentence is not involved. Rather, the question, negative, or imperative utterance is encoded by modality changes applied in the deep structure. The modality changes involve different kinds of communications one uses in addition to declarative statements. The first of these to be considered in the text is the imperative, which involves a request or order by the speaker to another person.

Unit 1: Adverbial Preposing

Objectives
- Identify adverbials in sentences by specifying the type and indicating those that are shifted
- Write sentences using the same adverb in different positions

Reference was made in chapter 2 to the movability of adverbials. This characteristic of adverbials allows them to occur in different places in a sentence, provided that they need not remain in the predicate as complements of the verb. Ordinarily, the adverbials that can be preposed, or moved to a position before the verb, are those designating time, frequency, and manner.

In language curriculums for hearing-impaired or other children who experience difficulties in acquiring language, a sentence pattern approach to syntax may be used.

When this is the case, teachers attempt first to develop in the child a knowledge of subject-verb relationships and the corresponding semantic relationships. The teacher gradually introduces adverbials, beginning with locative meaning and then temporal meaning after the child understands the subject-verb-object concept. The adverbials are usually kept at the end of the sentence, possibly because the locative is used first and there are more restrictions as to its movability. Children, however, should be exposed to the meaningful use of preposed adverbials because of the difficulty in specifying rules as to when and to what position adverbials may shift.

Adverbial preposing is common with the time adverbials.

basic sentence: Susan is arriving *now.*

adverbial preposing: (a) *Now* Susan is arriving.
                     (b) Susan is *now* arriving.
                     (c) Susan *now* is arriving.

The adverbial *now* is shifted (preposed) in (a) to the beginning of the sentence, in (b) between the auxiliary and the verb, and in (c) before the auxiliary. Not all adverbials of time will shift to more than one position as *now* does.

Tomorrow it may rain.
*It *tomorrow* may rain.
On Monday, Grandmother will arrive.
*Grandmother will *on Monday* arrive.

As discussed in chapter 2, the adverbials of frequency are shiftable and more often come before the verb than at the end of the sentence.

The baby cries *often.*
Often the baby cries.
The baby *often* cries.
The baby will *often* cry.

The one-word adverbials of frequency more readily shift to different positions than do those that are noun phrases or prepositional phrases.

Every morning the boys are late.
*The boys *every morning* are late.
On Saturday mornings, my father plays golf.
My father, *on Saturday mornings,* plays golf.

Although it is permissible to shift the prepositional phrase (as in *My father, on Saturday mornings, plays golf*), we would tend not to because we must pause both before and after the adverbial.

The one-word adverbials of manner (*politely, quickly, sadly*) also are shiftable to positions other than at the end of the sentence.

> *Quietly*, the boys left the room.
> The boys *quietly* left the room.
> The boys should *quietly* leave the room.

Adverbials of manner that are prepositional phrases introduced by *with* or *by* are not as readily shiftable. In some instances, they may not be shifted, especially when the adverbial involves the semantic case *instrument*.

> ***By train* the boys arrived.
> **With a hairpin* Mary opened the door.

There are more restrictions applied to the movability of locative adverbials than to those of the other adverbial groups. The sentences *At the movies, the girls ate popcorn* and *Behind the door, the girls were giggling* have permissible adverbial shifts. However, when the verb implies action or movement to a place or from a particular source, the adverbial does not shift; it remains in the predicate as a complement of the verb. In the following sentences, the locative adverbial should not be shifted.

Sally took her mother *to the doctor*.	**To the doctor* Sally took her mother.
The children ran *behind the door*.	**Behind the door* the children ran.
Jack brought the horses *out of the barn*.	**Out of the barn* Jack brought the horses.

Hargis (1977) cited two classes of adverbials that function as sentence adverbials and that may occupy the same positions as the adverbials of manner. The first group is called **modal** adverbials and the second, **evaluative** adverbials. The meanings implied by the two groups are different. The modal adverbials, such as *apparently, clearly,* and *probably,* infer a degree of likelihood; whereas the evaluatives, such as *fortunately, strangely,* and *interestingly,* imply a judgment about something that is assumed to be true. Some of these same adverbials can be used as adverbials of manner. The differentiation is in the meaning conveyed.

Jane behaved *strangely* in school.	(adverb of manner)
Strangely (enough), Jane behaved in school.	(evaluative adverb)

In the first sentence, *strangely* indicates how Jane behaved. In the second sentence, the adverbial denotes a judgment as to Jane's apparently satisfactory behavior. The word *enough* occasionally is used with some of the manner and evaluative adverbials so as to better differentiate the meaning.

As can be seen, it is difficult to spell out rules for the movability of adverbs. A native user of the language can try out adverbials in different positions and decide which to use on the basis of what sounds right. But that same person can only run into difficulties when trying to state a rule for a particular use. This characteristic of the adverbials adds another complex dimension to syntax and meaning in our language and, when mastered, brings added facility with the language.

Turn to Exercise 16 for practice in recognizing and using preposed adverbials.

Unit 2: Intensifiers

Objectives

- Define intensifier
- State another term used to designate an intensifier
- Identify intensifiers in sentences and indicate if the qualified word is an adjective or adverb
- Differentiate intensifiers from adverbials in sentences

A group of words, which you may have learned were adverbs, are designated in modern grammar as **intensifiers** or **qualifiers**. These are words that are additions to sentences and that stress or qualify the meanings of adjectives or adverbs. Syntactically, it can be said that intensifiers signal an adjective or an adverb, as determiners signal nouns. The use of an intensifier is a transformation; it involves the addition of a word or words to a sentence.

The following list includes some of the commonly used intensifiers. The sentences show how intensifiers can be used.

a bit	pretty
a little	quite
enough	rather
exceedingly	so
extremely	somewhat
highly	too
indeed	very

Jane is a little homesick.

That man walks rather slowly.

Those girls are old enough.

Bob leaned over too far and fell into the water.

In the first and third sentences, the intensifiers *a little* and *enough* qualify the meaning of the adjectives *homesick* and *old*. In the other two sentences, the intensifiers *rather* and *too* qualify the meaning of the adverbs *slowly* and *far*. Although the majority of intensifiers precede the adjective or adverb that they modify, note that *enough* follows the adjective.

As can be seen in the sentences below, there is a continuum as to the degree of qualification or intensity that can be implied for a particular attribute or manner.

John is *a bit* fat.

John is *rather* fat.

John is *quite* fat.

John is *extremely* fat.

At times, two intensifiers can be combined—*a bit too* fat, *quite* fat *indeed, so very* fat.

The intensifiers *too* and *very* often appear early in samples of preschool children's language. Dependent upon its use by the family or among the child's associates, *pretty*, as in *pretty* hot and *pretty* old, could be used by a young child. Often in stories the traits possessed by the characters are stressed using *very*—a *very* wicked witch, a *very* sly fox. The story of the Three Bears makes repeated use of the intensifiers *too* and *just*—*too* hot, *too* cold, *just* right, *too* soft, *too* hard, etc.

The use of intensifiers, although not difficult, does add a degree of complexity to the language young children use. Children must, however, have a range of adjectives and adverbials in their lexicons.

Turn to Exercise 17 for practice in recognizing intensifiers.

Unit 3: Indirect Object Preposing

Objectives
- Specify a restriction governing the indirect object
- Label sentences with indirect objects as grammatical or ungrammatical
- Differentiate basic sentences in which the indirect object can be preposed from those in which it cannot

Indirect objects were introduced in chapter 4 in the discussion of Pattern 2 sentences with transitive verbs that can have both direct and indirect objects. The basic sentence form when there is an indirect object is $NP^1 + V + NP^2 + Adv$. The adverbial, with the preposition *to* or *for*, contains an NP that is the indirect object. The noun in the NP is human or animate and is the recipient or beneficiary of whatever object is given, presented, read, etc.—*The teacher read a story to* **the children**, *Bob got some milk for* **the cat**.

The alternative or transformed indirect object sentence is used equally as much (if not more) as the basic sentence form. Young children may use this form in a request such as *Gimme the ball*. It is possible that children hear the alternative form more than the basic sentence form in requests made of them—*Bring Mommy your shoes, Give Daddy the matches, Give the baby his rabbit*. Although these sentences are in the request form, the differences in the positioning of the constituents can be easily seen. The indirect object comes after the verb and precedes the direct object. This is the reason that in some texts an additional sentence pattern is given: $NP^1 + V + NP^3 + NP^2$. The NP^2 refers to the direct object and the NP^3 is the indirect object. The following sentences adhere to this pattern.

> Paul told his friends a joke.
> Mother made Dad a pie.
> The committee awarded Mary the prize.
> Jill sent Tim a gift.

Indirect object preposing involves two operations. The preposition, *to* or *for*, is deleted and the indirect object is moved to a position before the direct object. The first sentence in the list above resulted from the deletion of *to* and the shifting of *his friends* before *a joke*.

A limited group of transitive verbs may have both direct and indirect objects. When confronted with sentences with prepositional phrases with *to* or *for* as adverbial elements, the alternate form (i.e., indirect object transformation) can be a test as to whether or not the human or animate noun in the phrase is an indirect object.

> Susan brought some cookies for *Mother*.
> Susan brought *Mother* some cookies.

Since this sentence can be stated in both ways, *Mother* is the indirect object, the recipient of the cookies.

Note the following sentences:

> The boys watered the garden for *Mother*.
> *The boys watered Mother the garden.

The handler walked his dog to *the judge.*
*The handler walked the judge his dog.

In the first set, the grammatical sentence implies assistance. The boys assisted their mother by watering the garden. In the second set, the judge is a locative case, the place to which the dog was walked. Neither *walk* nor *water* can have an indirect object.

Some verbs that may have indirect objects may be used to indicate a beneficiary who receives assistance. Therefore, in the basic form, the use of *for* plus an NP could be ambiguous when out of context—*Mary read the story for Mother.* If Mary reads the story to her mother, then *Mother* is the indirect object, and *Mary read Mother the story* would convey the same meaning. If however, Mary read the story to someone else (e.g., to the children) because mother was unable to do it, then the transformation could not be applied because the meaning would be different. This could also be the case in a sentence such as *Dad bought that gift for Mother.* If Mother were unable to go out and get the gift, which was for someone else, this meaning would not be conveyed in *Dad bought Mother that gift.*

The examples in the preceding paragraph constitute a restriction on the use of the preposed indirect object sentence (i.e., the meaning must imply a recipient of some thing rather than the receiver of assistance). Another restriction on indirect object preposing is that it may not be used when the direct object is a personal pronoun.

The committee awarded *it* to Mary.
*The committee awarded Mary *it.*
Mary sent them to *him.*
*Mary sent *him* them.

In the case of the verb *ask,* which may have an indirect object, the transformation or alternative form is obligatory.

John asked the teacher a question.
*John asked a question to the teacher.

The verb *tell,* the meaning of which children may confuse with *ask,* can be used with either indirect object sentence form, the basic form, or the form with the preposing.

Jack told the secret to Susan.
Jack told Susan the secret.

Edith Fitzgerald, who devised the Fitzgerald Key, apparently considered the "straight language" form of indirect object sentences to be subject + verb + indirect object + direct object, as can be seen by the order of the key headings in Figure 2.

	Verb	Indirect Object	Direct Object
Who: What:	=	What: Whom:	Whom: What:
Tom	handed	Tim	the ball.

Figure 2
Fitzgerald Key Headings

Both Fitzgerald (1926) and Pugh (1955), however, advocated that the child experiencing difficulties in language development should understand the subject-verb-direct object relationship prior to being expected to comprehend and produce indirect object sentences.

As both sentence forms are used in reading materials, as there are restrictions in the use of each form, and as there are also restrictions on the use of *to* or *for* with the particular transitive verbs taking indirect objects, children in programs of language development must be exposed to both forms of the indirect object sentence.

Turn to Exercise 18 for practice using indirect object preposing.

Unit 4: Imperatives

Objectives
- Specify the form of the verb used in the imperative
- Identify the imperative transformation in sentences
- Identify the noun phrase elaborations, modality changes, and transformations in given sentences

The **imperative sentence** form, the first of the modality changes to be considered, is an often used pattern. One of the important functions of language is that of directing or controlling the behavior of others. Although as adults we learn more polite or softened ways of requesting another to do something for us, the imperative form is an economical way of getting the idea across. Many of the directions given to us are in the imperative form.

Road signs: Drive slow(ly)
Recipes: Add the milk alternately with the flour.
Directions: Attach the handlebars as shown in Diagram E.

In the imperative (request) sentence form, the subject *you* is not used and, if the request is positive, only the base form of the verb is used. Some examples follow:

> Be a good girl.
> Open the window.
> Please close the door.
> Pass the salt, please.

The word *please* in the last two sentences does not change the sentences syntactically. It is merely an addition that the speaker uses as a device to soften the request. The imperative form, with the subject *you* omitted and the base form of the verb, is the same in all three sentences.

When the imperative is negative, *don't* is often used—*Don't go out of the yard, Don't let the cat out of the house.* The use of the negative adverbial *never* implies a strong imperative—*Never play with matches.*

Indirect requests, those not involving the imperative form, are often used by adult speakers. These can be in the form of questions with modal auxiliaries. For example,

> Can you open a window?
> Would you close the door?
> Shouldn't you go to bed now?

None of the example sentences uses the imperative form, but the intent of the speaker can be to request or direct someone to do something. The imperative form is also not used in the following way, although the intent of the speaker would be the making of a request—*You sit down here, You water the plants.*

It may be difficult to determine if children are using the syntactic imperative form. At a two- and three-word level, children tend to use the null form of the verb, and they may not have a subject for the verb. This necessitates always recording what is going on at the time the utterance occurs so as to know the intent. Young children, however, make frequent use of imperative kinds of utterances beginning with pointing and other nonverbal means of getting what they want or need. When they begin to use the imperative form, it is the direct imperative—*Put the dogs here*—that is used.

Turn to Exercise 19 for practice in recognizing imperative sentences.

CHAPTER 9
Verb Phrase Complexities

Complexities in the verb phrase arise with the addition of auxiliary verbs, contractions, and negations. The *be*, modal, and *have* auxiliaries were introduced earlier in the text, and the difficulties associated with their use, both syntactically and semantically, were explained. The auxiliary *do* is considered in this chapter since its inclusion in a verb phrase constitutes a transformation. A second modality change, *negation*, is also presented, as is another transformational operation, *contraction*.

Unit 1: *Do*-Support

Objectives
- Specify the present and past forms of the *do* auxiliary
- Specify the form of the verb used with the *do* auxiliary
- Use the *do* auxiliary to express emphasis or contradiction in sentences
- List the kinds of sentences (other than positive declarative) requiring *do*-support for marking verb tense
- Change positive declarative sentences to negatives or questions using *do*-support

The *do* auxiliary is inserted in sentences for the purpose of marking the tense of the verb when the verb is simple present or past and the modality is interrogative or negative. It is also used for emphasis in positive declarative sentences, as in the following:

Does the baby walk?
When *did* your guests arrive?
Those boys *do* not study.
Mary *does* look beautiful.

In the sample questions, *do* must be inserted. Without *do*, the questions would be *The baby walks?* and **When your guests arrived?*

Although *The baby walks?* is grammatical, and it asks a question, it does not have the syntactic form of a question. However, the declarative sentence **Those boys not study* without the word *do* would be ungrammatical.

The auxiliary *do* carries no meaning and must not be confused with the verb *do*, as in *John does his homework every night*. When used in a declarative sentence, the *do* auxiliary serves to emphasize or to contradict, as in *Mary does look beautiful tonight, Those boys do study,* and *John didn't eat anything*. The *do* auxiliary also occurs in the form contracted with *not*, as in the last sentence in the group. In the first sentence, note that *do* is inflected for the third singular present tense. Without the *do* auxiliary, the verb in the sentence would be *looks*, the third singular present tense form.

The three forms of the auxiliary *do* are *do, does* (both present tense forms), and *did* (past tense form). Note the clues to the use of the *do* auxiliary plus the base form of the verb to substitute for the finite present and past verb forms.

Finite Verb Form	***Do*** + *Base Form*
play + Ø: I (they) *play* tennis.	do + Ø: I (they) *do play* tennis.
play + -s: He *plays* tennis.	do + (e)-s: He *does play* tennis.
play + -ed: We *played* tennis.	do + past: We *did play* tennis.

The *do* auxiliary is acquired relatively late by hearing children. According to Streng (1972), the *do* auxiliary is difficult for hearing-impaired children. This would be due in part to the lack of meaning carried in the auxiliary and in part to the necessary prerequisite knowledge of the inflectional rules for the present and past tense verbs.

Further references to the use of the auxiliary *do* will be included in the units on contractions and negatives in this chapter, and in the following chapter with questions.

Turn to Exercise 20 for practice in identifying and using the do auxiliary.

Unit 2: Negation

Objectives

- Specify the position in the sentence that *not* occupies when the verb is *be* or when the verb has one or more auxiliaries
- Indicate types of sentences for which *do*-support is also required when making sentences negative
- Write the negative of positive sentences containing one or more auxiliaries

In English there are various ways of expressing negation. Some adverbials and some determiners carry a negative element. The negator *not* and the contraction of an auxiliary with *not* negate the sentence or verb phrase. There are a number of derivational prefixes that negate words. Examples of these methods of expressing negation are included in the following list of sentences.

determiner:	Juan has *no* money.	
	Juan has *little* money.	(not much)
adverbial:	Terry *never* studies.	
	Terry *seldom* (*rarely*) studies.	(not often)
negator:	Sally is *not* upset.	
	Sally could *not* come.	
negative contraction:	The boys are*n't* coming.	
	The boys could*n't* come.	
derivational prefix:	This job is *im*possible.	
	This job is *un*rewarding.	

There are still other ways of expressing negation. In the unit on indefinite pronouns, we discussed three negative pronouns compounded with the negative determiner *no: no one, nothing,* and *nobody.* Many of the adjectives in English have an inherent negative connotation. For example,

thin	=	*not* fat
small, little	=	*not* large or big
ugly	=	*not* pretty or beautiful
dirty	=	*not* clean
short	=	*not* tall or long

Bloom (1970) pointed out three aspects of meaning in negatives as used by the children she studied. A child may use *all gone* or *no* to express **nonexistence** when the object referred to no longer exists, is not where it was, or may never have existed. A second semantic aspect is that of **rejection**, the use of *no* to indicate refusal of some object or participation in some activity—*no* milk, *no* sleep. The third aspect of meaning, **denial**, is used when the child asserts a contradiction or denial of something said by another—*no kitty* (i.e., That's not a kitty; that's a dog). The child uses these forms of negation prior to learning about the negative modality nodes with *not,* the correct syntactic use of which requires the *be, do, have,* and modal auxiliaries.

Elaboration of a sentence with the negator (i.e., the insertion of *not* in a sentence or verb phrase), unlike the *do* transformation, carries meaning, as do all the other forms of negation. The following meanings may be expressed in sentences with *not*.

nonexistence:	Daddy is *not* in the garage.
rejection:	I do *not* care for potatoes.
refusal:	I will *not* go to the party.
denial:	Mary can*not* sing.

It is difficult to indicate the meaning in sentences out of the context of discourse. However, the above sentences could serve as examples of the various semantic notions that can be expressed.

To generate syntactically correct negative sentences with *not*, one must have the rules for the copula *be*, as well as the rules for auxiliary use in verb phrases. Note the placement of *not* in Pattern 3, 4, and 5 sentences with the copula *be*. The negator *not* is placed after the verb and before the following constituent when the finite forms of *be* are used—*John is not happy, I am not a nurse, The boys are not in the gym.*

The following negative sentences contain auxiliaries.

Sally *is* not coming.
Those boys *may* not go.
Dad *has* not seen a movie in years.
The mail *may* not *have* arrived.
That child *should* not *be* walking in the road.
The dishes *had* not *been* washed.

Can you derive a rule for the placement of the negator in a verb phrase with an auxiliary, or auxiliaries, that would hold for all verb phrases other than with the finite forms of the copula *be*? The first three sentences have one auxiliary and the last three have more than one. A rule stating that *not* is inserted between the auxiliary and the verb would not fit the verb phrases in the last three sentences, since a second auxiliary intervenes before the verb. The rule would be that *not* is inserted after the auxiliary carrying the tense of the verb phrase. This is always the first auxiliary in the verb phrase.

The verb phrases in the preceding sentences have modal auxiliaries and/or progressive or perfect aspect. In each case the tense is carried in the auxiliary. When negativizing sentences with simple present or past verbs, the *do*-support transformation must be applied so that the sentences have an auxiliary to carry the tense.

*Mother not *bought* a dress.

Mother *did* not *buy* a dress.

*Those boys not *play* football.

Those boys *do* not *play* football.

Negative sentences requiring the *do*-support in addition to the *not* insertion are more difficult than negative sentences containing only a *be* or modal auxiliary. This is because of the use of a rule in addition to that of the negative insertion. An exception to this could be the use of the negative contraction *don't* as in *I don't want that.*

The negative contractions, which will be given in more detail in the next unit, are more natural to use in communication and occur more often than do the uncontracted forms of the auxiliary plus *not*. Children learning the language must learn both the contracted and uncontracted forms—*isn't* = is not, *can't* = cannot, *haven't* = have not, *don't* = do not, etc.

The negator *not* may also occur in noun phrases preceding the determiners. *Not* serves to negate the determiner or noun phrase and thus alters the meaning of the phrase.

Not many people came.

Not one student failed the test.

Not much of the house was damaged.

The negator is also used in sentences containing both a positive and a negative proposition—*Jane likes John, not Bob* or *Jane likes John, but she does not like Bob.*

When analyzing a sample of a student's language, we look for the devices that are used for the negative modality. The very young child can negate by shaking the head, turning away, or making a facial expression before the time any negative forms are used. As the child acquires language, we look for instances of *not*, the negative contraction, the expression *No!*, the determiner *no*, the negative indefinite pronouns, and the negative adverbial *never*.

Russell, Quigley, and Power (1976) pointed out retardation in the acquisition of negation in hearing-impaired children in whom the process of acquisition is much the same as in hearing children, but considerably delayed. This could very well be the case in other children who experience language delay. Russell, Quigley, and Power also allude to the problems this delay can cause in reading comprehension. Negatives appear with high frequency in beginning reading materials, which could be encountered prior to the time at which some children have even minimal understanding of the forms of negation in English.

Turn to Exercise 21 for practice in identifying and using different forms of negation.

Unit 3: Contractions

Objectives

- Write contractions for given noun phrases plus a copula verb or auxiliary
- Specify the type of auxiliary contained in given contractions
- Identify the contracted *be* as the *be* verb or *be* auxiliary
- Write contractions for verbs or auxiliaries in negative sentences
- Write the negative form of positive sentences using contractions
- Indicate the transformation used to generate given negative sentences
- Identify the modality changes, noun phrase elaborations, and transformations in given sentences

Positive contractions of the copula *be*, the *be* auxiliary, the modal *will*, and the *have* auxiliary; and the negative contractions for some auxiliaries in each of these groups and for the *do* auxiliary make up a finite list of contractions permissible in English.

The Copula *Be*

The forms of the copula that are contracted, other than in most negative contractions, are usually attached to personal pronouns. The features of person and number must be observed so that there is agreement of the noun phrase and the verb.

I'm a boy.	[I + *am*]
He's sick today.	[He + *is*]
We're (They're) here.	[We/They + *are*]

The contraction of *is* also is attached to singular nouns (e.g., *Jane's a girl*). This use of the contraction with nouns is usually restricted to spoken language. The printed contraction form can be confusing to a child because of the similarity to the possessive form.

Be Auxiliary

The contractions of the *be* auxiliary are the same as for the copula.

I'm sleeping.	[I + *am*]
She's leaving.	[She + *is*]
They're playing.	[They + *are*]

Again, as with the copula, the *be* auxiliary contraction (e.g., *Jane's* crying) is more often attached to nouns in speech than in writing.

Modal Auxiliaries

The modal auxiliary *will* is contracted as *'ll* and is appropriately used with the personal pronouns—*I'll, he'll, we'll, you'll, they'll.* The only other modal that is contracted with pronouns is *would,* as in *I'd like to go.*

The contraction of the *have* auxiliary with the personal pronouns occurs in speech as follows:

I've seen that movie.	[I + *have*]
He's caught a fish.	[He + *has*]
She'd left her coat.	[She + had]

The *'s* and *'d* contractions are not usually found in formal writing.

The positive contractions serve to provide easier articulation of a pronoun or noun with an auxiliary. Speech is streamlined since one can articulate two morphemes in a single syllable.

Negative Contractions

Negative contraction occurs with the copula *be;* the *be, have,* and *do* auxiliaries; and some modal auxiliaries. The forms of the copula *be* or the *be* auxiliary that are negatively contracted are *is, are, was,* and *were.* There is no negative contraction for *am,* although one may hear the dialectal form *ain't,* which is also used with second and third person pronouns or with nouns.

All three forms of *have* and of *do* may be contracted with the negative. The modals contracted with *not* are *can, will, could, should,* and *would.* The form *shan't* is a colloquial negative contraction for *shall.* The modals *must* and *might* have no negative contractions given in the dictionary. The form *mustn't* is heard in spoken language, but it is not found in the written form, as is also the case with *mightn't.*

The negative contractions are listed below according to category of auxiliary.

be	*modal*	*have*	*do*
isn't	can't	haven't	don't
aren't	won't	hasn't	doesn't
wasn't	couldn't	hadn't	didn't
weren't	shouldn't		
	wouldn't		

As indicated before, children will use some of the negative contractions prior to their acquisition of the rules for *not* in the verb phrase. The negative contractions *don't, won't,* and *can't* are acquired early and may be used prior to the acquisition of the particular auxiliaries which they represent. Children appear to learn these negative contractions as single morphemes and use them to negate prior to learning the auxiliary plus *not.*

The appropriate use of contractions by a child indicates that the child is operating with sets of rules for contractions and for negatives. In the case of *doesn't* and *didn't,* in addition to using the negative contraction, the child is also using the *do*-support transformation. Often in the case of *don't,* as in *I don't want that,* it cannot be assumed that the child is using the *do*-support because the contraction *don't* appears much earlier than the other negatively contracted forms of *do.* Should the child use *don't* to begin questions, however, one could cite this as an instance of *do*-support.

Turn to Exercise 22 for practice in identifying and using contractions.

CHAPTER 10

Question Modalities

There are two major types of questions in the English language: **yes-no questions** and **wh-questions**. Included in the yes-no questions are **tag questions**, which may be considered a third type because of the difference in syntactic structure from other yes-no questions. Semantically, however, there are two forms, distinguished by the response that is expected by the questioner. For one group of questions, the expected response can be either *yes* or *no*. For the other large group, the *wh-*questions, some specific information may be requested—*Who____? Where____? Why____?* etc.

For communication competence, an individual must be able to ask as well as to comprehend questions and, thus, be able to respond to questions. Very young children may use rising intonation, facial expression, and/or gesture to ask questions long before they can generate even the simplest full syntactic question forms. An early question form may be *What's that*, which for some children is not the question as stated, but an utterance such as *Z'at?* used with a pointing gesture for the purpose of eliciting a name for something from an adult. From *Z'at?* children may proceed to using something like *What dat?* prior to the form *What's that?* as modeled by an adult. In the process of learning questions, they will generate forms that they may not have heard used by an adult, but which represent intermediate steps of complexity, as in *Why not doggie eat?*

Streng, Kretschmer, and Kretschmer (1978), state that mothers use more yes-no questions with very young children and more *wh-*questions with older children. A young child in the preoperational state (2 years 6 months to 7 years) uses both *wh-* and yes-no questions, especially questions beginning with *Why, What, Is,* and other yes-no forms. The authors suggest that hearing-impaired children in the early stages of language development need the question *What's that?* for purposes of labeling the important people, objects, and events in their environment, thus enabling them to gain vocabulary. They propose that *wh-*questions (e.g., *Why?*) with which children elicit information, be given high priority and that a child not be held to a full question form while in the process of acquiring the basic semantic relationships and phrase structures of declarative form sentences.

Unit 1: Yes-No Questions

Objectives

- List the three types of questions in English
- Write examples of echo questions that are yes-no type questions
- Change Pattern 3, 4, and 5 sentences to yes-no questions
- Change given sentences to yes-no questions indicating the inversion as copula, *be*, modal, or *have* auxiliary
- Identify the need for *do*-support, auxiliary, or copula inversion in generating a yes-no question for given statements
- Indicate the transformation(s) and/or modality changes needed to generate given questions and statements

A speaker who asks a yes-no question expects a response of at least *yes* or *no*. The speaker may use the syntactic structure of a declarative sentence with intonation and facial expression, thus creating an interrogative yes-no utterance—*The girls are arriving today? Mary is sick?* Questions of this type demand no more syntactic knowledge than that required for a basic sentence. All constituents of the sentence are in the same order, so that the changes are semantic and phonological rather than syntactic. Semantically, the meaning is changed from declarative to interrogative. Phonologically, a rising intonation indicates that the utterance is a question.

A young child may use this form of yes-no questioning prior to acquiring the syntactic rule for the yes-no question—*You read a story now?* or *My Daddy is (Daddy's) coming home?* Questions such as these may be called **echo questions**, although in the true sense of the term, they are not echo questions. A child or adult may use the form in initiating a communication or changing topics, without the other person having referred to the topic at all. However, when one person has made a statement such as *Jane stayed home today because she's sick*, the other person may, in the true sense, use an echo question—*Jane stayed home today?* or *Jane is sick?* The intent of the adult using echo questions may be to check on what has been said or to express surprise or disbelief.

When doing a syntactic description, echo questions must be differentiated from yes-no questions that use the more complex yes-no form. This is because echo questions have the same syntactic form as declarative statements. The use of this type of questioning would be indicated in the pragmatic and phonological analyses, and the child would not be credited with using the syntax for a yes-no question.

The syntactic forms for yes-no questions are not all equally complex. From easiest to most difficult, the order of difficulty as determined by the rules needed to generate each is copula verb or auxiliary inversion, *do*-support plus auxiliary inversion, tag question.

Copula Verb or Auxiliary Inversion

In yes-no questions with copula verb or auxiliary inversion, the *be* verb or the auxiliary carrying the tense is inverted before the subject and begins the question.

copula inversion:
- *Is* Grace sick?
- *Was* Jim in school today?
- *Are* those girls cheerleaders?

be aux inversion:
- *Were* the children studying?
- *Are* the boys helping their father?

modal inversion:
- *Can* Barbara come to the party?
- *Should* we leave the dog at home?
- *Will* the game be in Washington?

have inversion:
- *Have* the electricians finished their work?
- *Has* Bob raked the yard?

The addition of auxiliaries to verb phrases will increase complexity in any sentence regardless of the form, declarative or interrogative. Complexity in the yes-no questions, then, will depend in part on the difficulty level of the auxiliaries in the verb phrases. The same rule of auxiliary inversion is used in all, however.

When there is more than one auxiliary in the verb phrase, only the auxiliary marking the tense is inverted.

Will John *be living* in New York all year?
Has that motor *been running* long?
Could the band *have been practicing* in the auditorium?

These yes-no questions are more complex than the preceding ones because of the use of more than one auxiliary in the verb phrase.

Do-Support and Auxiliary Inversion

The necessity of the transformational rule of *do*-support in addition to the auxiliary inversion for the question when the verb is simple present or past results in increased complexity. In analyzing a sample of language, the occurrence of both complexities should be noted. Some examples of questions requiring the use of both auxiliary inversion and *do*-support are

> *Did* Dad rake the yard?
> *Does* that clock chime?
> *Do* elephants eat hay?

The equivalent echo question for the first question would be *Dad raked the yard?* Since the auxiliary for past is affixed to the verb in *raked* and cannot be shifted, the *do*-support rule must supply an auxiliary to carry the tense.

> Dad *did* rake the yard?
> *Did* Dad rake the yard?

It is for yes-no questions with the *do* auxiliary that children first really need the *do*-support rule. They will use the negative contractions, especially *don't*, in negative declarative statements prior to acquiring the *do*-support rule. Language samples of young children may contain yes-no questions requiring the auxiliary inversion rule only, along with echo yes-no questions that do not have the question syntactic form because the *do*-support rule has not yet been acquired.

> Can I go outside?
> Is the baby sleeping?
> You want a cookie? (Do you want a cookie?)

Turn to Exercise 23 for practice in identifying and using yes-no questions.

Unit 2: Tag Questions

Objectives
- Supply tag questions for given declarative statements
- Indicate either *yes* or *no* as the response the speaker would expect to given tag questions
- Specify the modality changes and transformations necessary to generate given tag questions

The most difficult and the last to be mastered of the questions in English, including the *wh*-questions, are the **tag questions**. To generate syntactically appropriate tag questions, one has to employ a number of rules. Look at the following questions and determine the complexities involved in them that would account for the difficulties children experience in acquiring this type of question.

John is arriving soon, isn't he?
The boys are going to a move, aren't they?
The girls won't come, will they?
Mary hasn't seen that movie, has she?

A statement plus a question tag constitutes a yes-no tag question. The person asking the question expects a response of yes to some questions and no to others; the syntactic form of the question varies accordingly. If the answer expected is yes, the questioner uses a positive statement plus a negative tag, as in the first two questions. The reverse is true when a negative response is expected; i.e., a negative statement precedes a positive question tag.

A tag is a partial question containing the auxiliary that would begin the yes-no question and the subject. The other words in the question are deleted since the information is already contained in the statement. To generate a syntactically correct tag question, the child must first be able to use the yes-no auxiliary inversion rule and, thus, one would expect to find simple yes-no questions in that child's language sample. The rules for personal pronoun referencing are also necessary. The noun phrase is given in the statement, and a personal pronoun that is appropriate as to person, number, and in some cases, gender, must be selected. The rules for negative contractions are necessary and the child must know the auxiliary makeup of the contraction. Note in the third example above the use of won't, which must become will in the tag. In addition to all of the above, the rules of positive plus negative or the reverse must be added so as to indicate the expected response.

When a tag question has a simple present or past tense form in the positive statement, the question becomes more complex because of the necessity of the do-support transformation.

Those boys love food, don't they?
Jane leaves at 1:00 p.m., doesn't she?
The package arrived, didn't it?

The tag must contain the do auxiliary in the same tense and person as the verb in the statement and the same number as the subject. If one analyzes the question Those boys love food, don't they, the following would be listed as the modality changes and transformations necessary for generating the question: yes-no question, do-support, negation, contraction, auxiliary inversion, pronominalization (personal), and deletion (of identical elements).

Note the last transformation listed. **Deletion** is used in other complex structures, but tag questions are the first in which you have encountered it. In a tag question, identical elements are deleted. In the question *Those boys love food, don't they*, the full question in the first tag would be *Don't they love food?* The words *love food* in the verb phrase are deleted because they are not necessary.

Tag questions need not involve the negative contraction. However, the uncontracted auxiliary plus *not* is a much more formal use. In this case, the *not* remains after the pronoun—*David is working, is he not? Julia arrived, did she not?*

All of the transformations mentioned make the generation of tag questions complex. This, in part, accounts for their being late in the pattern of question acquisition. The communicative intent of yes-no tag questions, however, is not that of getting information, of getting approval, or of making a request as with other yes-no questions. The majority of the time, tag questions are used when the questioner knows the answer or when the questioner wants affirmation of the statement preceding the tag.

Mention was made in the unit on imperatives of the use of yes-no questions to direct the behavior of others. In these instances, the interest of the speaker is not to seek confirmation, reaffirmation, or information, and a *yes* or *no* response is not expected. Compliance is, however, expected since the speaker is using a more polite or subtle means of getting another person to do something. The questions may take different forms, such as

Will you open a window?
Can you open a window?
Would you like to open a window?
It's rather stuffy in here, isn't it?

When one considers (a) the various ways to use yes-no questions in the communication situation and (b) the syntactic difficulty of such questions, it is not surprising that hearing-impaired children demonstrate delay in the acquisition of questions. Quigley, Wilbur, and Montanelli (1974) reported that their 18-year-old deaf subjects did not demonstrate mastery of questions equivalent to that of the 10-year-old hearing subjects. This could also be the case in children experiencing language delay from other causes.

Quigley et al. also pointed out that in a representative basal reading series, yes-no questions were used in the first primer. These questions occurred approximately 8 times per 100 sentences in the third primer and first-grade reader. One could anticipate that even the simplest reading materials would present difficulties for a child whose acquisition of questions and other complex syntax is delayed.

Turn to Exercise 24 for practice in using tag questions.

Unit 3: *Wh*-Questions

Objectives

- Identify the sentence constituent replaced by given *wh*-words
- Identify the PRO-form used for each *wh*-word and selected determiners
- Write *wh*-questions from sentences containing PRO-forms
- Identify auxiliary or copula inversion and *do*-support in given *wh*-questions
- Write echo *wh*-questions
- Rank *wh*-questions in order of difficulty based on the different rules needed to generate the question
- Indicate the transformations and modality changes needed to generate given *wh*-questions
- Identify the modality changes, noun phrase elaborations, and transformations in given sentences

There is a broader range of *wh*-questions than of yes-no questions, as well as a wider variety of forms that the questions take. Syntactically the *wh*-questions, as a whole, are more complex than the yes-no questions, excluding tag questions.

A speaker asking a *wh*-question is seeking some specific information, such as identification of a person; a location; the time, duration, or frequency of an activity; a reason; a recounting of events; or even a full set of directions as to how to do something.

Wh-Questions without Inversion

Wh-questions begin with either a *wh*-word or with a preposition immediately preceding a *wh*-word. The only interrogative word not beginning with *wh* is *how*. Some *wh*-questions require only the insertion of the *wh*-word for the part of the sentence or phrase in question, so that these are among the least syntactically complex of the *wh*-questions.

Who is sick?	(Someone) is sick.
What hit me?	(Something) hit me.
Whose dog bit Jean?	(Someone's) dog bit Jean.
Which boxes are heavy?	(Some) boxes are heavy.

The sentences to the right of the *wh*-questions illustrate the declarative form of the question with a **PRO-form** substituted for what is unknown. As can be seen, the *wh*-word in the question clues the listener to the information sought. The PRO-forms indicate the type of word or constituent that the *wh*-word replaces. In the first two sentences the replaced constituent, which is the subject, is a noun phrase. In the third question, the *wh*-word replaces a genitive determiner or noun, and in the fourth, a determiner, both appearing in the subject noun phrase. Thus, in *wh*-questions in which the *wh*-word represents the subject or a determiner or other modifier of the subject, the auxiliary or copula inversion transformation is not necessary.

Wh-Questions with Inversion

When the information sought pertains to an adverbial or to the noun phrase that is the direct object, auxiliary or copula inversion must occur. This, then, adds syntactic complexity to the question.

	What?
What is Tina making?	Tina is making (something).
Where is Pete?	Pete is (somewhere).
Why is the dog barking?	The dog is barking (for some reason).
How can Bill study all night?	Bill can study all night (somehow).

In the first question, the *wh*-word is an interrogative pronoun used as the NP^2 in the question. This can be seen in the sentence with the PRO-form *something*.

NP^1 V   NP^2
Tina / is making / (something).

If the auxiliary inversion rule were not used, the question would be ungrammatical— **What Tina is making?*

In the rest of the questions, the *wh*-words are interrogative adverbs; each replaces an adverbial element. Again, as in the first question in the group, auxiliary inversion is needed because the *wh*-word functions as a constituent other than the subject.

Wh-Questions with *Do*-Support

Wh-questions become more syntactically complex when the *do*-support transformation must be applied for the auxiliary inversion. As in the yes-no questions, there must be an auxiliary for the inversion when the verb is in the simple present or past tense.

	Jeff broke (something).
do-support:	Jeff did break (something).
aux inversion:	Did Jeff break (something/what)?
wh-question:	What did Jeff break?

Wh-Questions with Prepositions

When the answer the questioner is trying to elicit involves the indirect object in a sentence or a location, time, or reason, the question may begin with a preposition. Such questions may use preposition plus auxiliary (or copula) inversion. Some examples follow.

Information Desired	Question	Response
to/for + IO:	To whom did Mother send a gift?	Mother sent a gift to (someone).
	For whom is Ted buying the ring?	Ted is buying the ring for (someone).
Locative:	To what city are the Browns moving?	The Browns are moving to (some city).
Temporal:	At what time is the meeting?	The meeting is at (some-time).
Reason:	For what did Cris buy the cake?	Cris bought the cake for (something).

Questions like those in the previous group may begin with the *wh*-word with the preposition left at the end of the sentence. The questions, then, have only the auxiliary inversion.

Who(m) did Mother send the gift to?
What city are the Browns moving to?
What did Cris buy the cake for?

This is a more informal type of question, and it may be the form preferred by speakers. Books of usage usually recommend that the preposition be shifted to the beginning.

The *why* question is often used as an equivalent for *What . . . for*, so that the last question could be *Why did Cris buy the cake?*

The previous units on *wh*-questions have concentrated on the word orders and the syntactic rules for the word orders in the *wh*-questions. Some mention was made of the clues that the question word gives the listener as to the answer that is being sought by the questioner. All of the different kinds of *wh*-questions were not presented. The following groupings are presented to summarize and to point out various difficulties involved in *wh*-questions.

Questions Eliciting Noun Phrase, Determiner, or Modifier Responses

	Who made the cake?
NP:	What caused the fire?
	To whom did you give the book?
NP with Det	*Which boy* do you like?
and/or	*Whose book* do you have?
Modifier:	*How many checks* did you write?
	What kind of bread did you buy?
	How much milk did you get?
	What (color) shirt did you buy?

The last question could ask for other attributes such as size, sleeve length, or style. In the last six questions the underlined noun could be omitted with a deletion transformation when it already has been identified and is known by the person being questioned, as in *How many did you write?* or *What color did you buy?*

Other *wh*-questions seeking modifier case responses may begin with *how*. These are questions with linking verbs, as in *How does (NP) look (feel, smell, taste, sound)?*

Questions Eliciting Adverbial Responses

There is a *wh*-word, or words, for each of the adverbial types, some of which were presented previously.

Where:	locative
When (What time):	temporal
Why:	reason, cause
How long:	duration
How often:	frequency
How:	manner, *with* + instrument

Questions beginning with prepositional phrases, except when containing an indirect object, are used to elicit adverbial responses—*In what city, At what time, To what state,* etc.

Questions with *how* followed by an adjective may also elicit information about an attribute—*How big (tall, heavy, cold, etc.).*

Questions Eliciting Verb Phrase and Sentence Responses

The *wh*-question with the verb *do* elicits information regarding the verb phrase, so a full sentence response may be required. The sentence using a PRO-form could be *John (What . . . do)*. Some examples of *wh*-questions with the verb *do* include

What did Gabrielle *do?*
What will the coach *do* now?
What has that dog *done?*
What is Dad *doing?*

The *do*-support transformation is used in the first sentence along with the verb *do*. In the other sentences, only the auxiliary inversion rule is needed with the *wh*-question modality.

A common question that is asked often (one that might require a summarization or recounting of events) begins with, or may in its entirety be *What happened?*

What happened at school today?
What happened after the meeting?
What happened to Jill?

Echo *Wh*-Questions

In *wh*-questions, as well as in yes-no questions, one may use the echo question. Again, the echo question requires no additional modality node elaboration or transformational rule. The *wh*-word is used for what the individual wants repeated for reaffirmation or wants to express surprise about.

Helen did *what?*
The Johnsons went *where?*
The boys are leaving *when?*
That plant is *how* tall?
Mother wants *what kind of* apples?

Although these questions are among the easiest syntactically of the *wh*-questions, they represent an adult communicative act and are not used by young children. As with other echo questions, the speaker was not the initiator of the topic and is responding to what another has said. The intent of the question may be to check on what one has heard or to get repetition of some specific information that is surprising or almost unbelievable.

The appropriate use of the different types of *wh*-questions requires considerable semantic, as well as syntactic, competence. Streng (1972), in commenting on the difficulty of *wh*-questions, mentioned the necessity of the acquisition of concepts of space, time, causality, and other complex relationships for the generation of the *wh*-question forms other than those asking *Who* _____, *What is* _____, etc.

In considering the question types in English: yes-no, tag, and *wh*-questions, Russell, Quigley, and Power (1976) cited research indicating that hearing children demonstrate good understanding of question types by the age of 10 years. The pattern of difficulty for comprehension of questions (easy–difficult) was yes-no questions, *wh*-questions, and tag questions. The same pattern of difficulty was found in hearing-impaired children. Quigley, Wilbur, and Montanelli (1974), whose research has been cited, also found that *who* as a subject was easier than *when* or *who* as an object. As with other aspects of syntax, hearing-impaired children exhibited delay rather than deviance in question acquisition.

Quigley, Wilbur, and Montanelli analyzed the occurrence in a basal reading series of *wh*-questions and yes-no questions, as mentioned previously. They found that *wh*-questions first were used in the second primer. These questions occurred 11 times per 100 sentences both in the second and third primers. Children with delayed language acquisition can be expected to have difficulty comprehending both major types of questions in their early reading experiences.

Turn to Exercise 25 for practice in identifying, using, and analyzing wh-questions.

CHAPTER 11

Particle Movement and *There* Transformation

The **particle movement** (prt movt) and **there transformation** are operations involving a rearrangement of words in basic sentences, and, in the case of *there*, the addition of a word. The meaning relationships in the sentence, for the most part, remain the same after the transformation.

Unit 1: Particle Movement

Objectives

- Identify given sentences in which the particle movement transformation was applied
- Identify the feature of the verb and particle needed for the particle movement transformation
- State the condition(s) under which the particle movement transformation is obligatory
- Differentiate particles from prepositions in given sentences
- Indicate when the particle movement transformation is appropriate for given sentences

The particle in a two-word verb may be shifted away from the verb to a position following the object of the verb. This operation is called **particle movement**. The particle movement transformation is optional in subject-verb-direct object sentences with particles, except when the direct object, the NP^2, is a personal pronoun. In this case the transformation is obligatory.

	Mary *put out* the fire.
optional prt movt:	Mary *put* the fire *out*.
	*Mary put out it.
obligatory prt movt:	Mary *put* it *out*.

In the second sentence in each pair, the prt movt transformation is used, and in the second set, the transformation is obligatory. The movement of the particle is away from the verb so that it follows the noun phrase that is the object of the verb. The first set of sentences illustrates the optional use of the prt movt. In the second set, the object of the verb is the personal pronoun *it*; therefore, the particle must be shifted away from the verb. The particle is also shifted around demonstrative pronouns, as in

> *Pick* that *up.*
> *Throw* this *out.*

The particle movement is obligatory when a reflexive pronoun is the NP^2, although the use of reflexives as objects of verbs with particles does not occur as frequently as does the use of the personal pronouns.

> Jane *let* herself *out.*
> The thief *turned* himself *over* to the police.
> I *dried* myself *off.*

By way of review, note that in the sentence *Mary put the fire out, out* does not indicate location. Together with the verb, the two morphemes have a different meaning. Neither *put* nor *out* retains its own meaning, and the combined words *put out* mean extinguish.

The following sentences contain examples of a word used as a particle in one instance and a preposition in the other. The word *off* is used in a transitive verb sentence frame in the first sentence. In the fourth sentence, *off* is a preposition introducing an adverbial prepositional phrase in an intransitive verb frame. There is a perceptible difference in the intonation and stress patterns of the two sentences when the particle is not moved.

> $V + prt + NP^2$:   Tom / *turned off* / the ignition.
> prt movt: Tom *turned* the ignition *off.*
> $V_i + Adv$:   Tom / *turned* / *off* the road.
>   *Tom *turned* the road *off.*

The sentence *Tom rolled the blinds down this morning* has a particle movement, as can be seen by shifting the particle back with the verb—*Tom rolled down the blinds this morning.* In the sentence *Tom rolled the barrel down the hill*, this is not possible—*Tom rolled down the barrel the hill.*

Adverbials of manner may not be placed between a verb and a particle. However, they may occur between a verb and a preposition.

$V + prt + NP^2$	$V + prep\ phr$
Mother *hung up* the clothes quickly.	John *walked out* the door slowly.
*Mother *hung* quickly *up* the clothes.	John *walked* slowly *out* the door.

The particles in subject-verb-object sentences are the only particles with which particle movements may occur. The verb plus particle is transitive as there is a direct object. The particle may not be shifted away from either intransitive or linking verbs. There are only a few linking verbs that pattern with particles and a limited number of intransitive verbs that pattern with particles. As there is a relatively large number of verb + particle combinations that are transitive, and these are the instances in which the particle movement is applicable, the transformation may occur rather frequently.

Turn to Exercise 26 for practice in recognizing particle movement.

Unit 2: *There* Transformation

Objectives

- State the conditions under which the *there* transformation is applicable
- Indicate given sentences to which the *there* transformation could be applied
- Indicate *there* in given sentences as an adverb or the result of the *there* transformation
- Identify the modality changes, noun phrase elaborations, and transformations in given sentences.

The ***there* transformation** in traditional grammar is called the **expletive**. The transformation involves shifting the full copula verb (with auxiliaries) and adding *there* to begin the sentence. The word *there* is used as a sentence introducer. *There* carries no meaning, but allows for stress to be placed on other words or parts of the sentence. It is not to be confused with the adverbial *there*, meaning *in that place,* or for drawing attention to or pointing out something.

A Pattern 5 sentence, which usually contains a locative adverbial, may be transformed with *there* if the NP that is the subject contains a nondefinite determiner. The following sets of sentences show a Pattern 5 sentence on the left and the same sentence transformed with the *there* transformation on the right.

Pattern 5 Sentences	***There** Transformation*
Some apples are in the refrigerator.	There are some apples in the refrigerator.
Two boys are in my office.	There are two boys in my office.
Many people were at the game.	There were many people at the game.
A mouse could be in the cupboard.	There could be a mouse in the cupboard.
More boys should have been at the party.	There should have been more boys at the party.

Each of the basic sentences on page 104 has a subject noun phrase with a nondefinite determiner—*some, two, many,* etc. Note that the verb *be* and the auxiliaries used with it are inverted before the NP in the transformed sentence—*There could be a mouse in the cupboard.*

When sentences such as those listed are spoken, *there* and the verb are not stressed. The noun phrase has a higher pitch contour and is stressed, while falling intonation is used for the adverbial.

In the following sentences, *there* has a locative meaning and is an adverbial that has been shifted, as is shown in the sentences on the right.

The dog is there.	There the dog is. or There is the dog.
My purse is there, on the table.	There my purse is, on the table.
Those boys are there.	There those boys are.
The mouse is there.	There the mouse is.

Except for the second sentence on the right, there is no adverbial following the noun phrase, so that it is more easily determined that the *there* transformation has not been applied. Also in the sentences, the determiners in the NPs are definite: *the, my, those.* In each of the sentences, *there* could receive stress when spoken, and the meaning would be more apparent as locative or pointing out something.

The sentences on the left show the sentence before the adverbial shift. The adverbial *there* is a constituent in the basic sentence. In sentences with *there* transformations, the *there* is an addition to a sentence that contains an adverbial. In all the sentences on the right, the copula could be shifted to a position after *there*, as indicated in the first sentence.

The *there* transformation is not limited to Pattern 5 sentences with a locative adverbial. It may also be applied to some sentences with adverbials that have other meanings, such as temporal—*There were two meetings last night.*

Another instance of the application of the *there* transformation is in sentences with verb phrases containing a *be* auxiliary plus a verb with progressive aspect.

Several children were playing in the street.	There were several children playing in the street.
Many people are arriving this afternoon.	There are many people arriving this afternoon.

In such transformations, only the *be* auxiliary is moved around the subject so that it follows *there*. When identifying these transformations in sentences, it is sufficient to call them *there* transformations and not indicate the auxiliary and copula changes.

The *there* transformation is difficult for individuals who cannot hear, as one depends on stress patterns to discriminate sentences with *there* transformations from sentences with a different meaning, that of locating or drawing attention to something or someone. Since in some cases the *there* transformation may be more natural to use or may be preferred to the more basic form of the sentence, hearing-impaired children should be exposed to it early and sufficiently often to gain competence in both comprehending and using the transformation.

Turn to Exercise 27 for practice in identifying the there transformation.

CHAPTER 12

The Passive Transformation

The passive is used extensively in writing. One cannot pick up a newspaper without being confronted by passives in headlines, in news features, and, especially, in the sports pages. One finds such headlines as

Million A Year in Overtime *(was) Paid.* . . .
Job Trainee Says Pay *(was) Issued.* . . .
Tigers *(were) Destroyed* by Bruins

Within the text of a news story, one may find a paragraph such as the following:

The Tigers *were destroyed* by the Bruins in a game that *was played* under the lights at the Arena. Although Johnson *had been put* in at quarterback as a last ditch effort, it was too late. The game already *had been lost* in the third quarter when the Bruins *were allowed* to score three times. The Tigers *were overwhelmed* by the Bruins at their best.

The italicized verb phrases are all passive voice. An individual not understanding the structure of the passive could derive the wrong information concerning some of the facts of the story. Having arrived at a level of being able to understand the subject-verb-object relationships in sentences, one could, by using the clues of word order (**surface order strategy**), get the information that *the Tigers destroyed the Bruins, Johnson put in the quarterback,* and *the Tigers overwhelmed the Bruins.*

Unit 1: Passive Voice

Objectives
- State the feature of the verb needed for the passive transformation
- Specify the tense and voice of active and passive verb phrases
- Specify passive sentences as reversible or nonreversible

The passive is an operation on a Pattern 2 sentence with a transitive verb. Only verbs with the feature [+transitive] can be transformed to passive voice. In many instances, the meaning relationships of the sentences that can be transformed are

Agent—action—patient; however, the other meanings that can be expressed in Pattern 2 sentences also may be found in passive sentences.

Rules for Passive Voice

In the full passive sentence, a number of rules must be used to get to the surface structure (the passive form) from the deep structure (subject-verb-object or Agent—action—patient). The rules in the following list must be used in generating a passive sentence to express an Agent—action—patient relationship.

Agent—action—patient
The girl kissed the boy.
1. Patient or object, *the boy*, becomes the subject of the sentence
2. *Be* auxiliary is inserted in the verb phrase: past + *be* = was
3. *-en* is affixed to the verb: *-en* + kiss = kissed
4. *by* is added and is followed by the NP, which is the agent or subject, *by the girl*

These changes result in the sentence *The boy was kissed by the girl*, which retains the same meaning as the original sentence in the active form. If one uses a surface order strategy in interpreting the passive sentence and focuses on the order of the stressed words in the passive sentence, *boy kissed girl*, then one misinterprets the meaning. This is often the case in young children and in language-delayed children prior to the time that they understand the significance of the clues to the passive: the *by* and the *be* auxiliary with the verb.

Reversible and Nonreversible Passives

One reason that some passives can be more readily misinterpreted than others is that the original meanings expressed are reversible. It is possible in the preceding example that the boy could have kissed the girl. If one gets this meaning from the passive sentence, which is semantically reversible, it is not surprising. Note what happens when the relationships are nonreversible.

active: Mr. Smith painted the house.
passive: The house was painted by Mr. Smith.
(active):   *The house painted Mr. Smith. (surface order strategy)

A passive sentence such as the above would not make sense if one used a surface order strategy. The noun phrases, *Mr. Smith* and *the house*, cannot be interchanged and result in a sentence that is semantically appropriate or that makes a realistic or probable statement. In *The girl kissed the boy* or *The boy was kissed by the girl*, the noun phrases could be substituted one for the other (i.e., reversed). The resulting sentences would make statements that were probable, realistic, and appropriate.

In the following list, which of the passive sentences are reversible and which are nonreversible?

1. A Honda was hit by a Chevette.
2. The rat was killed by the kitten.
3. John's TV was stolen by thieves.
4. The baby was bathed by the nurse.
5. The bear was wounded by the moose.

The third and fourth sentences are nonreversible and the others are reversible. It is possible and realistic that a Chevette could be hit by a VW, that a kitten could be killed by a rat, and that a moose could be wounded by a bear. However, TVs can't steal thieves, and it is highly unlikely that nurses would be bathed by babies.

Turn to Exercise 28 for practice in identifying and using passive sentences.

Unit 2: Passive Sentences with Other Complexities

Objectives

- Write the active equivalent of nontruncated passive sentences
- Specify the information from passive sentences that a reader using a surface order strategy could receive
- State that which is deleted in truncated passives
- State a condition under which passive sentences would be in truncated form
- Specify passive sentences as truncated or nontruncated, as reversible or nonreversible, and as the informal passive when appropriate
- Identify the voice and tense of verb phrases in a paragraph
- Identify the passive sentences in given active and passive sentences
- Identify all modality changes, noun phrase elaborations, and transformations in sentences with and without passive verb phrases

Truncated Passives

The passive sentences that were used as examples in the previous section were in the full form. A further transformation, deletion of *by + the agent* (or NP[1]) may be applied to some passives. This results in sentences such as the following:

The boy was pushed into the river.
PL 94-142 was passed in the 1970s.
John's jokes were not appreciated.
The work will be completed by Saturday.
Our team was defeated by only three points.

Passives with the *by + NP[1]* deletion are called **truncated passives.** The agent or experiencer, as would be the case in the third sentence, is not included in the sentence because it is either unknown or unimportant. The last two sentences contain *by* phrases. What is the function of these phrases? Do they contain the agent? *By Saturday* is an adverbial denoting the time by which the work will be completed. In the last sentence, *by only three points* is an adverbial designating the margin by which the team was defeated by its opponents. Thus, in these sentences, as well as in the others, there is a deletion of the *by + NP[1]*.

The active and passive forms of the first sentence would be as follows:

active: *Someone* pushed the boy into the river.
passive: The boy was pushed into the river *by someone.*
pass + del: The boy was pushed into the river.

The pattern of a passive sentence cannot be analyzed because the subject is not the NP1, but the NP[2]. Therefore, any passive sentence would have to be changed to the active form for analysis. If one uses analysis as a teaching strategy, a passive sentence with which a child has difficulty can be written in the active form so that the appropriate relationships in the sentence can be seen.

It is recommended that teaching materials be written in the active form, with the passive gradually introduced after the child has a good grasp of the subject-verb-object sentence. Also, the full passive should be used rather than the truncated form until a child grasps clues to the passive from the *be* auxiliary + *-en* + V and from *by.*

Passives with Indirect Objects

The meanings in sentences with both direct and indirect objects can be expressed in four ways. Consider the following basic sentence and the transformations that can be applied to it.

Basic sentence:	The principal gave medals to the winners.
passive:	Medals were given to the winners by the principal.
ind obj preposing:	The principal gave the winners medals.
pass + ind obj preposing:	The winners were given medals by the principal.

For true flexibility with language, the individual should be able to get the same basic information from all four sentences as well as the nuances of the different emphases possible when one form is selected over another. In addition to the four forms already indicated, the two passive forms can be truncated by deletion of *by the principal* if the person who presented the medals is not of importance—*Medals were given to the winners,* and *The winners were given medals.*

Passives with Other Complexities

When the passive is combined with complexities such as questions, pronominalizations, and other operations on a single sentence, or when passive sentences express more than a single proposition, the difficulty is increased. If one lists all the complexities for the sentence *Shouldn't she have been sent money by her guardian,* the list would have to include

pronominalization—*she* (nom, fem, sing, 3rd pers)
agreement in gender and number of gen det—*her*
perfect aspect in verb
negative contraction of modal
passive (reversible) + indirect object preposing
yes-no question with aux inversion

Passive Verb Forms

As previously indicated, verbs must have the feature [+transitive] to be transformed to the passive voice. Verb phrases may be either active or passive voice if the verb is transitive; all other verbs have only active voice. When the verb phrase is changed to the passive it must contain a *be* auxiliary and the *-en* form of the verb. The tense and aspect must be the same as in the active.

The majority of the verbs in Pattern 2 sentences are transitive; however, a small number of verbs that are followed by NPs are not [+transitive]. Some of these verbs, which are sometimes referred to as middle verbs (Roberts, 1968), are *have, want, cost, contain,* and *resemble.* When *weigh* and *measure* are followed by noun phrases such as *ten pounds* or *three feet*, respectively, they are not transitive. Thus, the following sentences cannot be passive sentences.

> *Some apples were wanted by John.
> *Forty dollars was contained by the wallet.
> *A new house is had by the Browns.

The verb *have* in the informal sentence *A good time was had by all* is passive. Also, *have* is used idiomatically, as is the verb *take* in sentences like *Bob was taken by that realtor,* and *Bob was had by that realtor.* The verb *have,* when it denotes possession, however, is not [+transitive] and does not change to passive voice.

In generating a passive sentence, the verb must agree in number with the NP that is the subject, so that the number may be different from that of the active form—*A raccoon was eating the apples,* but *The apples were being eaten by a raccoon.* The verb phrase in the passive sentence is also past tense and progressive aspect, as it is in the active sentence. Verb phrases in the passive voice, then, may carry the meanings of both progressive and perfect aspect. They may also contain modal auxiliaries and be used to express the additional meanings of these auxiliaries. Following are examples of different forms that passive voice verb phrases may take.

Active	*Passive*	*Tense/Aspect*
evaluates	is evaluated	simple present
discussed	was discussed	simple past
is, was fixing	is (was) being fixed	pres or past progressive
have (had) destroyed	have (had) been destroyed	pres or past perfect
can (could) catch	can (could) be caught	pres or past + modal
may (might) have opened	may (might) have been opened	pres or past + modal + perfect

The verb in each of the above passive verb phrases has the *-en* affix. Also, each verb phrase has a *be* auxiliary, although it varies in form depending upon the aspect and the other auxiliaries used.

An alternative passive is the **informal**, or **got, passive**, which substitutes a form of *get* for the *be* auxiliary. In the following sets of sentences the informal passive is contrasted with the regular passive.

Informal Passive	*Regular Passive*
Tom is getting married.	Tom is being married.
A man got shot.	A man was shot.
Those boys may get caught by the police.	Those boys may be caught by the police.

Turner and Rommetveit (1967), in an investigation of the development of the passive, found that hearing preschool children used *got* passives more frequently than *be* passives. Power (1971), in studying deaf children's acquisition of passive voice, found that all or the majority of subjects at the age levels from 9–10 to 17–18 rejected *got* passives as grammatical or "good" sentences. He attributed this to their being taught that such sentences were "bad" English.

Russell, Quigley, and Power (1976) stated that research indicates that the passive voice is difficult for hearing children, and it may not be mastered until the age of 8 or 9. Young hearing children were found to use a surface order strategy in interpreting meaning, and they had more difficulty with reversible than with nonreversible passives. Research studies also indicate that deaf children use surface order strategy in interpreting passives until a much later age than do hearing children. At ages 17 and 18, almost 40 percent of the subjects used by Power and Quigley (1973) incorrectly interpreted passive sentences by using a surface order strategy. Nonreversible passives were more difficult than reversible, and passives with a *by* + *agent* deletion were by far the most difficult.

Russell, Quigley, and Power stated that "many deaf children appear not to have grasped the meanings of passive voice markers up to 10 years after the point at which virtually all hearing children have done so" (p. 96). Sentences in the passive appear as early as in first-grade reading texts and are used relatively frequently at all levels of reading texts. This presents problems in comprehension to the reader who has not mastered this syntactic form.

Turn to Exercise 29 for practice in recognizing and using passive sentences.

CHAPTER 13

Language Analysis II and Review

Objectives

- Demonstrate the performance required in objectives for Language Analysis I
- Identify the following modality changes in the sentences in the syntactic description of the analysis:
  a. Negative
  b. Imperative
  c. Yes-no question
  d. *Wh*-question
- Identify in the syntactic description the following transformations:
  a. Auxiliary inversion
  b. Pronominalization (personal, indefinite, reflexive, demonstrative)
  c. Contraction
  d. *Do*-support
  e. Adverbial preposing
  f. Particle movement
  g. Intensifier
  h. Indirect object preposing
  i. There
  j. Passive
  k. Deletion
- Determine the frequency of occurrence of the transformations and modality changes in a given sample
- State the semantic descriptions of one, two, and three proposition sentences having noun phrase elaborations, modality changes, and transformations
- Determine the total number of propositions in the sample and the number of propositions per utterance

Review: Units 7-12

- Identify the basic pattern of given sentences with and without modality changes and simple transformations
- Identify features of nouns, verbs, etc. in sentences
- Identify determiners, prepositions, adverbs, adjectives, noun adjuncts, intensifiers, pronouns, and particles in given sentences

- Identify the tense, voice, and aspect of verb phrases
- Identify specific modal, *be* and *have* auxiliaries, and/or list designated auxiliaries
- Identify descriptions of specific pronouns: personal, reflexive, indefinite, and demonstrative
- Identify passive sentences as reversible or nonreversible, and as truncated or nontruncated; write the active equivalent of passive sentences
- Identify adverbial type as location, temporal, manner, etc.
- Identify noun phrase elaborations, modality changes, and transformations in given sentences
- Identify the semantic relationships in given sentences

The first set of chapters presented basic sentences and complexities in noun and verb phrases. The second set dealt with additional complexities that result from modality changes and from single base transformations, operations involving single sentences. Most of the complexities to this point have been in single proposition sentences, with the exception of those with additional propositions because of the noun phrase elaborations: adjective, noun adjunct, and possessive determiners or nouns. The remainder of the chapters will deal with complexities resulting from the combining of sentences or elaborations that produce complex sentences of more than one proposition.

You should be able to identify basic sentences and the constituents that make up such sentences. This knowledge will enable you to chart a child's development of the different types of sentence frames. It will also help you to control your language when working with curriculums using basic sentence patterns in the beginning stages of language development for children who exhibit difficulties or delay in language acquisition.

Learning the various noun and verb phrase modulations, noun phrase elaborations, modality changes, and transformations will help you to assess a child's language development, to judge the complexity of the language in teaching materials (both commercial and teacher-made), and to control the language you use, when necessary. With this knowledge and with the knowledge of more complex syntax presented in the following chapters, you should have the basic information on English grammar needed to deal with the syntactic aspect of language analysis and language programming.

In the first twelve chapters, all of the types of form class and structure words, with the exception of conjunctions, were presented. You should now be able to identify form class words: nouns, verbs, adjectives, adverbs; and structure words: determiners, pronouns, prepositions, auxiliaries, intensifiers. These are classifications used in language arts series as well as in some of the available language curriculums for children with special language needs.

Basic semantic information has been presented so that you may be able to stress this important aspect of language. The ability to determine the semantic relationships a child comprehends and expresses and to expand these through your language programming is more important than stress on the syntactic relationships. Within the syntactic frame of S-V-O ($NP^1 + V + NP^2$) many meanings are possible. This is only one example that indicates the importance of meaning over syntax.

A practice test for the second portion of the text, which incorporates information from all the chapters thus far, begins on p. 141 in the workbook.

In doing an analysis of a child's language sample, all the complexities indicated in the syntactic description, and the frequency of occurrence of each, can be determined. Again as a means of review, a hypothetical sample, contrived so as to present the complexities presented in the text to date, will be analyzed.

The following section includes those structures to be tabulated in the syntactic description, if such structures occur in the sample.

Syntactic Description

Noun Phrase Modulations

regular plurals
irregular plurals
articles
prearticles
demonstratives
other determiners

Verb Phrase Modulations

irregular past
regular past
regular third person
irregular third person
modal aux
copula (contracted, uncontracted)
progressive aspect
have aux
perfect aspect
particle
be aux
preposition

Elaborations in NP

possessive determiner
possessive noun
adjective modifier
noun adjunct modifier

Modality Changes

negation
imperative
yes-no question
wh-question

Transformations

pronominalization
  personal
  reflexive
  indefinite
  demonstrative
auxiliary or copula inversion
contraction
do-support
adverbial preposing

Transformations (continued)
intensifier
reflexive intensifier
reflexive intensifier movement
indirect object preposing
particle movement
there
passive
deletion

Although a full syntactic description is given as an example, this is not necessary for the teacher or clinician in a real work situation. A summary indicating the frequency of occurrence of the various modulations, elaborations, etc., should be included in the report of a language analysis. This can be done by using a tabulation sheet (see Figure 3). This tabulation sheet can be modified so as to include the various complexities to be presented later in the text.

A semantic description is included and you will receive practice in determining the frequency of occurrence of the various noun, verb, modifier, and adverbial cases. In the semantic description, the same noun and adverbial cases will be used as in the last analysis, except that intensifiers will be included in adverbial cases. This time, the use of **ordinals** and **cardinals**, if any are used, will be indicated as **modifier cases** in the semantic description.

Again, it must be stressed that the language sample that will be analyzed is not a complete sample and it is not representative of a language level. Children generating questions, passives, etc., would also be using two or more proposition sentences with some rather complex modality changes, conjoinings, elaborations, and transformations. The sample was contrived so as to provide practice in analyzing the syntactic structures presented thus far in the text. The sentences themselves, however, are typical of what would be found in samples of children's language, along with even more complex sentences.

Language Sample
Subject: Bobby

1. Can you get this top off for me?
2. Put another circle here. (Direction to another person)
3. His daddy bought animal cookies for a snack.
4. I gave my mommy some cookies.
5. Do you like soda?
6. Now there's not one toy on the floor.
7. I'll show you something.

8. Those fish aren't in dirty water.
9. Where did Daddy hurt himself?
10. Is that tree very green?
11. When was Billy's dog killed?
12. Mommy made that herself.

Syntactic Description

Sentence   *Pattern*

1. Can you get this top off for me?
      You can get this top off for me. $NP^1 + V + NP^2 + Adv$

   VP modulation: modal auxiliary
                       particle
                       preposition (*for*)

   NP modulation: demonstrative determiner (+near)
   Modality change: yes-no question
   Transformation: personal pronominalization (2)
                       auxiliary inversion
                       particle movement

2. Put another circle here.
      (You) put another circle here. $(NP^1) + V + NP^2 + Adv$

   NP modulation: −def article
   Modality change: imperative

3. His daddy bought animal cookies for a snack. $NP^1 + V + NP^2 + Adv$

   VP modulation: irregular past
                       preposition (*for*)

   NP modulation: ∅ article
                       −def article
                       regular plural

   NP elaboration: possessive determiner
                       noun adjunct

4. I gave my mommy some cookies.
      I gave some cookies (to) my mommy. $NP^1 + V + NP^2 + (Adv)$

   VP modulation: irregular past
   NP modulation: −def article
                       reg plural

   NP elaboration: possessive determiner
   Transformation: personal pronominalization
                       indirect object preposing

5. Do you like soda?
   You like soda. $NP^1 + V + NP^2$
   NP modulation: Ø article
   Modality change: yes-no question
   Transformation: *do*-support
                    auxiliary inversion
                    personal pronominalization

6. Now there's not one toy on the floor.
   One toy is on the floor now. $NP + V_{be} + Adv + Adv$
   VP modulation: copula (contracted)
                    preposition (*on*)
   NP modulation: +def article
                    cardinal
   Modality change: negation
   Transformation: adverbial preposing
                    there
                    copula inversion
                    contraction

7. I'll show you something.
   I will show something (to) you. $NP^1 + V + NP^2 + Adv$
   VP modulation: modal (contracted)
   Transformation: personal pronominalization (2)
                    indefinite (1)
                    indirect object preposing
                    contraction

8. Those fish aren't in dirty water. $NP + V_{be} + Adv$
   VP modulation: copula
                    preposition (*in*)
   NP modulation: demonstrative determiner
                    irreg plural
                    Ø article
   NP elaboration: adjective modifier
   Modality change: negation
   Transformation: contraction

9. Where did Daddy hurt himself?
   Daddy hurt Daddy somewhere. $NP^1 + V + NP^2 + Adv$
   NP modulation: Ø article
   Modality change: *wh*-question
   Transformation: *do*-support
                    auxiliary inversion
                    reflexive pronominalization

10. Is that tree very green?
    That tree is very green. $NP + V_L + Adj$

    VP modulation: copula (uncontracted)
    NP modulation: demonstrative
    Modality change: yes-no question
    Transformation: copula inversion
                      intensifier

11. When was Billy's dog killed?
    Someone killed Billy's dog sometime. $NP^1 + V + NP^2 + Adv$

    VP modulation: be auxiliary
    NP modulation: Ø article
    NP elaboration: poss noun
    Modality change: wh-question
    Transformation: auxiliary inversion
                      passive
                      deletion

12. Mommy made that herself.
    Mommy (Mommy) made that. $NP^1 + V + NP^2$

    VP modulation: irregular past
    NP modulation: Ø article
    Transformation: demonstrative pronominalization
                      reflexive intensifier movement

Syntactic Summary

Sentences	Frequency of Occurrence	Comments
Pattern 1	0	
Pattern 2	9	adverbials (5)
Pattern 3	1	
Pattern 4	0	
Pattern 5	2	adverbial (1)
Verb Phrase Modulations		
irregular past	3	
modals	2	can, will (contracted)
copula	3	is, are
particles	1	
prepositions	4	in, on, for

	Frequency of Occurrence	Comments
Noun Phrase Modulations		
regular plural	1	
irregular plural	1	
articles	10	Ø article, (the), another, some, a
demonstratives	3	this, that, those
Noun Phrase Elaborations		
possessive determiner	2	
possessive noun	1	
adjective	1	
noun adjunct	1	
Modality Changes		
negation	2	not, negative contraction
imperative	1	
yes-no question	2	
wh-question	2	location and time *wh*-word
Transformations		
pronominalization		
personal	6	I, you, me
indefinite	1	something
reflexive	2	himself, herself
demonstrative	1	that
do-support	2	do, did
auxiliary or copula inversion	6	in questions and *there*
contraction	3	modal *will* and *is*, negation
adverbial preposing	1	time adverbial
intensifier	1	very
indirect object preposing	2	verbs—give and show
reflexive intensifier movement	1	
there	1	with *be* and adv place
particle movement	1	
passive	1	truncated
deletion	1	

Semantic Description

Sentence	*Description*
1. Can you get this top off for me?	Agent—action—patient—beneficiary
2. (You) Put another circle here.	Agent—action—complement—patient—location
3. His daddy bought animal cookies for a snack.	
Daddy bought cookies for a snack	Agent—action—patient—reason
(someone) has a daddy	Possessor—process—patient
the cookies are animals	Entity—stative—equivalent
4. I gave my mommy some cookies.	
I gave some cookies to mommy	Agent—action—patient—beneficiary
(Bobby has) a mommy	Possessor—process—patient
5. Do you like soda?	Experiencer—process—patient
6. Now there's not one toy on the floor.	Entity—stative—location—time
7. I'll show something to you.	Agent—action—patient—beneficiary
8. Those fish aren't in dirty water.	
those fish are in water	Entity—stative—location
the water is dirty	Entity—stative—condition
9. Where did Daddy hurt himself?	
Daddy hurt Daddy somewhere	Agent—action—patient—location
10. Is that tree very green?	Entity—stative—intensifier—color
11. When was Billy's dog killed?	
Someone killed the dog sometime	Agent—action—patient—time
Billy has a dog	Possessor—process—patient
12. Mommy made that herself.	Agent—action—complement—intensifier

Semantic Summary

Number of utterances:	12
Number of propositions:	17
Propositions per sentence:	1.4

Noun cases	Frequency of Occurrence
Mover	0
Agent	8
Experiencer	1
Patient	10 or 11
Entity	5
Equivalent	1
Possessor	3
Beneficiary	3
Complement	1 or 2
Verb cases	
Action	8
Process	4
Stative	5
Modifier cases	
Condition	1
Color	1
Cardinal	1
Adverbial cases	
Location	4
Time	2
Reason	1
Intensifier	1

Syntactic Structures	Utterances												Total
	1	2	3	4	5	6	7	8	9	10	11	12	
Verb Phrase Modulations													
irregular past			1	1								1	3
regular past													
regular third person													
irregular third person													
modals	1						1						2
copula						1		1		1			3
progressive aspect													
perfect aspect													
particles	1												1
prepositions	1		1			1		1					4
Noun Phrase Modulations													
regular plural			1										1
irregular plural								1					1
articles		1	2	1	1	1		1	1		1	1	10
demonstratives	1						1		1				3
cardinals						1							1
prearticles													
Noun Phrase Elaborations													
possessive determiner			1	1									2
possessive noun											1		1
adjective								1					1
noun adjunct			1										1

Figure 3
Tabulation Sheet for a
Syntactic Description

Syntactic Structures	Utterances												Total
	1	2	3	4	5	6	7	8	9	10	11	12	
Modality Changes													
negation						1		1					2
imperative		1											1
yes-no question	1				1								2
wh-question										1		1	2
Transformations pronominalization: personal	2			1	1		2						6
reflexive									1			(1)	2
indefinite							1						1
demonstrative												1	1
do-support				1			1						2
auxiliary or copula inversion	1			1	1		1	1	1				6
contraction						1	1	1					3
adverbial preposing						1							1
intensifier										1			1
indirect object preposing			1				1						2
reflexive intensifier													
reflexive intensifier movt											1		1
there						1							1
particle movement	1												1
passive											1		1
deletion											1		1

Figure 3 (continued)

Turn to Language Analysis II Exercise for practice analyzing a language sample.

CHAPTER 14

Coordination

Complex sentences containing two or more propositions are primarily derived by means of operations. These operations include conjoining, relativization, complementation, and nominalization. Thus far, you have dealt with complex sentences containing two propositions that were derived with operations such as adjective or noun adjunct embeddding (a *beautiful* day, a *paper* hat), or genitive inclusion (*his* dog, *Mary's* sister). The operation covered in this chapter is **coordination,** which results from the use of coordinating and correlative conjunctions and conjunctive adverbs. Through coordination, two or more propositions may be expressed in one sentence.

Unit 1: Conjoining with Coordinating Conjunctions

Objectives
- List the operations used to combine two or more propositions into a single sentence
- List three coordinating conjunctions
- Define clause and independent clause
- State a condition that must exist if sentences without deletions are conjoined with *and*
- Combine sentences that can be conjoined with *and* + pronominalization
- State the conditions under which identical elements may be deleted in conjoined sentences
- Specify the conjoined constituents in sentences conjoined with *and*
- Specify the deleted words in conjoined sentences with deletions
- Write sentences using words that require conjoined noun phrases.
- Order the difficulty of sentences conjoined with *and*
- State the conditions under which sentences may be conjoined with *but*
- Appropriately conjoin pairs of sentences with *and* or *but*
- State an alternate conjunction that can be used for *but*
- State the conditions under which two sentences may be conjoined using *or*

- State an additional operation that must be performed in the second sentence when conjoined with *nor*
- Identify the coordination in sentences as *conjunction, disjunction,* or *alternation*
- Appropriately conjoin pairs of sentences with *and, but, or,* or *nor*
- Identify the words deleted from sentences conjoined with *and, but,* and *or*

Conjoining with *And*

The most commonly used form of coordination is the conjoining of elements with the **coordinating conjunction** *and.* If two sentences have identical parts, the nonidentical parts may be conjoined with *and,* so long as it is clear to the listener or reader what has been deleted. This means, then, that noun phrases, verbs, adverbials, and adjectives all may be conjoined so as to streamline the communication. The identical elements, which may be noun phrases, noun phrases plus verbs, etc., must have the same or similar structure. Figure 4 illustrates some of the ways in which sentences may be joined with a deletion of identical parts.

In all of the examples in Figure 4, the italicized identical elements in the second sentence are deleted, and the nonidentical parts in each sentence are conjoined. Thus, each of the sentences on the right is derived from coordination with *and* plus deletion. Except for the sentence with conjoined subjects, the coordination of sentences with identical subjects may occur with a pronominalization of the subject in the second sentence of the conjoined pair without reduction of the other identical elements. Except for the last example, in which the entire predicates are conjoined, the intent could be additional stress or clarity of the nonidentical or identical parts. For example,

The baby stumbled, and she fell.
Luis is tall, and he is strong.
Dana bought the groceries, and he walked home.

As can be seen in the three example sentences, the operations used to derive each sentence are coordination with *and* plus pronominalization using a personal pronoun. Pronominalizations in sentences conjoined with coordinating conjunctions are always forward pronominalizations, with the referent of the pronoun being the subject or another noun phrase in the first part of the sentence.

In traditional grammar, such sentences as those cited are called **compound sentences** because they are made up of two independent clauses. A **clause** is defined as a group of words containing an NP + VP that is part of a sentence. Clauses in sentences conjoined with the coordinating conjunctions are considered to be **independent clauses**, since each could stand alone as a sentence and one is not subordinate to the other. Therefore, both *The baby stumbled* and *she fell* are independent clauses. In analyzing such sentences syntactically, one would give the pattern of each independent clause.

Conjoined Subjects	*Jane* slept all morning. *Joan* slept all morning.	Jane and Joan slept all morning.
Conjoined Verbs	*The baby* stumbled. *The baby* fell.	The baby stumbled and fell.
Conjoined Direct Objects	*Mother bought* bacon. *Mother bought* eggs.	Mother bought bacon and eggs.
Conjoined Indirect Objects	*Dad gave money to* Jean. *Dad gave money to* Josie.	Dad gave money to Jean and Josie.
Conjoined Predicate Nominatives	*Sally is a* nurse. *Sally is a physical* therapist.	Sally is a nurse and a physical therapist.
Conjoined Adjectives	*Luis is* tall. *Luis is* strong.	Luis is tall and strong.
Conjoined Adverbials	*Chloe drives* skillfully. *Chloe drives* carefully.	Chloe drives skillfully and carefully.
Conjoined Objects of Prepositions	*Mr. Bean drove to* Chicago. *Mr. Bean drove to* Omaha.	Mr. Bean drove to Chicago and Omaha.
Conjoined Predicates	*Dana* bought the groceries. *Dana* walked home.	Dana bought the groceries and walked home.

Figure 4

**Optional Ways to Conjoin Sentences
by Deleting Identical Elements**

Two sentences with no elements in common can be conjoined with *and*. In this case, the two sentences must have a logical semantic relationship, which may be temporal (e.g., *The baby stumbled, and she fell; Tom sold his car and bought a motorcycle).* Examples of conjoined sentences that do not have identical parts but do have a temporal relationship would be *The man approached the house, and Mother locked the door; Mary broke her engagement, and the family was shocked.*

When the relationship is not temporal, the two sentences must be related and must have an approximate value, so that the propositions are equally important bits of information—*Jane was knitting a sweater, and Sue was making a dress* and *Bob cleaned the house, and Mary worked in the garden.*

Another form of coordination with *and* is used when the two sentences to be conjoined have identical parts in the VP. In this case, the verb in the second clause is deleted and *so* or *too* is inserted. When the verb in the first clause is the simple present or past tense, the *do*-support transformation is also applied. When *so* is used, the auxiliary inversion rule must be applied and the verb is deleted.

Mary bought a house, and so did John.
Jim can go, and so can Tom.
Tina lost her way, and Ann did, too.
Toby plays golf, and Tina does, too.

This form of coordination can be a preferred form for those sentences that may be ambiguous. If the first sentence in the list were *Mary and John bought a house*, it could have two meanings: each could have bought a house or they could have bought one house together.

Hargis (1977) cited instances of obligatory conjoined noun phrases. Words such as *same, different, alike, together, mix,* and *combine* may require conjoined noun phrases. Examples of coordination of this type follow. In sentences such as these, there are no deletions.

Jim and his brother play together.
Wanda parked between a bus and a truck.
Mother mixed the flour, salt, and shortening.
Her purse and shoes are the same color.

The syntactic difficulty of coordination of propositions with *and* is dependent upon the number of operations necessary for the conjoining. If pronominalization and/or *do*-support is required, this would increase the complexity. Additional complexity could be the result of deletion. The following sentences are presented in order of difficulty, with the easiest first.

The girls mowed the lawn, and the boys cleaned the house.

Jack felt weak, and he had a headache.

Tina lost her way, and Ann did too.

Conjoining with *But*

In coordination with *and*, the relationship of the propositions is termed
conjunction, and the propositions are concurrent or consecutive in time.
Coordination with *but* is called **disjunction** because one proposition is contradictory,
unexpected, or in contrast to the other.

Jim is twenty-five, but he is immature.

Mary slept for eight hours, but she looks tired.

The sun was warm, but the snow wasn't melting.

Disjunction can be more difficult than most of the forms of conjunction. One
reason for the difficulty is the semantic contrast. Also, a negative verb or word may be
required in one of the two clauses and a positive one in the other. A disjunctive form
of coordination may also be reduced when one of the propositions is in contrast to the
other, and a negative contraction is used in one of the clauses.

Jane can dive, but Jim can't.

The boys don't dance, but the girls do.

Mary and I want to go, but we can't.

Except for the auxiliary inversion rule, the sample forms of disjunction present
most of the same kinds of difficulties that are found in tag questions. Wilbur, Quigley,
and Montanelli (1975) found that deaf children had much greater difficulty with
sentences conjoined with *but* than those conjoined with *and*, showing little
improvement over the years from 10 to 18. A steady improvement was found in
conjoining with *and*; the authors stated that, for deaf students, this was among the
easiest of the more complex structures.

An alternative conjunction that can be used in disjunctive conjoining is *yet*. The
same conditions are necessary as for *but*.

That boy slept all morning, yet he seems tired.

Tom worked all night, yet he didn't finish his paper.

Conjoining with *Or* and *Nor*

Another form of coordination that is difficult is **alternation**. In alternation, the
sentences are combined with or without reduction through deletion, and the conjunctions
or or *nor* are used.

The conjunction *or* is used when one of the propositions is a consequence or an alternative of the other.

The boys should leave, or they will be late.
Jane will buy a Buick or an Oldsmobile.
Bob can't sing or dance.

Sentences conjoined with *nor* are more difficult and require the generation of more rules than sentences with *or*. When there is a negative in the first clause and *nor* is used, the copula verb or auxiliary inversion rule must be applied.

Mother wasn't angry, nor was she upset.
Jane can't cook, nor can she sew.
Bill hasn't paid you, nor should he.

Both clauses in the three sample sentences also contain negation; *nor* is a negative conjunction that replaces *not* (*he should not pay you*). In the last sentence, there is also an instance of deletion of identical elements (*pay you*).

***Turn to Exercise 30 for practice in conjoining sentences with** and, but, yet, or,* ***and** nor.*

Unit 2: Conjoining with Correlative Conjunctions

Objectives
- List pairs of correlative conjunctions
- Differentiate sentences having correlative conjunctions from sentences having coordinating conjunctions
- Specify the conjoined constituents in sentences conjoined with correlative conjunctions
- Derive sentences using the appropriate correlative conjunction from sentences conjoined with *and, or,* or *nor*

Sentences may be conjoined with paired words called **correlative conjunctions**. The relationships of conjunction, disjunction, or alternation may be expressed in such sentences depending upon which of the conjunctions is used. The paired correlative conjunctions are *both . . . and, either . . . or, neither . . . nor, not . . . but,* and *not only . . . but also.*

When subjects are conjoined with *both . . . and*, the identical elements are deleted and, when appropriate, the verb is changed to the plural.

$$\left.\begin{array}{l}\text{Jack is sick.}\\\text{Jill is sick.}\end{array}\right\}\quad\text{Both Jack and Jill } \textit{are} \text{ sick.}$$

$$\left.\begin{array}{l}\text{Mother plays bridge.}\\\text{Dad plays bridge.}\end{array}\right\}\quad\text{Both Mother and Dad } \textit{play} \text{ bridge.}$$

The same elements may be conjoined with the correlative conjunctions as with the coordinating conjunctions.

Jane is both beautiful and intelligent.
Dad bought both a suit and a coat.
That student computes problems both quickly and accurately.

In using the correlative conjunctions rather than the coordinating conjunction *and* in the above sentences, one can add emphasis to the conjoined elements. The sentences convey approximately the same meaning as when *and* is used alone and given added stress.

Jane is beautiful *and* intelligent.

The meaning in some of the sentences with *both . . . and* is more that of disjunction than conjunction. Approximately the same meaning can be conveyed with *not only . . . but (also)* as with *both . . . and*. The *also* is placed in parentheses in the sentences to indicate that it may be deleted.

Jane is not only beautiful, but (also) intelligent.
Dad bought not only a suit, but (also) a coat.

Sentences with *not . . . but* can be a shortened or alternative means of combining sentences expressing a contradiction.

$$\left.\begin{array}{l}\text{Tom didn't win the prize.}\\\text{Mary won the prize.}\end{array}\right\}\quad\text{Not Tom but Mary won the prize.}$$

$$\left.\begin{array}{l}\text{That child is not shy.}\\\text{That child is immature.}\end{array}\right\}\quad\text{That child is not shy, but immature.}$$

The propositions in such conjoined sentences are mutually exclusive, and express a disjunctive relationship, as does *but* when used alone—*That child is not shy, but she is immature.* When the conjoined elements are subjects, note that the negator *not* is inverted before the subject, and all other elements in the predicate are deleted. In conjoining two propositions as in the first pair in the preceding example, there may be a separation of the subjects, with the positive proposition stated first.

Mary won the prize. ⎫
Tom didn't win the prize. ⎭   Mary won the prize, not Tom.

When both propositions are negative, the negative conjunctions *neither* and *nor* are used. The relationship in this instance is that of conjunction, and the two propositions could be conjoined with *and*, although this would entail both a longer and redundant sentence, such as *Jim can't swim, and Bob can't swim.* Instead, these two propositions can be conjoined with *neither . . . nor—Neither Jim nor Bob can swim.* This sentence represents a less formal, and possibly a less difficult, way of expressing a conjunctive relationship than when *not* is retained and only *nor* is used—*Jim can't swim, nor can Bob.*

Alternation can be expressed using *either . . . or* rather than with *or* alone.

Either Jim or Bill can drive tonight.
Your keys must be either in your purse or in the car.
Bob wants either a hamster or a gerbil.

Turn to Exercise 31 for practice conjoining sentences.

Unit 3: Conjoining with Conjunctive Adverbs

Objectives:

- List conjunctive adverbs that may be used to join related sentences
- Write alternative sentences having the same meaning from given sentences with conjunctive adverbs or coordinating conjunctions
- Identify the modality changes, conjoinings, elaborations, and transformations in given sentences

In writing and in somewhat formal spoken communication, the coordination of propositions may also be accomplished through the use of **conjunctive adverbs**, rather than with the coordinating conjunctions *and* and *but*. Conjunctive adverbs function as both conjunctions and adverbs: they link sentences, and they may shift around in the second sentence. Examples of such coordinators are *however, nevertheless, therefore, consequently, moreover,* and *subsequently.*

The propositions that are coordinated must be related in that they exist concurrently or one is subsequent to or a consequence of the other. The meaning may also infer a contrast or a somewhat unexpected occurrence.

Mother felt ill; *however,* she cleaned the house.
A storm was predicted; *therefore,* we canceled our trip.
Tim broke his engagement with Fiona; she continued to date him, *nevertheless.*
Congress recessed; the senator's proposal, *subsequently,* was not introduced.

When propositions are combined with conjunctive adverbs in writing, a semicolon is used to separate the clauses. The conjunctive adverb may shift to a medial or final position in the second clause. It is set off with a comma when at the beginning or end of the clause and with two commas when in the middle of the clause.

Some of the coordinating and subordinating conjunctions may be used to join propositions, resulting in approximately the same meaning as when the conjunctive adverbs are used.

conjunctive adverb:	Mother felt ill; *however,* she cleaned the house.
coordinating conjunction:	Mother felt ill, *but* she cleaned the house.
subordinating conjunction:	*Although* mother felt ill, she cleaned the house.
conjunctive adverb:	Congress recessed; *subsequently,* the senator's proposal was not introduced.
coordinating conjunction:	Congress recessed, *and* the senator's proposal was not introduced.
subordinating conjunction:	*Since* Congress recessed, the senator's proposal was not introduced.

The coordination in this chapter involves conjoining with either coordinating conjunctions, correlative conjunctions, or conjunctive adverbs. When two full sentences occur with one of these coordinators, they are considered independent clauses. Other forms of coordination, which involve the subordination of one of the clauses (propositions) to the other, are introduced in the following unit.

Turn to Exercise 32 for practice using conjunctive adverbs.

CHAPTER 15

Subordination

Propositions may be linked in the surface structure to express meaning relationships such as time, location, manner, concession; cause and effect relationships; and conditional relationships. The resulting sentences will consist of an independent clause and a dependent clause introduced by a subordinating conjunction.

Since there are a number of important relationships that may be expressed, and since these relationships represent concepts acquired at varying stages, conjoining with **subordinating conjunctions** has been separated into three units: adverbial clauses (time, location, etc.), conditional clauses, and causal clauses.

Unit 1: Adverbial Clauses—Time, Location, Manner, Concession

Objectives
- Define dependent clause
- Identify the subordinating conjunctions and the dependent clauses in sentences
- Specify the relationships or meanings in sentences joined with subordinators
- Label the constituents of sentences with adverbial clauses
- Indicate whether adverbial clauses in given sentences are preposed
- Identify adverbial clauses in sentences as denoting time, duration, manner, location, or concession

When one proposition indicates the time, location, or manner in which another proposition occurred, the two may be linked with such subordinating conjunctions as *when*, *where*, and *as if*. The subordinator introduces a **dependent clause**, which may not be used alone as a sentence. In all instances, the two propositions, if not syntactically expressed with a subordinator, could be uttered or written one after the other. Conjoining with a subordinator allows a language user to convey more information in one sentence, as was the case with sentences conjoined with coordinating and correlative conjunctions and conjunctive adverbs.

Adverbial Clauses of Time

When one of the propositions indicates the time at which the other occurred, the duration or frequency subordinating conjunctions (e.g., *when, whenever, after, before, as, until, while,* and *since*) are used to join the two. Some of the subordinators may contain more than one word—*as soon as, as long as,* and *now that.*

Time:	Mother cried *when the boys left.*
	Chun walks the dog *before he eats dinner.*
Duration:	Betty has played golf *since she was nine years old.*
	Mother shopped *until Dad got off work.*
Frequency:	The baby cries *whenever the doorbell rings.*
	Fernando will talk about politics *as often as anyone will listen.*

In all of the sentences, the first clause is independent and the second is dependent. *When the boys left,* as well as the other dependent clauses, cannot be used alone as a sentence. These clauses serve as adverbials in the sentence, stating the time, place, etc., of the action of the main verb in the independent clause. One can analyze the structure of sentences with dependent clauses as follows:

$$NP^1 \qquad V \qquad NP^2 \qquad\qquad Adv$$
Betty / has played / golf / since she was nine years old.
$$NP \qquad V \qquad\qquad Adv$$
Mother / shopped / until Dad got off work.

Adverbial clauses of time may be shifted to the front of the sentence, as is the case with temporal phrases. This may be done when one wishes to put more emphasis on the time or duration.

Until Dad got off work, Mother shopped.
Before he eats dinner, Chun walks the dog.
$$(or)$$
Before Chun eats dinner, he walks the dog.

When the two clauses contain the same subject, the pronominalization transformation is applied. The pronominalization may be forward or backward if the referent of the pronoun is clear to the listener or reader. In the second sentence, the pronominalization is backward: the pronoun occurs in the first clause and its referent, *Chun,* is in the second clause. Forward pronominalization, as in the third sentence, is easier to comprehend for those having problems with pronoun reference. Also, there is less opportunity for confusion about the referent. In the second sentence it is possible that the *he* refers to the dog.

Children use adverbial clauses of time that begin with *when* prior to subordinating with *before, after,* and *until.* The use of *when* clauses, however, is preceded by earlier forms of expressing temporal order, such as through coordination with *and, or,* and *then* (Kretschmer & Kretschmer, 1978).

Adverbial Clauses of Location

An adverbial clause may indicate location, in which case the subordinating conjunctions *where* and *wherever* may be used.

Jack put the box *where Sue wouldn't find it.*
Tad parked the camper *where it would be safe.*
The dog left dirty footprints *wherever it walked.*

There are restrictions on the movement of locative clauses using *where*; therefore, the adverbial preposing transformation often may not be applied. Those clauses introduced by *wherever* are less restricted as to movement.

Adverbial Clauses of Manner

Adverbial clauses of manner introduced by the subordinators *as if* and *as though* also involve the meaning of comparison. Such clauses are not shiftable and must remain in the verb phrase.

Tom is walking *as if he had a stiff leg.*
Jane talks *as though she has something in her mouth.*
The girl cried *as if her heart were breaking.*

When the subject in the dependent clause is singular, the plural form of the verb or auxiliary represents more formal usage, as is shown in the third sentence. When *as* is used as the subordinator, there may be a deletion of the verb—*That boy walks as an old man would (walk).*

In cases of comparison, another means of combining the propositions is with a phrase introduced with *like—That boy walks like an old man.* The addition of an auxiliary or verb after a phrase with *like* is not necessary. The use of *like* as a preposition is considered to be more appropriate than its use as a subordinating conjunction.

Adverbial Clauses of Concession

The most commonly used subordinators for adverbial clauses expressing concession are *although* and *though*. As shown in the second sentence, adverbial clauses of concession may be preposed.

Sue cleaned the house *although she was tired*.
Though she preferred a Buick, Camille bought a Chevrolet.

Approximately the same meanings expressed in adverbial clauses with *although* or *though* can be expressed by conjoining sentences with the coordinating conjunction *but* or with a conjunctive adverb.

Camille preferred a Buick, but she bought a Chevrolet.
Camille preferred a Buick; nevertheless (however), she bought a Chevrolet.

It is difficult to say whether or not the meaning of concession is as clearly communicated when a different syntactic form is selected. However, the examples do indicate the flexibility of language for a communicator who has the rules for the various operations necessary for generating complex sentences.

Turn to Exercise 33 for practice recognizing and using adverbial clauses.

Unit 2: Causal Clauses

Objectives

- List words that introduce causal clauses
- List a word that introduces effect clauses
- Identify the dependent clause in sentences as one of cause or effect

An important meaning relationship that can be expressed in various ways in English is that of cause and effect. The ability to both comprehend and produce utterances denoting causal relationships is dependent upon a certain level of cognitive development and linguistic competence. One way of expressing causality or reason is to use an adverbial phrase of reason introduced with *for—Mother went to the store for coffee* or *That cake is for the party*. Such phrases answer the question *Why?* or *What . . . for?* Another way to express such relationships is to add a clause that gives either the cause or the effect or consequence of an action or event.

Cause Clauses

The words *because, since,* and *as* are used to introduce dependent clauses that give the cause or reason for the propositions in the independent clauses to which they are joined. The independent clauses explain the effect of the **causal clauses.**

    (effect)   (cause)
The teacher left school *because he was ill.*
The boys were upset *since they lost the game.*
Holly canceled her trip *as the roads were impassable.*

The conjunction *for* is rarely used to introduce causal clauses in speaking, but it may be found in written materials—*All the people loved Alfred for he was a kind man.*

The use of conjunctions other than *because* may cause difficulties in comprehension of sentence meaning. Temporal clauses are also introduced by both *since* and *as,* so that some sentences are ambiguous. Note the ambiguities in the following sentences:

The boys have been upset since they lost the game.
The children could pick up acorns as they are walking through the woods.

The dependent clauses in the sample sentences could answer questions beginning with *How long* and *When,* or they could state the reasons *Why.* It would be preferable in sentences such as these to introduce the clauses with *because* when the relationship is causal. Children, however, must be exposed to the different conjunctions for introducing causal clauses as they will often meet them in reading texts.

Causal clauses introduced by *because, since,* and *as* may be preposed. Both forward and backward pronominalization may occur when the subject NPs are the same.

Because Bill was tired, he went to bed at 8:00 p.m.
Since she had worked hard, Sharon received a raise.

The words *so that* and *in order that* are also used to introduce adverbial clauses denoting cause or reason. In the case of *so that,* the *that* may be deleted without changing the meaning of the clause.

My brother practices every day *so (that)* he can make the first team.
Melissa bought a car *in order that* she could drive to work.

Causal relationships may be expressed in sentences with phrases denoting the cause. Such phrases are introduced by *because of, due to,* or *on account of.*

Traffic was heavy because of the holiday.
The meeting was canceled due to lack of a quorum.
Jim resigned on account of his illness.

Effect or Consequence Clauses

Clauses denoting the effect or consequence in causal relationships are introduced by *so* or *so that*, with the cause stated in the first clause.

(cause)   (effect)
Mary was tired, *so she went to bed early.*
Joe wrecked his car, *so that he has to ride the bus.*

Clauses that begin with *so* and denote a result or consequence may not be shifted; nor can backward pronominalization be used. Also, these clauses do not function adverbially as do clauses with *because, since,* etc. The use of *so* denoting an effect or consequence is analogous to the use of the coordinating conjunction *and* (plus *so*) or to the conjunctive adverbs *therefore* and *consequently,* and the meaning conveyed is about the same.

Mary was tired, and she went to bed.
Mary was tired, so she went to bed.
Mary was tired, consequently, she went to bed.

A clause introduced by *so,* as in *Mary was tired, so she went to bed,* does not function as an adverbial in the sentence. *So* is used to connect two independent clauses. All the previous sentences would have to be syntactically analyzed as two sentences.

Because of the different ways in which *so* is used in causal relationships, and because of its use as an intensifier, it may pose difficulties in the comprehension of meaning and in the learning of the possible syntactic forms for expressing causality. As has been described, *so* can introduce a clause in a cause and effect sentence. It can also be used as an intensifier. At times when used as an intensifier, *so* may be followed by a clause introduced by *that* to express a causal relationship.

Mary was *so* tired!
Mary was *so* tired *that* she went to bed early.
Jim worked *so* slowly *that* he didn't finish his paper.

In sentences with *so . . . that,* the *so* intensifies an adjective or an adverb and the *that* clause acts as a complement, completing the meaning of the adjective or adverb. This elaboration of the adverb or adverbial adds a second proposition through the process of complementation.

It should be clear from this unit that competence in comprehending and expressing causal relationships is complex and dependent upon both cognitive and linguistic maturity. The child who responds, "Because," to a *Why* question has much to learn before being able to comprehend and express the various ways of denoting causality.

Turn to Exercise 34 for practice in identifying causal clauses.

Unit 3: Conditional Clauses

Objectives
- List words or co-occurring words that introduce conditional clauses
- Add conditional clauses to independent clauses
- Identify sentences as having an adverbial clause of time, duration, place, or concession; a cause or effect clause; a conditional clause; or a conjunctive adverb
- Analyze sentences with conjoinings by means of coordinating or subordinating conjunctions
- Identify the modality changes, conjoinings, elaborations, and transformations in given sentences

Another type of adverbial clause is the **conditional clause**. Conditional clauses state a condition that is relevant to the consequence stated in the independent clause. Most commonly, conditional clauses are introduced by *if.* They are shiftable and may begin a sentence. When a conditional clause with *if* is at the beginning of a sentence, *then* may co-occur with it and introduce the second or main clause.

We'll arrive at 10:00 *if the plane is on time.*
If the plane is on time, we'll arrive at 10:00.
If you finish your work, *then you may go outside.*

As with the other adverbial clauses, both forward and backward pronominalization may be used; however, forward pronominalization is preferred for clarity.

Other words that may be used to express a conditional relationship are *so long as, provided that,* and *unless.*

Students cannot graduate *unless they have a C average.*
John is going to Hawaii *provided that he saves enough money.*
The boys will mow the lawn *so long as they are paid.*

Note the future aspect or possibility expressed or implied in sentences with conditional clauses and the frequent use of the modal auxiliaries.

Conditional clauses with *if* are less difficult than those with the other clause introducers and can be expected to be understood and generated earlier.

Most of the complexities in this chapter, including adverbial clauses of time, place, manner, and concession, and causal and conditional clauses, represent the expansion of an adverbial to a clause. In this way, two propositions are joined, creating one sentence that can express two or more pieces of information depending upon other complexities used in the sentence. The general pattern of sentences with subordinate clauses is $NP^1 + V + (\quad) + Adv$. The subordinate clause is labeled as Adv.

NP^1 V_i Adv
Paul / bathed / before dinner was ready.
NP^1 V NP^2 Adv
We / put on / the storm windows / because winter was coming.
  NP   V   Adj   Adv
Jane / will be / happy / if she is accepted at Harvard.

A number of the adverbial clauses may be preposed and may occur at the beginning of the sentence. All adverbial clauses are accomplished by a form of conjoining with subordinating conjunctions. These clauses serve to incorporate two or more propositions in a single sentence. In those cases in which the adverbial clause comes first in the sentence, there is an adverbial preposing transformation in addition to the conjoining with a subordinating conjunction—*When Sue was in Europe, she purchased many gifts for friends.* The complexities in this sentence are adverbial clause of time, adverbial preposing, and pronominalization using a personal pronoun.

The process described in this chapter was subordination (i.e., the conjoining of sentences with subordinating conjunctions). The previous chapter dealt with conjoining of sentences with coordinating conjunctions. Conjoinings represent the first of the processes for combining sentences in order to communicate more information in a single sentence.

Turn to Exercise 35 for practice in recognizing subordinate clauses.

CHAPTER 16

Relativization

The previous two chapters dealt primarily with complex sentences involving the process of conjoining with either coordinating or subordinating conjunctions. A second operation for relating propositions is **relativization,** in which one proposition is embedded into a main or core proposition. Relativization provides added information or specificity to the noun in the main proposition, and, in many instances, makes clear to the listener the topic of conversation.

Unit 1: Relative Clauses

Objectives
- List the relative pronouns and the relative adverbs
- Explain the function of a relative clause in a sentence
- Identify relative clauses in sentences and their noun referents in the matrix sentences
- Write the matrix and insert sentences for sentences having a relative clause
- Write sentences having a relative clause for matrix and insert sentences
- Identify the syntactic environment of relative clauses, the constituent each relative pronoun replaces, and whether the clause is prep-fronted
- Specify the information from sentences with relative clauses that a reader using a surface order strategy would receive
- Explain the difference in meaning in a pair of identical sentences, one having a restrictive and one a nonrestrictive relative clause
- Identify restrictive and nonrestrictive relative clauses

Clauses with Subject Pronouns

One of the syntactic forms of relativization is the addition of a **relative clause** as a postnominal modifier of a noun phrase. The main proposition is encoded in the **matrix sentence** and the relative clause is embedded into it following whichever NP it modifies or elaborates. A full relative clause is introduced by a **relative pronoun,** such as *who, whom, which,* or *that,* or the relative possessive *whose.* When the clause is related to a noun in an adverbial phrase, the NP is expanded with a preposition followed by a relative clause beginning with *which* or *whom.*

The easiest of the relative clauses for young children or children with language difficulties is a relative clause that modifies the last NP constituent in the matrix sentence. The relative pronouns *who, which,* and *that* are used as the subjects in these clauses; these clauses have **subject relativization**.

> Jane didn't see the man *who was standing in the shadows.*
> Skydiving is a sport *that is dangerous.*
> The man told a story *that was funny.*

A child who comprehends and expresses S-V-O relationships and who applies a surface order strategy will have much less difficulty interpreting sentences with relative clauses in the final position than with clauses in the medial position. The subjects of the verbs appear in close proximity to the predicates. A child hearing or reading the third example sentence would get the information *man told story; story funny.*

In order to use the different relative pronouns, a child must possess certain rules: *who* can occur only with NPs that have the feature [+human], *which* is used with only [−human] referents, and *that* can be used in place of either *who* or *which.*

It is important to understand that a relative clause expands a noun phrase; it does not function as a sentence constituent, as does an adverbial clause.

> NP^1 V NP^2
> Jane / didn't see / the man who was standing in the shadows.

The NP^2, or direct object, in the sentence above is *the man who was standing in the shadows.* The noun phrase has a definite article, a head noun, and a relative clause modifier of the noun (i.e., a postnominal modifier).

> (+def art)   (head noun)   (relative clause)
>   the   man   who was standing in the shadows.

The two underlying sentences are *Jane didn't see the man* and *The man was standing in the shadows.* The first sentence expresses the main proposition; it is called the **matrix sentence**. The second sentence provides specificity and more clearly identifies one of the **arguments** (nouns) of the sentence (in this case, *the man*). This is the **insert sentence** that is embedded into the matrix. The matrix and insert sentences have identical noun phrases.

> Matrix: Jane didn't see *the man.*
> Insert: *The man* was standing in the shadows.
>   who
> Jane didn't see the man (the man) was standing in the shadows.

The appropriate relative pronoun replaces the identical NP in the insert sentence, which is inserted after the NP that is its referent in the matrix sentence. In relative clauses such as this, the relative pronoun is the subject of the clause, since it replaces the subject of the insert sentence.

The relative clause may be medial; that is, it may expand or be a modifier of a noun other than the one at the end of the matrix sentence. For example,

$$NP^1 \qquad\qquad V \qquad NP^2$$
The boy *who was late to class* / makes / good grades.
Matrix: The boy makes good grades.
Insert: The boy was late to class.

$$NP \qquad\qquad V_L \quad Adj$$
The books *that are in the cabinet* / are / very old.
Matrix: The books are very old.
Insert: The books are in the cabinet.

A child who understands the S-V-O relationship but does not understand the function of relative pronouns can misinterpret the meaning in such sentences if using a surface order strategy. The child could obtain the following information from the first sentence—*the boy was late* and *the class makes good grades*. The child could interpret the second sentence to mean that *the cabinet is very old*.

Medial relative clauses may cause difficulty for children who are progressing normally in language development. These clauses are less readily processed by adults than are those in the final position (Sheldon, 1977). Quigley, Smith, and Wilbur (1974) reported that 41 percent of their oldest hearing subjects (10 years old) misinterpreted the meaning in medial relative clauses.

Clauses with *Whose*

The relative word *whose* functions as a possessive determiner in a noun phrase because it replaces a possessive noun modifier in the phrase. Clauses with *whose* may be either final or medial, and they modify or elaborate a noun phrase as do other relative clauses.

The children felt sorry for Don *whose dog ran away.*
The family *whose house burned down* received help from the Red Cross.

The matrix and insert sentences for the first sentence are as follows:

Matrix: The children felt sorry for Don.
Insert: Don's dog ran away.

The relative clause with *whose*, in addition to representing the second proposition in the deep structure, also represents a third proposition with the relationship of Possessor—process—patient (*Don had a dog*).

Clauses with Object Pronouns

In all of the preceding examples of sentences with relative clauses, the relative word was the subject or was in the subject of the clause.

```
NP          Vᵢ            Adv
who / was standing / in the shadows
     NP          Vᵢ
whose dog / ran away
```

These two sample clauses contain examples of subject relativization; that is, the subject or a possessive in the subject is relativized.

The relative pronoun may replace the object or NP^2 in the insert sentence. This results in clauses that are more difficult to interpret correctly. Consider the following examples:

> Bob is dating the girl *whom he met at a party last month.*
> Dad hid the present *which he bought for Mother.*
> The ring *that Mary lost* was valuable.

In all of these sentences, the relative pronoun is the object of the verb in the clause; it replaces an NP that is the object of the insert sentence. Clauses in the example sentences, then, are said to have **object relativization**.

Matrix: Bob is dating *the girl.*
                    (object)
Insert: Bob met *the girl* at a party last month.
Matrix: *The ring* was valuable.
                    (object)
Insert: Mary lost *the ring.*

To relativize the insert sentence, two (or three) operations are necessary: a relative pronoun replaces the identical NP and the relative pronoun is moved to the front of the clause.

Insert: Mary lost *the ring.*
rel pro: Mary lost *that*
rel pro movt: *that* Mary lost

When the insert sentence has two shared nouns rather than only one, a pronominalization transformation is also necessary.

Insert:	*Bob* met *the girl* at a party last month.
rel pro (and pronominalization):	*he* met *whom* at a party last month
rel pro movt:	*whom* he met at a party last month

Russell, Quigley, and Power (1976) stated that studies of both hearing and hearing-impaired subjects indicated that clauses with object relative pronouns were more difficult than those with subject pronouns.

An added difficulty in understanding sentences with clauses having object pronouns may result from the optional deletion of the relative pronoun. This will be discussed further in the second unit of this chapter.

Bob is dating the girl (whom) he met at the party last month.
Dad hid the present he bought for Mother.
The ring Mary lost was valuable.

All of the above sentences contain the operations relative pronoun insertion, rel pro movement, and rel pro deletion.

Clauses with Prepositions

The relative pronoun may replace an indirect object or the object of a preposition in a phrase that is a location, time, etc., adverbial in the insert sentence.

The girl *to whom he gave his fraternity pin* dates other boys.

Matrix: *The girl* dates other boys.
                                              IO
Insert: He gave his fraternity pin to *the girl.*

Jane often returns to the town *in which she was born.*

Matrix: Jane often returns to *the town.*
Insert: She was born in *the town.*

Quigley, Steinkamp, Power, and Jones (1978) called relative clauses such as those in the preceding sentences **prep-fronted**. Prep-fronted means that the preposition and the relative pronoun have been moved to the front of the clause. The operations used to generate sentences with prep-fronted relative clauses include the following:

clause: he gave his fraternity pin to *the girl*
rel pro insertion: he gave his fraternity pin to *whom*
rel pro + prep movt: *to whom* he gave his fraternity pin

The relative pronoun *that* may not be used in *prep-fronted* relative clauses. However, when only the relative pronoun is moved to the front of the clause, *that* can replace the noun phrase.

The girl *that* he gave his fraternity pin *to* dates other boys.
The girl *to whom* he gave his fraternity pin dates other boys.
Jane often returns to the town *that* she was born *in*.
Jane often returns to the town *in which* she was born.

When the preposition is not moved, native speakers may elect to use *who* rather than *whom*, although they use *whom* when the preposition precedes the pronoun— *The men who he gave the money to left town* or *The men to whom he gave the money left town*. The relative pronoun may, or may not, be deleted when the NP replaced by the relative pronoun is the object of a preposition that is not shifted.

The man (   ) he gave the money to left town.
Jane often returns to the town (   ) she was born in.

Clauses with *Where* and *When*

Relative clauses introduced by *where* and *when* represent an alternative means of relativizing insert sentences in which the relative pronoun would replace the object of a preposition in an adverbial of place or time. In this case, the *where* and *when* function as adverbials and may be referred to as **relative adverbs**. You will find that some texts include these words in their lists of relative pronouns. Examples of clauses with relative adverbs follow.

My family made a trip to Mt. Vernon where Washington had lived.
Matrix: My family made a trip *to Mt. Vernon*.
Insert: Washington had lived *at Mt. Vernon*.
rel adv insertion: Washington had lived *where*
rel adv movt: *where* Washington had lived

Marge arrived at noon when I was out to lunch.

Matrix:	Marge arrived *at noon*.
Insert:	I was out to lunch *at noon*.
rel adv insertion:	I was out to lunch *when*
rel adv movt:	*when* I was out to lunch

In these examples, the appropriate relative adverb is inserted for the shared adverbial (NP in the Adv) in the insert sentence; it is moved to the front of the clause, and the clause is inserted after the adverbial (or the NP in the adverbial) that is the referent in the matrix sentence.

Clauses with relative adverbs can be distinguished from location and time adverbial clauses since (a) there is always a referent immediately preceding the relative adverb and (b) the clause is part of an NP or prepositional phrase rather than an added sentence constituent. Note the differences between the adverbial clauses and the relative adverb clauses in the following sentences.

$$NP^1 \qquad V \qquad\qquad\qquad NP^2$$
rel adv: Mary / loved / the state where she lived as a child.

$$NP \qquad V_i \qquad\qquad\qquad Adv$$
rel adv: Joe / arrived / in the morning when we were asleep.

$$NP^1 \qquad V \qquad NP^2 \qquad\qquad Adv$$
adv cl: Mother / leaves / her keys / where she can't find them.

$$NP \qquad V_i \qquad\qquad Adv$$
adv cl: The men / jog / when the weather is pleasant.

Restrictive and Nonrestrictive Clauses

All of the relative clauses that have been used thus far have been **restrictive clauses.** Restrictive clauses restrict the meaning of the NP that they modify. They are used to more clearly identify the person, place, or thing referred to. **Nonrestrictive clauses** provide additional information, but they are not necessary to identify or clarify who or what is referred to. In writing, nonrestrictive clauses are easily identified because they are set off by commas. In speech, the intonation pattern of the sentence is different, with pauses used where the commas appear in writing.

nonrestrictive:	My brother, *who is an engineer*, will be in Washington next week.
restrictive:	My brother *who is an engineer* will be in Washington next week.

In the first sentence, the nonrestrictive clause provides the listener or reader with additional information. This clause is encoded as a separate sentence. When one takes the meaning into account, it is not really tied to the NP as a postnominal modifier would be. In the second sentence, the relative clause is an integral part of the noun phrase. The clause specifies which brother is meant because the speaker has more than one. This meaning is not conveyed in the sentence with the nonrestrictive clause.

In some sentences, the semantic difference in clauses that are restrictive as opposed to nonrestrictive appears greater.

| restrictive: | Multihandicapped children *who are retarded* should not be mainstreamed. |
| nonrestrictive: | Multihandicapped children, *who are retarded,* should not be mainstreamed. |

Can you see a difference in the meaning of the two sentences? The first sentence implies that only those multihandicapped children who are retarded should not be mainstreamed. The second sentence implies that all multihandicapped children are retarded and that they should not be mainstreamed.

The following sentences also convey different meanings.

| restrictive: | Dogs *that* can be trained make good pets. |
| nonrestrictive: | Dogs, *which* can be trained, make good pets. |

In the first sentence, the individual is stating that only those dogs that can be trained make good pets, while the second sentence infers that all dogs can be trained. This set of sentences points out a restriction in nonrestrictive clauses: the relative pronoun *that* may not be used in a nonrestrictive clause.

Relative clauses, whereas they are complex in themselves, may be embedded in questions, imperatives, expletive sentences, etc., and may contain other complexities, such as passives. Consider the following sentences:

Did you find the book you were looking for?
Give Jean the gift that Mary gave you.
The horse that was kicked by the man ran into the field.

The last sentence, which contains a passive, is an example of a type of sentence that is often misinterpreted by children who use an S-V-O surface order strategy. Because of the indirect object transformation, the second sentence would have three noun phrases in a row if *that* were deleted. This sentence contains a second indirect object transformation and pronominalization in an imperative sentence. The first sentence is a yes-no question with *do*-support, auxiliary inversion, deletion of the relative pronoun, and personal pronominalization.

The embedding of relative clauses is a recursive process; that is, one relative clause may be embedded after the other beyond the limit at which the information can be decoded easily.

This is the boy that hit the girl that kicked the dog that chased the cat that ate the mouse that had a nest in the house that the boy lived in.

In the example, one long noun phrase containing six embedded relative clauses follows the word *is*. Rarely does one find this many embeddings; however, it is not unusual to find two or three relative clauses in a single sentence in basal reading texts for young children.

Turn to Exercise 36 for practice identifying and using relative clauses.

Unit 2: Elaborations from Relative Clause Reductions

Objectives
- Indicate the words deleted in sentences with relative clause reductions
- Identify *-ing* phrases, *-en* phrases, prepositional phrases, and appositives in sentences that contain relative clause reductions
- Identify and label prenominal modifier(s) in sentences
- Expand sentences having pre- or postnominal modifiers to sentences with a relative clause before relative clause reductions
- Analyze sentences with relative clauses and relative clause reductions and coordinating and subordinating clauses
- Write noun phrases correctly ordering specified adjectives and determiners
- Indicate the operation(s) needed to generate sentences with relative clauses or relative clause reductions
- Identify the modality changes, conjoinings, elaborations, and transformations in given sentences

Thus far, most examples of elaboration of noun phrases by means of relativization have contained complete relative clauses. The operations involved in these relativizations have been insertion of a relative pronoun only, insertion and movement of the relative adverb or object relative pronoun, or movement of the preposition and/or relative pronoun. As a result of one or more of these operations, a relative clause expands one of the noun phrases in a sentence. In identifying complexities in sentences with full relative clauses (e.g., *Bob loves the cat that he found in the park*), we shall note the relative clause elaboration and the (relative) pronominalization. If we are looking at a language sample, the notation of a relative clause elaboration and of a pronominalization indicates that the child used a complete relative clause and an appropriate relative pronoun. In the example sentence, we see that the [−human] feature of *cat* has been observed in the appropriate use of the relative pronoun *that*.

Relative Clause with Deletion

When the relative pronoun replaces a direct object or object of a preposition, it may be deleted. This leaves the clause intact except for the relative pronoun.

Jerry bought all the books *he needed for the semester.*
The town *the girls lived in during the year* was ten miles from the school.
The girl *Jack gave a ring to* left town.

The subject, the verb, and adverbials that modify the verb, other than the one containing the relative pronoun, remain in the clause. In all of the sentences, the pronoun (*that*), if it had been inserted, would have been moved to the beginning of the clause. When noting the complexities of this type of elaboration, cite the modifier as a relative clause and indicate a deletion transformation (in this case, that of a relative pronoun).

The following elaborations of noun phrases (participle, prepositional phrase, and adjective modifiers) result from relative clause reduction and involve different operations. Each of these could be expanded into a full relative clause; however, we often use only a phrase or a single word as a modifier. It will not be necessary to specify the operations (other than the passive) used to derive the elaborations and transformations in sentences. You should, however, be aware of how the modifiers could be expanded into relative clauses and of what the secondary proposition would be for each of the different types of modifier.

Participle Phrase Modifiers

The *-ing* and *-en* forms of the verb are called **participles**. Since they are verb forms, their use in the nonfinite form should indicate to you that they represent another proposition in the deep structure. One of the operations necessary to generate sentences with either a V-*ing* or V-*en* participle modifier is rel pro + *be* deletion.

~~who was~~
That man ₍standing near the bench₎ is the coach.

With the deletion of the relative pronoun and the *be* auxiliary, the subject noun phrase has a postnominal *-ing* participle modifier, *standing near the bench.*

When the relative clause is nonrestrictive and there is deletion of the rel pro + *be*, the participle modifier may be shifted before the NP it modifies.

> The child, weeping softly, walked out of the room. (rel pro + *be* deletion)
>
> Weeping softly, the child walked out of the room. (rel pro + *be* del + participle shift)

The NP elaboration in these two sentences is an *-ing* participle modifier from a relative clause reduction. The operations needed to generate the sentence are given in the parentheses.

In sentences with *-en* participle modifiers, there are additional operations. See if you can determine the additional operations in the following sentence.

> The gifts wrapped in foil were from Mary.

The propositions in this sentence are *the gifts were from Mary* and *someone wrapped the gifts in foil.* The sentence has an *-en* participle modifier, which is postnominal, that resulted from a passive transformation with agent deletion, and then a rel pro + *be* deletion (*the gifts were wrapped in foil by someone*).

In other sentences, the agent may not be deleted and the passive is easier to recognize.

> The team, defeated by their worst rivals, hurried to the showers.
>
> Exhausted by the long run, Tom slumped over at the finish line.

The second sentence contains a participle shift in addition to the rel pro + *be* deletion and the passive. However, in noting the complexities in a sentence, you need not indicate the rel pro + *be* deletion. Cite the elaboration as a participle modifier and the transformation as passive, or passive and deletion (of the agent).

Single-Word Participle Modifiers

When a single-word participle modifier elaborates a noun phrase, it is also the result of the operations rel pro + *be* deletion and participle shift. These operations need not be cited as transformations in noting complexities in sentences.

> The *leaking* gas could cause an explosion.
>
> The gas ~~which was~~ leaking could cause an explosion.
>
> Those *ironed* shirts should be on hangers.
>
> Those shirts ~~that were~~ ironed should be on hangers.

More than one *-en* or *-ing* participle may occur in an NP as modifiers. The order may vary unless there is some logical sequence in the actions denoted in the participles.

Glowering, yelling, pushing shoppers surged toward the door.
The tow truck hauled away the *dented battered* car.

Each modifier of the noun adds to the number of propositions expressed in the sentence. The sentence describing the shoppers contains four verbs and thus, contains the following propositions:

shoppers surged toward the door
the shoppers were glowering
the shoppers were yelling
the shoppers were pushing

Adjective Modifiers

Adjective modifiers are considered to result from the same type of operations as participle modifiers, i.e., rel pro + *be* deletion and adjective shift.

The children teased the *shaggy* dog.
The children teased the dog ~~which was~~ *shaggy*.

It is important to differentiate an adjective modifier from a participle modifier. The semantic relationships expressed in one case will contain a stative verb, the other will contain an action or process verb. The adjective modifier denotes a particular attribute, and the *-ing* or *-en* participle describes an action or process. The following examples illustrate these differences.

adjective modifier:	A *huge* cat crawled under the steps.	
participle modifier:	A *shivering* cat crawled under the steps.	
	Propositions	*Semantic Relationships*
matrix:	a cat crawled under the steps	Mover—action—location
insert:	the cat was huge	Entity—stative—size
insert:	the cat was shivering	Patient—process

As you have done in the past in citing adjective modifiers, you need only identify these elaborations as adjective modifiers (not as a rel pro + *be* deletion or relative clause).

Prepositional Phrase Modifiers

Noun phrases may be elaborated with postnominal modifiers that are prepositional phrases. Syntactically, the prepositional phrases were Pattern 5 sentences. Prepositional phrase modifiers result from relative clauses with rel pro + copula (*be*) deletions. The prepositional phrase adds another proposition to the sentence, which is usually Entity—stative—location (time, beneficiary, or reason).

The book *on the table* is a biography.
The book ~~that is~~ *on the table* is a biography.

the book is a biography: Entity—stative—equivalent
the book is on the table: Entity—stative—location

Other examples of prepositional phrase elaborations are

The cake *for the party* is in the oven.
The dress *for the baby* was too big.
The meeting *at noon* should be short.

Sometimes a *with* or *without* phrase is used as a postnominal modifier. In sentences like the following, the proposition denotes a Possessor—process—patient or an Entity—stative—part relationship.

prep phr mod:	The boy *with measles* should be at home.
rel cl mod:	The boy *who has measles* should be at home.
prep phr mod:	The child *without (with no boots) boots* could catch cold.
rel cl mod:	The child *that has no boots* could catch cold.
prep phr mod:	Bill likes the girl *with red hair*.
rel cl mod:	Bill likes the girl *who has red hair*.

More than one prepositional phrase modifier often occurs after another, with each modifying a different noun. This results from a series of deletions—*The book on the table near the sofa in the den is a biography*. The subject of the sentence includes all of the words before *is*. This subject contains a series of NPs with prepositional phrase modifiers. Therefore, the NP contains a series of embeddings that were derived from relative clause reduction.

NP:	the book on the table near the sofa in the den
NP + rel cl:	the book which is on the table which is near the sofa which is in the den

Table 9
Relativization

NP + Relative Clause	Operations	Elaborations and Transformations
with full rel clause:		
the boy *who came late*	rel pro insertion	rel cl, pronominalization (who)
the boy *that Mary likes*	rel pro + movt	rel cl, pronominalization
the town *where Joe lives*	rel adv insertion + movt	rel cl
the time *at which they arrived*	prep + rel pro movt	rel cl, pronominalization (which)
the girl *whose dog is barking*	poss rel insertion	rel cl, pronominalization, poss modifier
the girl *Blake took home*	rel pro movt + del	rel cl, deletion
with *–ing* phrase:		
the girl *sitting at the window*	rel pro + *be* del	*–ing* participle modifier
giggling loudly, the girl	rel pro + *be* del + participle movt	*–ing* participle modifier
the *leaking* faucet	rel pro + *be* del, participle movt	*–ing* participle modifier
with *–en* phrase:		
the team *managed by Mr. Blue*	passive, rel pro + *be* del	*–en* participle modifier, passive
managed by Mr. Blue, the team	passive, rel pro + *be* del, participle movt	*–en* participle modifier, passive
the *broken* glasses	passive + del, rel pro + *be* del, participle movt	*–en* participle modifier, passive + deletion
with prepositional phrase:		
the books *on the table*	rel pro + *be* del	prep phrase modifier
with adjective:		
the *tiny* rug	rel pro + *be* del, adjective movt	adjective modifier
with appositive:		
George, *the coach*,	rel pro + *be* del	appositive elaboration

The words *which is* or *that is* could be inserted before each preposition in the sentence; however, this would not be an economical way of identifying which book (also, table and sofa) is intended.

Appositives

Appositives result from relative clause reductions with the deletion of the relative pronoun and the copula verb. The insert sentence has the pattern $NP^1 + V_{be} + NP^1$.

Mr. O'Leary, *a teacher in Hartford*, retired at 80.
Their dog, *a winner in many shows*, requires special food.

The appositives in the preceding sentences are in italics. Each could be expanded to a full nonrestrictive relative clause as follows:

Mr. O'Leary, who was a teacher in Hartford, retired at 80.
Their dog, which was a winner in many shows, required special food.

In form, an appositive is a noun phrase inserted after the noun phrase that is its referent. The complexity should be noted only as an appositive elaboration; it is not necessary to indicate the operations of rel pro + be deletion.

To summarize the information thus far in the chapter, Table 9 gives examples of the various kinds of relativization, the operations used to arrive at each one, and the elaborations and transformations contained in such complexities.

Order of Modifiers

Adjectives, participles, and noun adjuncts may all be embedded as noun phrase elaborations. In English, the order of adjectives, other modifiers, and determiners, when they co-occur, have a rather set pattern of occurrence. Fitzgerald, in her book *Straight Language for the Deaf* (1926), gave the following rule for the occurrence of cardinals and adjective modifiers: *How many: What kind of: What color: What:* (e.g., three large green apples). This rule does not cover all of the possibilities. The order of determiners has been discussed in a previous section. Noun adjuncts, when used with adjectives, occur immediately before the noun and after the adjectives that denote characteristics, size, shape, age, and color. Modifiers indicating place of origin also occur before noun adjuncts. Adjuncts referring to what something is made of precede those that refer to what something is used for (e.g., *wicker baby carriage, chiffon dinner dress*). Allen (1966) suggested a sequence that would result in noun phrases such as the following:

(the)   tall blue Chinese vase on the table that's in the hall

(a)   long hot summer day in July when the humidity is high

(the)   old black wool dress that you never wear

Attributes such as shape or age occur before color, and prepositional phrases and relative clauses occur after the noun. Ordinarily one does not use more than two or three adjectives or modifiers before a noun. When more than this are used, there may be some variation in the order of occurrence due to stress variations. However, orders such as those illustrated represent some of the set orders.

Relative Clauses and Other Modifiers in Reading Texts

Relative clauses or elaborations resulting from relative clause reductions occur with high frequency in reading texts. Note the occurrences in this passage from a story in Scott Foresman's *Reading Unlimited* series.

Early one morning Pancho loaded his burro with all the pots *his father had made* and all the plates *his mother had painted.* Then he set out for the market place. As he walked along, he thought how fine it would be to ride in a saddle *trimmed with silver, wearing the biggest hat in all Mexico,* and how happy he could make his Mother with the purse *filled with gold.*
The burro stopped at the turn *in the road,* and so did Pancho. Right in the middle of the road stood the bull *with the crooked tail.* The cowboy's *broken* lasso trailed from his horns, and he was angry.

(Hader & Hader, 1976, p. 38)

All the types of elaborations presented in this chapter, except for prenominal *-ing* participles and appositives, are contained in this short passage from a reader on a third grade level. One or more occur in each of the paragraphs, some of which are only one sentence containing other complexities.

Russell, Quigley, and Power (1976) indicated that relativized structures first appeared in the second primer of the reading series they analyzed. There was an increase in the frequency of occurrence in successive books in the series. The authors cited research that normally hearing and hearing-impaired children have difficulty with some types of relativized sentences, so that control of these structures in reading materials may also be necessary for hearing children.

For children to get all the information contained in a sentence or paragraph, they need receptive control of the various elaborations possible in noun phrases: relative clauses, clauses without the relative pronoun, participle phrases or participles, prepositional phrases, appositives, adjectives, and noun adjuncts.

Turn to Exercise 37 for practice in using and analyzing relativization.

CHAPTER 17

Comparatives

Objectives

- Identify in sentences regular and irregular adjectives and adverbs in the comparative and superlative degree
- Identify the optionally deleted words in the comparatives in given sentences
- Identify adjective and adverbial phrase elaborations with comparatives and specify the phrase as adjectival or adverbial
- Identify the NPs that contain comparatives in given sentences
- Analyze sentences containing comparative elaborations of adjectives or adverbs
- Identify specified complexities in sentences with comparatives
- Identify the elaborations, modality changes, conjoinings, relativizations, and transformations in sentences

The ability to use **comparatives**, both the comparative and superlative degrees, reflects a certain level of cognitive or conceptual maturity. Hargis (1977) commented on the importance of comparative constructions in communicating cognitive processes such as seriation and conservation. An understanding of comparatives is necessary in many mathematical problems, even in beginning arithmetic. Comparatives are used in expressing differences or similarities in quantity, quality, and size, and in comparing people or things as to certain other characteristics.

The term *comparative,* when referring to syntactic complexity, is an inclusive one referring to both degrees, the **comparative** and the **superlative**. For review of regular and irregular adjectives and the comparison of adjectives, you may want to go back to chapter 2, pages 21–24.

An important difference in the comparative and superlative form is that the **comparative degree** (with *-er* or *more*) is used in comparisons of two things, and the **superlative degree** (with *-est* or *most*) is used in comparisons involving three or more things. Thus, if only two kites are flying, an appropriate question to ask would be *Whose kite is higher?* This rule holds regardless of the form that comparative constructions take.

Syntactically, comparatives elaborate adjective or adverbial sentence constituents and adjectives in noun phrases. In a noun phrase, comparatives with *-er* and *-est, more* and *most* + Adj, and other more irregular comparatives (such as *better, best, most,* *least, worst, northernmost,* etc.) may be used in a *the . . . of* pattern. This pattern contains a prearticle in the NP, for example,

> *the longer of* the two boards
> *the smallest of* the seven children
> *the more beautiful of* the two watches
> *the most interesting of* the pictures

Each of the noun phrases has an adjective elaboration that is comparative in form. The adjectives *long* and *beautiful* are in the comparative degree, and *small* and *interesting* are in the superlative degree.

Comparatives also may be found in noun phrases as adjective elaborations following a null article, other articles, genitives, or cardinal determiners.

> Lesley likes *daintier* figurines.
> The two *tallest* boys in our class are on the team.
> Our *more difficult* tests are on Saturday.

Each of the above sentences has an adjective modifier elaboration and a comparative elaboration. The second sentence also contains a prepositional phrase modifier, and the third, a possessive determiner.

Comparative constructions may involve the elaboration of an adjective or adverb in the pattern Adj + comp + than + NP + del. This pattern is used to express differences in size, quality, quantity, characteristics (adjectives); or manner (adverbs). An adjective or adverb is elaborated with a comparative form and a complement clause introduced by the conjunction *than*. There is a deletion in these structures of the word(s) that would complete the clause.

Note the elaborations in the following sentences.

> Jack is *tanner than Mary.*
> (Jack is tanner than Mary is tan)
> Jack is *tanner than Mary is.*
> (Jack is tanner than Mary is tan)

The word *tan* in both sentences is an obligatory deletion; it would not be included in the sentence. The copula *is,* however, may or may not be deleted. In the cases where it is deleted, the deletion is optional. The full complement clause would be *than Mary is tan.* Both of the sentences are the same pattern: NP + V$_L$ + Adj. The adjective, which is a sentence constituent, is elaborated with the comparative morpheme *-er* and a clause with deletion. The propositions underlying the surface structure are *Jack is tan, Mary is tan.*

The adjective elaboration may also be a modifier of a NP as shown in the following sentences, all with the same meaning but with varied deletions:

Mother has larger feet than Bob.
Mother has larger feet than Bob has.
Mother has larger feet than Bob does.

In each of the three sentences there is a deletion. In the first, the deletion is *has large feet*; in the second, *large feet*; and in the third, *have large feet*. Each sentence has an adjective elaboration, a comparative elaboration, and a deletion. The last sentence also has *do*-support.

Adverbials in a sentence may also be elaborated with comparatives and *than* clauses with deletion.

Jim works more steadily than Joe.
(Jim works more steadily than Joe works.)
(Jim works more steadily than Joe does.)

The adverbial complement of the verb *works* is *more steadily than Joe* (. . .). The deletions are respectively: *works steadily, steadily,* and *work steadily.* Other examples of sentences with adverbial comparative elaborations follow:

More cunningly than a fox, the boy hurried through the woods.
Sally tries *harder than her sister does.*
Her brother tries *the hardest* (hardest).
Seth worked *the most diligently.*

In the first two examples, the adverbial comparative elaboration is in the comparative degree, and in the last two in the superlative. The adverbial in the first sentence is preposed. Since the first two examples contain the conjunction *than,* there is a deletion in each of these sentences.

The syntactic form of the comparative with *than* may be used to express similarities with a negative word appearing before the adjective.

This dress is *not older than* that one.
Tim is *no more intelligent than* his brother.
Dad found *no more mushrooms than* Mother did.

The patterns as + Adj + as + . . . + del and as + Adv + as + . . . + del are used to express similarities. In the following two sentences, comparatives with *as . . . as* are used to expand adjectives:

    NP V_L Adj
John / is / *as smart as* April (is).

             NP V_i Adv
A boy *as smart as* John (is) / should go / to college.

In the first sentence the comparative is used with an adjective sentence constituent. In the second, the adjective is a postnominal modifier of *boy*, derived from a relative clause reduction, *who is as smart. . . .* The complexities would be listed as adjective modifier, comparative elaboration, and deletion for the second sentence; and comparative plus deletion for the first. With or without the copula *is* in either sentence, there would be a deletion. The deletion would be *smart* or *is smart*.

    In the comparative form *as + Adv + as*, the adverbs are usually adverbs of manner, but may be adverbs of frequency such as *often* or *frequently*.

    Dan works *as steadily as* Debby (does).
    Dad visits Grandmother *as often as* Uncle Dick does.

    The use of the auxiliary (*does*) or the verb (*works*) after *Debby* in the first sentence is not necessary, so that the sentence would be complete without *does*. This is the case with comparative elaborations of adverbs of manner. With adverbs of frequency, the use of the auxiliary may be obligatory to avoid ambiguity. Without *does*, the second sentence could be interpreted to mean Dad visits Grandmother as often as he visits Uncle Dick.

    When an adjective in a comparison expands the direct object, the comparative may be expressed in two ways.

    NP^1 V NP^2
Sarah / has / as dark a tan as Sylvia (has).
                  or
Sarah has a tan as dark as Sylvia's.
The man bought as large a car as his neighbor's.
                  or
The man bought a car as large as his neighbor's.

If the adjective is used as a postnominal modifier, as in the second sentence in each pair, a verb or auxiliary is obligatory when the possessive is not used. The complete NP^2 in the last sentence is *a car as large as his neighbor's*, and the adjective phrase, as with other adjective modifiers, is derived from a relative pronoun plus *be* deletion: *a car which is as large as his neighbor's.* All four sentences are the same pattern as shown in the first. Note that the deletion in the first sentence is *(has) a tan*; in the second, the deletion is *tan*; and in the last two, the *(car) is large* is the deletion. The propositions in the deep structure are the same whether expressed as *Sylvia (has) a tan*, or *Sylvia's tan*.

The *as . . . as* comparative form may involve a noun phrase with a determiner denoting quantity. The pattern was as + det + N + as. . . is used in the following sentences:

> Larry received *as few gifts as* Billy.
> Our team won *as many games as* your team did.
> Mother doesn't need *as much milk as* the dairy delivered.

In the first sentence, the deleted words are *received few gifts*. The word *received* could be retained in the sentence. As you can see, the propositions for the sentence would be *Larry received few gifts* and *Billy received few gifts*. The other two sentences also have deletions since there is a deletion of the verb and/or the object of the verb.

There may be words or phrases denoting quantity preceding the comparison with *as . . . as*. This form is often found in arithmetic word problems that involve multiplication. The terms *twice, three times, four times*, etc.; and *one-quarter, one-half, two-thirds, three-fourths*, etc.; appear often. In comparisons such as these, differences rather than similarities are expressed—*Jill bought four times as many apples as Jack, Nancy eats half as much candy as Sarah.*

Comparisons are also expressed with the words *same* and *different*. *As* or *than* may or may not be used in the comparison, depending upon the clarity of the meaning; with the deletions, the speaker assumes that what is being compared is known to the listener.

> Mary bought the same color dress (as Jean did).
> June bought a different color dress (than Mary did).

Words such as *number, amount, kind, quantity, quality*, etc., when patterned with *same* or *different*, require that children have the concepts for such superordinate categories and for the features of nouns in the categories.

> Mother wanted a different *kind* of car than Dad bought.
> Joe had a different *number* of books than Bob did.
> Jean drank the same *amount* of *beer* as her boyfriend.
> This *container* holds the same *quantity* as that.
> This *material* is not the same *quality* as that is.

Mention was made of the use of comparatives in arithmetic, even at the beginning levels. Examples of questions and word problems in a first-level arithmetic book are given below. In addition to the use of the comparative, other syntactic complexities are often found in such problems.

1. Is the first dog larger than the second one?
2. Does the first box have more blocks than the second one?
3. Who is older, the boy or the girl?
5. Which animal has the longest neck?
5. Dean has 4¢. How much more does he need for a candy bar that costs 5¢?
6. Sue wants 7 books. She has 5 books. She needs _____ more books.
7. How many more blue boxes were there than red boxes?
8. 12 is how many more than 7?
9. Bob has 16 marbles. Jane has 9 marbles. If Jane had _____ more marbles, she would have as many as Bob.
10. When the mail carrier has 35 pounds of mail, he has how many less than 50 pounds?

Note the use of the conditional with *if* in (9) and the conditional intent in the adverbial clause with *when* in (10). In (5), a problem that would appear early in a first level because the computation is so simple, the language of the question is so complex that it makes the problem difficult. The complexities are as follows:

Dean has 4¢.

How much more does he need for a candy bar that costs 5¢?

Wh-question with *do*-support and auxiliary inversion

deletion of a noun after *more (money)*

rel clause expansion of NP

pronominalization (*he*) in the question with the referent in the sentence before

Children who have language difficulties, although they may very well be able to give the answer to *five minus four,* may be unable to deal with a word problem involving the same computation because of the complexity of the language.

Comparatives, then, involve both syntactic and conceptual difficulties. They are found in various syntactic forms and demand varying levels of syntactic competence and conceptual maturity for both comprehension and expression.

Turn to Exercise 38 for practice in recognizing and using comparatives.

CHAPTER 18

Language Analysis III and Review

Objectives

- Demonstrate the performance required in objectives for Language Analyses 1 and 2

- Identify in the syntactic description, the following:
  a. coordination - conjunction
  b. coordination - disjunction
  c. coordination - alternation
  d. coordination - conjunctive adverb
  e. coordination - correlative conjunction
  f. deletion in above conjoinings

- Identify in the syntactic description, the following conjoinings with subordinating conjunctions:
  a. adverbial clauses of time, location, concession, manner, duration, frequency
  b. preposed adverbial clauses
  c. forward and backward pronominalization in adverbial clauses
  d. cause and effect clauses
  e. conditional clauses

- Identify the following elaborations in the syntactic description:
  a. relative clause
  b. *-ing* or *-en* participle modifier
  c. prepositional phrase modifier
  d. appositive
  e. comparatives

- Determine the frequency of occurrence of the above elaborations and conjoinings in a given sample

- Give semantic descriptions of sentences containing more than one proposition

- Determine the total number of propositions in a given sample and the number of propositions per utterance

- Identify the syntactic pattern of given sentences with relativizations, conjoinings, comparatives, and other complexities

- Identify the specific types of conjoinings and relativizations listed in the preceding objectives for the language analysis
- Identify comparatives in given sentences
- Identify the modality changes, conjoinings, elaborations, and transformations in given sentences
- Identify the semantic relationships in sentences with one or more propositions

The preceding chapters introduced conjoinings, relativizations, and comparatives. With the exception of the noun phrase elaborations (adjective, noun adjunct, and possessive modifiers) these syntactic complexities are the first that involve processes by means of which two or more propositions may be expressed in one sentence. Also, these complexities make possible the expression of cause and effect relationships, conditions, temporal order or aspect of events, disparities, and the like. Not only is communication streamlined, but messages can be more effectively communicated.

Syntactically, the complexities operate in various ways. In conjoinings that involve coordination, two complete sentences may be joined, so long as there is a relationship between the two or an equivalence of information. Some of the conjunctions, disjunctions, or alternations resulting from two complete sentences contain pronominalization transformations, adding another complexity to the sentence—***Larry** came to the party, but **he** left early; Mother baked a **pie**, and Dad ate all of **it***.

Other conjoinings, particularly with *and, or,* and the correlative conjunctions, serve to expand noun phrases in sentences by adding another noun to a noun phrase. These conjoinings also expand adjectives, verbs, etc., by adding another of these constituents. Some examples follow.

Jane and Jill came to the party.
Grandma is coming *today or tomorrow.*
Bill *jumped and fell.*
Tom is *both athletic and artistic.*
Mother bought *a turkey, sweet potatoes, cranberries, and a pumpkin.*

In coordinations such as those listed, there are deletions of the identical words that one would use if relating the information in two or more sentences.

Conjoinings with subordinating conjunctions add information to adverbials. Rather than having a one-word, noun phrase, or prepositional phrase adverbial in a sentence, the adverbial may be a complete clause with a subject and predicate. Some of the adverbial clauses may be preposed, adding another complexity to the sentence. Each adverbial clause adds at least one more proposition to the sentence.

Relativizations elaborate noun phrases, that is, add either a pre- or postnominal modifier to a noun phrase. The noun phrase may be a sentence constituent: the subject, the direct or indirect object, a predicate nominative, or the object of a preposition in an adverbial phrase. The resulting modifiers may be full relative clauses, relative clauses with the relative pronoun deleted, prepositional or participle phrases, or appositives. Relativizations are important to clear communication because they serve to specify the topic to the listener.

Postnominal modifiers that are prepositional phrases or *-ing* or *-en* participle phrases and appositives result from relative clause reductions.

> *The dog barking at the mailman* is Tagger.
>
> The dog ~~that is~~ barking at the mailman . . .
>
> The sails, *torn to shreds*, hung from the mast.
>
> The sails, ~~which were~~ torn to shreds, . . .
>
> The girl *in that car* is my cousin.
>
> The girl ~~who is~~ in that car . . .
>
> Jim, *the head cheerleader*, was not at the game.
>
> Jim, ~~who is~~ the head cheerleader, . . .

At times the *-ing* or *-en* participle is moved to a position before the noun. This is usually the case when the participle is a one-word modifier—**Shattered** *glass covered the walk; The* **boiling** *water scalded his legs*. When the *-en* participle or participle phrase is a modifier through relative clause reduction, the verb in the insert sentence is passive and another transformation has been used. There may also be an agent deletion, as in *the shattered glass* (the glass was shattered by someone). With *-ing* participle modifiers, the verb in the insert sentence is progressive aspect.

Comparatives add information to adjectives and adverbs. The adjectives may be noun phrase elaborations, in which case they expand the information given in a noun phrase, or adjective complements of linking verbs. Some of the comparatives expand an adjective with a clause introduced by *than* or *as*. In the majority of comparisons, there is a deletion of words that are not necessary to clearly convey the information or that are redundant. Adjectives may be regularly or irregularly compared with *more* and *most*. It is important to remember that the comparative form indicates a comparison of two things and the superlative indicates a comparison of three or more. *Same* and *different,* which indicate comparative relationships, also involve one or more referents.

Conjoinings, relativizations, and comparatives are syntactic devices for conveying more meaning in a sentence. Thus, the language used in communication through the air or in writing becomes semantically more complex. We usually limit the length of our sentences in oral/manual communication situations, but this is not always the case in writing, especially in instructional materials or in other kinds of reading materials. The sentences used in newspapers and other periodicals and in leisure reading materials are usually very complex both syntactically and semantically. The reader must often extract considerable information from one sentence.

Mention has been made before of the skills needed by clinicians and teachers who are responsible for the language development of children and youth with delayed or deviant language. Such skills include analyzing the receptive and expressive language of the child, analyzing one's own language and the language of those in the child's immediate communicative environment, and analyzing the language of the teaching materials one uses or wishes to use.

In the past review chapters, the language analyses were of contrived samples representing language that could be found in a young child. There were no analyses involving the language found in teaching materials. Of special importance among teaching materials are the basal reading series.

There have been references in the text to some of the complexities found in first-, second-, and third-grade readers. Those who construct the basal readers assume that the beginning reader has some experience or information pertaining to the content and, more importantly, has knowledge of the syntactic constructions and the semantic relationships expressed in the materials. The average beginning reader, who is between six and seven years of age, is expected to understand and use much of the syntax of the adult. The child is also expected to possess quite a degree of competence in discourse, the ability to carry on a conversation, and the skill to use a series of sentences in relating information to others.

Children at the age of six or seven with delayed language due to hearing impairment or other causes may be able to express or comprehend only the simplest NP + VP structures. Russell, Quigley, and Power (1976) state that it is age 10 when hearing-impaired children have mastered the phrase structure rule of NP + VP, and age 12 when the broad aspects of word order and word use are mastered. Streng, Kretschmer, and Kretschmer (1978), Kretschmer and Kretschmer (1978), and Russell, Quigley, and Power (1976) have indicated that many hearing-impaired children will meet syntactic structures that they are unable to comprehend and/or produce if expected to learn to read using a basal reading series. Although in basal readers the introduction of new words is controlled, the introduction of increasingly complex syntactic structures and figurative and idiomatic language is not (Hargis, 1970). A developmental approach to the teaching of reading is recommended whereby children are presented first with the language they can comprehend; they are gradually introduced to more complex syntax based on the expected pattern of development.

Whether one wishes to undertake a developmental approach to the teaching of reading or not, there is always the problem of obtaining an appropriate instructional match of the reader to the teaching materials in reading or other subject areas. This is dependent upon (1) analyzing the language competence of the student and (2) analyzing the level of the instructional materials. The readability formulas in current use (Dale & Chall, 1948; Spache, 1953; Fry, 1968) do not take into account syntactic complexity, and there is some evidence that they are not useful measures in determining the appropriateness of reading materials for hearing-impaired children.

Streng, Kretschmer, and Kretschmer suggest a modification of the Syntactic Complexity Formula (SCF) developed by Granowski and Botel (1974). In using the adapted SCF, weights (1,2,3) are assigned to specified noun and verb phrase modulations and elaborations, as well as to conjoinings, relativizations, comparatives, and various transformations. Research is needed as to the applicability of this adapted formula, but it holds promise as a more appropriate way of judging the readability of materials for language-delayed children.

In examining instructional materials, the teacher or clinician should be able to pick out the various complexities and locate those the child does not understand or use. Thus, in this chapter, passages are presented to afford some practice in analyzing language in instructional material.

Following is a passage from the last of the readers at the second-grade level in Scott Foresman's *Reading Unlimited* series:

> The king heard his daughter laugh, and he ran to the window. When he saw the funny sight, the king laughed, too. Then Peter laughed, and so did the people who were stuck together.
>
> (*All in Free,* 1976, p. 44)

Can you locate the conjoinings, the adverbial clause, the relative clause, and the passive? In the third sentence, the conjoining with *and so* also includes *do*-support, and auxiliary inversion. There are two preposed adverbials, one of which is a clause. None of the sentences is a basic pattern, and each sentence contains two or more complexities.

The following passage, also from a second-grade reader, contains two adverbial clauses, one of which is preposed. Within the first adverbial clause is an appositive-like construction, *his daughter (who was) Miki.* The second adverbial clause is preposed and contains conjoined comparatives. The main clause in the second sentence contains another comparative that expands an adjective (*beautiful*) with the clause *than the one before.*

> The artist painted *every day* while his daughter Miki watched. As he used more and more color, each painting became more beautiful than the one before.
>
> (Hirsh, 1976, p. 18)

Following is an adaptation of a sentence found in a third-grade reader. The syntactic complexities have been maintained as in the original. Note the number of propositions expressed in the one sentence.

> The next day Bill wore the brightest shirt that he had and proudly sat on his bicycle trimmed with streamers as he rode in the parade.

The reader must get the following information from this one sentence:

>   Bill wore a shirt the next day
>   the shirt was bright(est)
>   Bill had (other) shirt(s)
>   Bill had a bicycle
>   Bill (or someone) trimmed the bicycle with streamers
>   Bill sat on the bicycle proudly (for some time)
>   Bill rode in the parade

Syntactically, the sentence contains two preposed adverbials, one comparative, two personal pronominalizations, one conjoining with *and* with a subject deletion, one relative clause with movement of the relative pronoun, one postnominal -*en* participle modifier, and one adverbial clause. There are two noun phrases expanded with a relative clause or through relative clause reduction. One is the direct object of the verb *wore*, and the other is the object of the preposition *on*.

DO:	the brightest shirt *that he had*
Obj. of Prep:	(on) his bicycle (that was) *trimmed with streamers*

If one analyzed passages from a book containing sentences such as this one, the complexity level would be high. There are more than 10 syntactic complexities, and there are 7 pieces of semantic information the reader can extract from the one sentence.

Considering that other syntactic complexities not presented thus far in this text also occur in reading texts at the second- and third-grade levels, one can see that seven- and eight-year-old children must have reached a high level of linguistic competence to be able to comprehend what they read. If children with delayed language are at the point where they comprehend only simple sentence frames (by age 10 or 12), they will surely meet with failure if expected to read language so far above their linguistic capabilities. This author agrees with the aforementioned authors who recommend a developmental approach to language for language-delayed children, i.e., controlling the syntax but maintaining the vocabulary and the conceptual level of the materials. This places a burden on the teacher or clinician because of the dearth of instructional materials available. It also demands skills in analyzing the syntactic complexity of both teacher-made or commercially available materials.

Analyzing the language of the child in informal communication settings seems a simple task after looking at paragraphs from reading materials. However, the language we use (and that children use) in communicating with others may also contain a number of syntactic complexities and convey a considerable amount of information in a single sentence or in a few connected sentences.

The practice language samples you will analyze in this chapter again are contrived samples, limited to the syntactic complexities that you have studied in the first 17 chapters.

When a child reaches the point of generating sentences such as those presented in the following sample, one would expect that child to be using a variety of noun and verb phrase modulations with little or no error, so this need not be tabulated and recorded. They are included in your analysis as a review. Also, in a syntactic description of a child's language one need not specify the different kinds of conjoining with the coordinating and subordinating conjunctions, or the specific kinds of relativizations or comparatives. This, however, would provide more information as to the child's linguistic capabilities in expressing alternation; disjunction; and causal, temporal, and conditional relationships; it would also indicate the various ways in which the child elaborates noun phrases.

Following is a sample preceded by a listing of those syntactic occurrences to be designated and tabulated. The noun and verb phrase modulations, modalities, and noun phrase elaborations listed on pages 116–117 are not given again, but you are expected to include them in the analysis. For this analysis, differentiate contracted (*I'm, he's*, etc.) copulas from the uncontracted (*am, is*, etc.) under verb phrase modulations. The conjoinings with coordinators and subordinators and other postnominal or prenominal modifiers and comparatives will be added to the elaborations as indicated in the following list. The operations used for modifiers resulting from relative clause reductions are not to be included. However, if a relative clause has a relative pronoun, specify the pronominalization; if there is a clause with only the relative pronoun deleted, cite the deletion. If there is a deletion in comparatives with *as . . . as* or *comp + than*, also cite a deletion.

Conjoinings:

Coordination: conjunction
disjunction
alternation
correlative
conjunctive adverb

Subordination: adverbial cl time, etc.
causal clause
conditional clause

Elaborations: relative clause
-ing or *-en* participle modifier
prepositional phrase modifier
appositive
comparative

Remember that in the majority of conjoinings and comparatives you have a deletion.

Bob (played tennis) and Carrie played tennis.
June is warmer than May (is warm).

Language Sample

Subject: Nancy

1. Did you see that big snowman that Tim and I made this morning when we were outside?

2. Our snowman is the biggest on the block, but it doesn't have a broom or a stick.

3. Last night you were sleeping, and I peeked out the window and saw all the stars twinkling in the sky.

4. Mr. Jackson, the mailman, brought me a package so I opened it, but it was for Mom.

5. If Bobby is as tall as Daddy is now, how tall will he be when he's old?

Syntactic Description

Sentence	*Pattern*
1. Did you see that big snowman that Tim and I made this morning when we were outside?	$NP^1 + V + NP^2$

VP modulation:	irreg past, uncontr copula
NP modulation:	dem (2), $\emptyset$ art
Modality:	yes-no question
Conjoining:	conjunction
Elaboration:	adjective, relative clause (2) (rel pro, rel adv)
Transformation:	*do*-support, aux invers, pers (3) and rel pronoun, del

Sentence	*Pattern*
2. Our snowman is the biggest on the block, but it doesn't have a broom or a stick.	$NP^1 + V_L + NP^1, NP^1 + V + NP^2$

VP modulation:	uncontr copula, prep
NP modulation:	−def art (2), +def art (2)
Modality:	negation
Conjoining:	disjunction (*but*), alternation (*or*)
Elaboration:	adj (*big*), comparative, poss det
Transformation:	pers pronoun, contraction, *do*-support, del (*snowman*), del (in alternation)

3. Last night you were sleeping, and I $NP + V_i + Adv, NP + V_i + Adv,$
   peeked out the window and saw all $(NP^1) + V + NP^2$
   the stars twinkling in the sky.

VP modulation:	*be* aux, progressive, reg past, irreg past, prep (2)
NP modulation:	ord, preart, +def art (3), reg plural
Conjoining:	conjunction (*and*) (2)
Elaboration:	-*ing* participle modifier
Transformation:	adv preposing, pers pronoun, indef pronoun, del (*I*)

4. Mr. Jackson, the mailman, brought $NP^1 + V + NP^2, NP^1 + V + NP^2,$
   me a package so I opened it, but it $NP + V_{be} + Adv$
   was for Mom.

VP modulation:	irreg past, reg past, uncontr copula, prep
NP modulation:	Ø art (2), +def art, −def art
Conjoining:	disjunction (*but*), *so* cl
Elaboration:	appositive
Transformation:	indirect object preposing, pers pronoun (4)

5. If Bobby is as tall as Daddy is now, $NP + V_L + Adj + Adv + Adv$
   how tall will he be when he's old?

VP modulation:	uncontr copula (2), modal aux, contracted copula
NP modulation:	Ø art (2)
Modality:	*wh*-question
Conjoining:	conditional cl, adv cl of time
Elaboration:	comparative
Transformation:	adv preposing, pers pronoun (2), aux invers, contraction, del (*tall*)

Syntactic Summary

Verb Phrase Modulations	Frequency of Occurrence	Comments
regular past	2	
irregular past	3	
uncontracted copula	5	were, is, was
contracted copula	1	is
be auxiliary	1	
modal auxiliary	1	will
progressive	1	
preposition	4	in, on, out, for

Noun Phrase Modulations	Frequency of Occurrence	Comments
articles	15	null (6), −def (3), +def (6), *a* and *the*
demonstrative	2	this, that
ordinal	1	last
regular plural	1	
Modality Changes		
yes-no question	1	with *did*
wh-question	1	*how* + adj
negation	1	*do* contr
Conjoinings		
Coordination		
conjunction	2	conjoined subject NPs conjoined sentences
alternation	1	conjoined object NPs
Subordination		
causal clause	1	*so* clause
adverbial clause	1	temporal
conditional clause	1	if
Elaborations		
poss det	1	our
adjective modifier	2	big, biggest
relative clause	2	that, when
-ing participle modifier	1	postnominal phrase
appositive	1	NP with no modifier
Transformations		
adverbial preposing	2	ondit clause (1)
pronominalization: personal	12	ʒou, we, I, it, me
pronominalization: relative	1	that
do-support	2	did, does
auxiliary inversion	2	
contraction	2	does, is
indirect object	1	
deletion	15	comp, alternation, conj

Semantic Description

Sentence	*Description*

1. Did you see that big snowman that Tim and I made this morning when we were outside?

(you) see that snowman	Experiencer—process—complement
the snowman is big	Entity—stative—size
Tim (Nancy) made that snowman this morning	Agent—action—complement—time (2)
Nancy/Tim were outside this morning	Entity—stative—location—time

2. Our snowman is the biggest on the block, but it doesn't have a broom or a stick.

the snowman is the (snowman on the block)	Entity—stative—equivalent—location
Nancy/Tim have a snowman	Possessor—process—patient
the snowman is big	Entity—stative—size
the snowman has a broom	Entity—stative—part
the snowman has a stick	Entity—stative—part

3. Last night you were sleeping, and I peeked out the window and saw all the stars twinkling in the sky.

(someone) was sleeping last night	Experiencer—process—time
Nancy peeked out the window	Experiencer—process—location
Nancy saw all the stars	Experiencer—process—complement
the stars were twinkling in the sky	Patient—process—location

4. Mr. Jackson, the mailman, brought me a package so I opened, it, but it was for Mom.

Mr. Jackson brought a package to Nancy	Agent—action—patient—recipient (beneficiary)
Mr. Jackson is the mailman	Entity—stative—equivalent
Nancy opened the package	Agent—action—patient
the package was for Mom	Entity—stative—beneficiary

5. If Bobby is as tall as Daddy is now, how tall will he be when he's old?

Bobby will be (how) tall sometime under some condition	Entity—stative—size—time—condition
Bobby is old	Entity—stative—age—time
Bobby is tall now	Entity—stative—size—time
Daddy is tall	Entity—stative—size—time

Semantic Summary

Number of utterances:	5
Number of propositions:	27
Propositions per sentence:	5.4

Frequency of Occurrence

Noun cases

Agent	6
Experiencer	4
Patient	3
Entity	15
Equivalent	
Possessor	1
Part	2
Beneficiary (Recipient)	2
Complement	6

Verb cases

Action	6
Process	5
Stative	15

Modifier cases

Age	1
Size	5
Ordinal	1

Adverbial cases

Location	4
Time	7

Turn to Language Analysis III Exercise for practice analyzing a language sample.

CHAPTER 19

Nominalization and Complementation

The previous chapters on coordination and relativization centered on two of the four processes used for relating propositions. Complex sentences, those which express more than a single proposition, may also involve **complementation** and **nominalization**. The last chapters deal with these two processes for relating propositions and include direct and indirect discourse and forms of complementation with the complementizers *that, if, whether, for . . . to*, Poss-ing, and nominalizations.

In basic, single proposition sentences, the noun phrase contains a noun with determiner modifications. In complex sentences, there may be elaboration of noun phrases by means of insertion of adjective, possessive, or noun adjunct modifiers or by means of relativization. Each of these elaborations adds a second proposition to the sentence, so that the speaker can communicate more than one piece of information to the listener. Another means of embedding a second proposition is by using nominalization.

In the process of **nominalization**, a sentence (proposition) takes on a particular form (an infinitive or participle phrase, or a noun phrase derived from a full sentence) and functions as the subject or object of the main verb, as a predicate nominative, or as the object of a preposition. In other words, nominalizations function as noun phrases in sentences. For example,

> *Swimming in the ocean* was fun for Tim.
> The children wanted *to collect shells.*
> Mary's idea was *to board the dog for the weekend.*
> Jim paid his tuition by *working nights at the hospital.*

The italicized phrases are all nominalizations, and they function as noun phrases in the sentences. As you can see, these are not det + N noun phrases, but consist of verbs (*swim, collect, board, work*) with other sentence constituents. They represent propositions that could be expressed by sentences such as

> Tim swam in the ocean.
> The children collect shells.
> Mary will board the dog for the weekend.
> Jim worked nights at the hospital.

A nominalized sentence may serve as either a complement of the verb, such as the direct object, or as a complement of a noun phrase or adjective. The term **complement** is used in the grammatical sense (that which is needed to complete). An infinitive nominalization either completes a sentence, i.e., is one of the sentence constituents, or completes a verb phrase, noun phrase, or adjective.

There are different forms of complementation, with different complementizers (*for . . . to, whether, that,* etc.) used to introduce the various forms. With complements of these types there is always an embedding of another proposition. This chapter deals with infinitive and participle nominalization and complementation, and the following ones deal with other forms of these same two processes for relating propositions.

Unit 1: Infinitive Nominalization and Complementation

Objectives

- Identify the voice and aspect of infinitive phrases
- Analyze the constituents of infinitive phrases that represent predicates of the five basic sentence patterns
- State the feature of verbs enabling them to be followed by infinitives as complements
- Identify the direct object of the main verb in a sentence as an infinitive phrase, NP + infinitive phrase, or accusative pronoun + infinitive phrase
- Identify those verbs that may be immediately followed by an infinitive complement as the direct object
- Write the propositions in the deep structure for sentences with infinitive phrases, NP + infinitive, or accusative pronoun + infinitive as direct objects, and write the semantic relationships for each proposition
- Differentiate from other listed verbs those that require an NP + infinitive complement
- Identify in sentences infinitive phrases with and without deletion of the marker *to*

In the sentence *Jack wanted to go to college*, the main proposition is *Jack want(ed) (something)*. The second proposition, *Jack (will) go (to) college*, is nominalized. It takes on the syntactic form of an infinitive phrase and is used to fill the empty slot designated by *something* in the core proposition. The infinitive phrase serves as the direct object, or complement, of the verb in the given sentence.

Infinitives are **verbals** (verb forms) and represent the action, process, or state in a proposition in the deep structure. They are usually introduced by *to* in the surface structure, except in those cases in which the *to* is deleted by means of either an obligatory or optional deletion.

Infinitives may be active or passive voice, and progressive, perfect, or perfect progressive aspect. This adds other complexities to the sentence.

to see	simple active infinitive
to be seeing	progressive active
to have seen	perfect active
to have been seeing	perfect progressive active
to be seen	passive
to have been seen	perfect passive

Infinitive phrases may contain all the constituents of predicates. Following are examples of infinitive phrases containing the constituents found in the predicates of basic sentences.

Pattern 1
V_i Adv
to sleep / all morning

Pattern 2
V NP^2 Adv
to have been playing / football / this fall

Pattern 3
V_L Adj V_L Adj
to be / happy; to feel / upset

Pattern 4
V_L NP^1 V_L NP^1
to be / a doctor; to become / a surgeon

Pattern 5
V_{be} Adv
to have been / at the lake

Verb Phrase Complements: Infinitive

Infinitive phrases most often serve as objects of a verb, either immediately following the verb or following a noun phrase that is the subject of the embedded sentence. One of the most frequently used forms of complementation is embedding of a proposition with the same subject as the main proposition.

The boys *like* to *swim* in the ocean. (*the boys* like something, *the boys* swim in the ocean)

Mary wanted to babysit for Mrs. Brown. (*Mary* wanted something, *Mary* babysits for Mrs. Brown)

The complementizer *for . . . to* introduces infinitive complements with an obligatory deletion of *for + the identical NP* when the subject of the infinitive is the same as the subject of the main verb—*The boys like (for the boys) to swim.*

In infinitive complementation of this type, there are restrictions as to the verbs that can be followed by infinitives. Only those verbs having the feature [+catenation] can have infinitive phrases as objects. Some of the commonly used verbs that carry the feature of **catenation** for infinitives are listed below. Note that you can test for catenation by using the question, *I ____ what?*

I like to eat.   I started *to eat.*
I want *to eat.*   I tried *to eat.*

Verbs with [+catenation]

agree	decide	intend	refuse
attempt	deserve	like	remember
beg	expect	love	start
begin	fail	need	threaten
cease	forget	plan	try
choose	happen	prepare	want
continue	hope	promise	wish

When an infinitive immediately follows the verb as the direct object, the subject of the infinitive is the same as the subject of the main verb. The propositions in sentences with infinitive embedding immediately following the verb may be illustrated as follows:

The children want to play outside.
proposition: the children want (*something*) Experiencer—process—complement
proposition: the children play outside Mover—action—location

The noun phrase, *the children*, is the subject of both the main verb *want* and of *play*, the verb in the embedded proposition. The phrase *to play outside* is a nominalization of *the children play outside*, and it is used as the complement (direct object) of the verb *want.*

Verb Phrase Complements: NP + Infinitive

Some of the verbs in the preceding list may be followed by a noun phrase plus an infinitive complement. In embeddings of this type, the subject of the embedded proposition is a person or thing other than the subject of the main verb—*Joe wants the boys to play football.* In this sentence, *Joe* is the subject of *wants*, and *the boys* is the subject of the infinitive containing the verb *play* in the embedded proposition. The proposition, *the boys play football*, is nominalized as *the boys to play football* and is used as a complement of the main verb *want*.

The verbs from the preceding list that may be followed either directly by an infinitive or by an NP + infinitive include *beg, choose, dare, expect, need, prepare, promise,* and *want*.

> Bill wants *to wash the car.* NP^2 = infinitive phrase
> Bill wants *Tom to wash the car.* NP^2 = NP + infinitive phrase

In the second sentence, the NP (*Tom*) plus the infinitive phrase functions as the object of the verb. Should a personal pronoun be used rather than its noun phrase referent, the pronoun must be the accusative case—Bill wants **me** *to wash the car* (accus pro + inf phrase).

A number of verbs require that an NP precede the infinitive phrase; these verbs may not be immediately followed by the infinitive. In most cases, the subject of the infinitive is an NP other than the subject of the main verb. For a few of the verbs, the subject may be the same, and a reflexive pronoun is used. Some other verbs requiring an NP + infinitive complement are given in the following list. In this case, you can use the test pattern *I _____ (Who/What) to What?—I taught Mary to swim; I tempted the child to eat.*

advise	direct	send
allow	forbid	teach
challenge	force	tempt
command	remind	warn

Dad may allow the boys to drive the car.

The teacher warned the children to obey the patrol boys.

Jane forced herself to eat the cake.

The propositions in the deep structure for the sentence *Dad may allow the boys to drive the car* are as follows:

> Dad (may) allow (*something*)   Experiencer—process—complement
> the boys drive the car   Agent—action—patient

When the embedded proposition expresses the relationship of Entity—stative—attribute, there may be an optional deletion of the full infinitive *to be*, as in *Harry found the book (to be) interesting* and *Talia considers herself (to be) intelligent*.

With some verbs, the deletion of *for* is optional when the subjects are different; with other verbs, *for* is obligatory in the sentence—*We intended (for) the dance to be in the gym; The Senator arranged for the girls to have lunch with him.*

A number of verbs that may have an NP + infinitive complement do not use the infinitive marker *to*. Some of the verbs after which there is an obligatory deletion of *to* in the infinitive phrase are *feel, hear, help, make, see,* and *watch.*

Mother felt something brush across her face.
The boys helped some friends paint their house.
Dad made John go to school.

The infinitive phrases in the example sentences are *to brush across her face, to paint their house,* and *to go to school.*

Multiple embedding of infinitives as complements in the verb phrase increases the complexity of sentences.

Dad likes *to have something to do in the evening.*
Jim made Tom *go get some wood.*
Joe intended *to ask Mary to go see a movie.*

In the last sentence there are three infinitive phrases: *to ask Mary to go see a movie, to go see a movie,* and *(to) see a movie.*

Infinitive complements of the majority of the types presented thus far are among the first to be used by young children. Examples of the first occurrences of complementation found in the sentences of young children would include *I wanna see that, I hafta go, I gonna build a bridge.* These sentences represent what Lee (1974) and others refer to as an **emerging use of infinitives** since the marker *to* is not used. Children appear to use *wanna, hafta,* and *gonna* as single-word auxiliaries. It is often recommended that one look for instances of infinitives in which the marker *to* is found prior to crediting a child with producing other than emerging infinitive complements. These types of complements, however, are among the most often used, and adults in informal conversation use the same elision in articulation rather than saying *I want to . . ., I have to . . .,* or *I'm going to. . . .*

Verb Phrase Complements: Quasi-Modal + Infinitive

Have to and *(be) going to* are **quasi-modals.** They are alternative ways of expressing *must* or *will (shall).* These quasi-modals include the *to* marker of the infinitive and introduce infinitive phrases into sentences as complements of the verb. Another quasi-modal, a substitute for *should,* is *ought to.* Sentences illustrating the equivalent meaning of the quasi-modals and modals follow.

The girls *are going* to leave soon. = The girls *will* leave soon.

I *have to* wash my hair. = I *must* wash my hair.

Shirley *ought to* stay home. = Shirley *should* stay home.

Sentences with quasi-modals cannot be considered to include an embedded proposition as there are not two verbs. The *be going to* and *ought to* are not verbs, but alternative auxiliaries. The main verbs in the three examples are *leave*, *wash*, and *stay*. The first two sentences would be analyzed as follows:

$$NP \qquad V_i \qquad Adv$$
The girls / are going to leave / soon.
$$NP^1 \qquad V \qquad NP^2$$
I / have to wash / my hair.

Verb Phrase Complements: Infinitives of Purpose

The infinitive of purpose is another instance of complementation in the verb phrase. In sentences with infinitive of purpose embeddings, the infinitive phrase functions as an adverbial of reason; it answers the question *Why.*

Why?

We / drove / to Baltimore / *to see a movie.*

To raise money for the trip the girls are having a bake sale.

Dick sold one of his cars *in order to pay the hospital bills.*

The last sentence contains a variation of the infinitive of purpose. The phrase is introduced by *in order to* rather than only *to.* Infinitives of purpose may be shifted to the beginning of the sentence by means of the adverbial preposing transformation, as is shown in the second sentence. In all of the examples, the subjects of the main verb and of the infinitive are the same. When the subjects are different, the *for . . . to* complementizer must be used. In the following sentence, *Jane* is the subject of *got* and *Dick* is the subject of *go—Jane got a job in order for Dick to go back to college.*

In determining the propositions in the deep structure for sentences with infinitives of purpose, the empty slot in the main proposition is an adverbial slot.

| someone drove to Baltimore *(for some reason)* | Mover—action—location—reason |
| someone saw a movie | Experiencer—process—complement |

As the infinitive of reason serves as an adverbial complement of the verb and does not function as a noun phrase, it is *not* a nominalization.

In testing for verbs that have catenation for infinitives when the subject is the same as or is different from the subject of the main verb, the infinitive phrase does not answer the question *Why*. Almost all verbs can be followed by infinitives of purpose, but they are not said to have catenation for infinitives. When a verb has catenation for infinitives, the infinitive is a direct object.

$$\text{NP}^2 \text{ or direct object}$$
I / want / *to see that movie.*

$$\text{NP}^2 \text{ or direct object}$$
Bob / wants / *Mary to see that movie.*

The verb *want* in the preceding sentences has catenation for infinitives. However, in the following sentences, the verbs *cries, ran,* and *covered* do not have catenation for infinitives. In these sentences all the infinitives are infinitives of purpose.

$$\text{Adv}$$
Billy / cries / *to get attention.*

$$\text{Adv}$$
Mom / ran / *to catch the bus.*

$$\text{Adv}$$
Dad / covered / the wound / *to keep it clean.*

Turn to Exercise 39 for practice recognizing and using infinitive complementation and nominalization.

Unit 2: Functions of Infinitives in Sentences

Objectives

- Write the propositions and the semantic relationships of the propositions for sentences with infinitive nominalization and complements, including infinitives of purpose and infinitives embedded in noun phrases
- Differentiate from other listed adjectives those that can be expanded by an infinitive complement which has as its subject the same NP as is the subject of the sentence
- Identify infinitive phrases in sentences indicating if each is the direct object, subject, predicate nominative, or adverbial of purpose
- Identify the main verb, the subject of the main verb, the infinitive verbal, and the subject of the infinitive
- Identify the syntactic function of infinitives presented in sentences

Infinitives as Predicate Nominatives

Infinitive phrases also serve as complements of the copula verb when they function as a predicate nominative (NP^1). The secondary proposition is nominalized as an infinitive phrase and inserted into the empty slot that would be occupied by a noun phrase (the predicate noun) after the stative verb *be*. This type of nominalization and complementation does not occur with high frequency because many speakers opt to use a participle (*-ing* form of the verb) rather than infinitive nominalization.

> NP^1 $\qquad\qquad\qquad$ V_L $\quad$ NP^1
> John's favorite exercise / is / *to jog around Haines Point.*
> NP^1 $\quad$ V_L $\qquad\qquad\qquad$ NP^1
> Jim's wish / was / *for his son to be admitted to Annapolis.*

The *for* of the *for . . . to* complementizer is obligatory when the subject of the embedded proposition is different from that of the main proposition, as in the second sentence. A preferred form of complementation for the first sentence would be the participle phrase *jogging around Haines Point.*

Infinitives as Subjects

Another instance of infinitive nominalization occurs when the secondary proposition becomes an infinitive phrase, or for + NP + Inf phrase, and functions as the subject of the sentence. The infinitive in the subject position, as shown in the first sentence below, is not used frequently. Most speakers prefer the participle nominalization.

> $\qquad\quad$ NP^1
> *To jog around the park* / is / John's favorite exercise.
> $\qquad\qquad$ NP^1
> *For Mary to have completed the paper on time* / was / a surprise.

The two propositions in the second sentence are

(*something*) was a surprise	Entity—stative—equivalent
and	
Mary completed the paper on time	Experiencer—process—complement—time

One can see in the first proposition that the empty slot was the subject, which, in the surface structure, is filled with an infinitive phrase.

Sentences like those above may undergo an *it-replacement* transformation, resulting in a sentence such as *It was a surprise for Mary to have completed the paper on time.* The *it-replacement* will be described further in the following chapter.

Infinitives as Adjective Complements

Infinitives may expand adjectives that are sentence constituents, provided that the adjective is one which has catenation for infinitives. Some of these adjectives are

afraid	happy	sorry
eager	ready	wise

The girls were *eager* to go to New York.

Jason was *wise* to wear a coat.

The adjective constituent of the first sentence is *eager to go to New York*. The two propositions in this sentence are *the girls were eager* and *the girls go to New York*. It can be seen that the subject of the main verb and of the infinitive is the same: *the girls*.

When the subject of the infinitive is different from the subject of the main verb, as can be the case after some adjectives, the *for . . . to* complementizer is used—*The girls were eager for Grandma to come.*

Adjectives such as *easy, hard,* and *impossible* may be expanded by infinitives—*The problem was hard to solve, The map was easy to read.* In cases such as this, the subject of the infinitive (some person or people) is not given. The propositions in the first sentence are *the problem was hard* and *someone solve the problem.* The subject of the major proposition is different from the subject of the main verb.

This is also the case with a large number of adjectives, which when modified by an intensifier may be elaborated with infinitive complements. The intensifier can be one that precedes or one that follows the adjective.

That cake is *too* beautiful to eat.

The weather is warm *enough* to set out the plants.

The box was *rather* heavy for Bobby to carry.

In all three of these sentences, the subject of the infinitive is different from the subject of the sentence.

Infinitives as Noun Phrase Complements

Infinitives may be embedded in noun phrases elaborating the noun phrase and providing for the combining of two (or more) propositions in a single sentence. The *for . . . to* complementizer is used with the *for* + NP deletion in those instances when the subject of the embedded proposition is understood or is the same as the subject of the main proposition. When the subjects are different, the *for* is obligatory in the sentence.

The plan *to go to Jones Beach* sounds exciting.

The boys made an attempt *to be polite.*

This year is the time for us *to invest in a house.*

Mary was excited about the opportunity *for her brother to intern in New York.*

As can be seen in the preceding sentences, a noun phrase in any position in a sentence may be elaborated by embedding another proposition by means of infinitive complementation. The subject of the first sentence is *The plan to go to Jones Beach.* The noun *plan* is elaborated with an infinitive complement. In the last sentence, the embedding is in the noun phrase that is the object of the preposition *about.*

In the first sentence, the subject of the infinitive is not indicated, and in the second, the subjects of both propositions are the same, so that *for* plus NP is deleted. In the third sentence, the intent is to specify *us* as the people who should invest in a house. If the sentence read, *This year is the time to buy a house,* the intended subject of *buy* could refer to people in general.

A different means of noun phrase complementation with infinitives involves the use of a preposition plus relative pronoun movement. For example,

Sandy wants *a dog with which to play.*

Jim met *a man to whom to sell his tools.*

The noun phrases with the embedded infinitives and relativizations are italicized in the sentences. In both sentences, the prepositions have been moved before the relative pronoun. Without the relative pronouns, the preposition would not be shifted, but would remain at the end of the sentence.

Sandy wants a dog to play with.

Jim met a man to sell his tools to.

Summary of Syntactic Functions of Infinitives

Table 10 serves as a summary of different ways in which infinitives function when embedded either as nominalizations and/or complements. It also illustrates some added complexities when certain transformations occur.

The range of infinitive complementation is very broad. It ranges from a simple infinitive complement in a sentence like *I want to go,* to multiple embeddings or to infinitive phrases containing a variety of modulations, conjoinings, and transformations. Although not recommended, one can embed multiple infinitives in a single sentence— *For Dad to buy a car that wasn't fit to drive two miles made Mother cry and ask what he was going to do next to upset her.* This sentence has six embedded infinitive phrases with the verbs (*buy, drive, cry, ask, do,* and *upset*), in addition to modulations, relativization, conjoining, and transformations.

Sentences with infinitives do not have to be as long as the example; nor should they have multiple embeddings to cause difficulty for children with language problems.

Table 10
Some Syntactic Functions of Infinitives

Sentences	Syntactic Functions
The kitty wants *to eat*.	simple inf compl of verb (obj of verb)
Jane wants Mommy *to read a story*.	NP + inf compl of verb
Bobby wants *me to go*.	accus pro + inf compl of verb
Billy made *the dog roll over*.	NP + inf compl + del of *to*
The dress is *for Mary to wear to the dance*.	*for . . . to* complement of verb *be*
Trisha's goal is *to become captain of the team*.	predicate nominative, compl of V$_{be}$
The team is going (has, ought) *to leave soon*.	inf compl with quasi-modal
My sister is going to New York *to buy her wedding gown*.	inf of purpose (adv in sentence)
Mother was *happy to see Aunt Ida*.	adj + inf compl of linking verb
Sally is *too nervous to drive*.	intensifier + adj + inf compl
To become captain of the team is his goal.	inf nominalization as subject
For Tom to have flunked out of school upset Dad.	inf nominalization as subject (with obligatory *for*)
It upset Dad *for Tom to have flunked out of school*.	inf nom as subj + *it*-replacement
Mark has *an opportunity to go to Stanford*.	inf complement of noun
Brace needs a friend *with whom to share secrets*.	NP complement + prep + rel pro + inf compl
The medics ought *to be given a medal for bravery*.	quasi-modal + passive inf compl, deletion (of agent)
Father asked Sam *to go help Tim rake the leaves*.	multiple inf compl with deletions of *to*

The use of perfect or progressive aspect or passive voice in a single infinitive complement introduces complexity.

When the modality of the embedded proposition is negative, *not* precedes the infinitive after certain verbs—*Meg tries not to eat too much candy; We advised David not to leave.*

When there is a noun phrase intervening between the main verb and the infinitive with an identical NP as the subject, young children misinterpret the meaning. Examples of such sentences are *Steve has many friends to play with* and *The children promised the teacher to be quiet.* These sentences may be interpreted as though the noun phrase closest to the infinitive is the subject of the infinitive. Young children, as mentioned before, use the minimal distance principle (i.e., a surface order strategy) in interpreting meaning. In the case of relative clauses, a sentence such as *The dog that bit the boy ran away* may be interpreted in part to mean that *the boy ran away.* In the second sentence, the interpretation might be that *the teacher should be* or *was quiet.* C. Chomsky (1969) found that children between 6 and 9 years of age had difficulty comprehending sentences with the verb *promise* similar to the one above. Limber (1973) cited infinitive complements such as those in both sentences to be late in acquisition.

Young children with normal language development, however, use a number of different types of infinitive complements early and with high frequency. It is important, then, that the teacher or clinician be aware of both the pattern of development and the pattern of complexity of infinitive complementation to develop skill in the use of infinitives in children with language difficulties. Also, reading texts make much use of the different kinds of infinitive complementation, so that if children experiencing language problems are to comprehend even the beginning books in a reading series, they must develop competence in this often used aspect of syntax.

By way of further summary, note the analysis of sentences with some of the various kinds of infinitive structures.

NP^1 V NP^2
Billy / heard / the phone ring only once.

NP^1 V NP^2
June / wants / to live in Colorado where she can ski.

NP^1 V NP^2 Adv   Adv
Mother / is going to bake / a cake / for Tom / tomorrow.

NP^1 V_L Adj
To leave during rush hour / would be / unwise.

NP V_i Adv   Adv
The girls / are going / to Francine's / to study for finals.

NP V_L Adj
Jerry / was / too upset to study.

NP_1 V_L NP^1
April / is / the month to come to Washington.

Other instances of infinitive complementation will be presented in the following chapter on indirect discourse and embedded imperatives and questions.

Turn to Exercise 40 for practice analyzing and using infinitive complementation and nominalization.

Unit 3: Participle Nominalization and Complementation

Objectives

- Analyze the constituents in participle nominalizations
- Differentiate from among listed verbs those that may have only participle complements and those that may be followed by both infinitives and participles, or infinitives alone
- Identify participle phrase nominalizations in sentences and identify their functions
- State the propositions in sentences containing participle nominalization
- Identify the subjects of participle nominalizations, i.e., the subject of the embedded proposition
- Identify in given sentences the modality changes, conjoinings, elaborations (including participles and infinitives), and transformations

The progressive **participle**, *V-ing*, may also be nominalized. A *V-ing* phrase can function as a noun phrase in the subject position, a complement in the verb phrase, or as a noun phrase in other positions in sentences. You may be more familiar with the term **gerund**, which is used to designate a participle functioning as a subject, object, predicate nominative, or object of a preposition.

Since participles are verb forms, as are the infinitives, they may be followed by any of the constituents found in basic sentences.

Pattern 1	V_i Adv swimming / in the ocean
Pattern 2	V NP^2 buying / a car
Pattern 3	V_L Adj V_L Adj feeling / happy; being / happy
Pattern 4	V_L NP^1 V_L NP^1 becoming / a chemist; being / a witch
Pattern 5	V_{be} Adv being / in the dark

The *-ing* participle, with or without the constituents shown in the examples, is the most often used participle nominalization. The participle is the *-ing* inflected form of the copula or another verb. Occasionally the auxiliary *being* is used to form a nominalized passive participle that may be nontruncated or truncated.

Being defeated by their strongest rival upset our team.
The baby likes *being bathed*.

The italicized words in each sentence are a participle phrase; the phrase is used in the first sentence as the subject and in the second as the object of the verb.

As with infinitive complements, verbs must have catenation for participles in order to be immediately followed by participles as direct objects. Some verbs, however, have catenation for both infinitives and participles. These verbs include the following:

attempt	continue	hate	like	prefer	start
begin	dislike	hesitate	love	propose	try
cease	dread	intend	neglect	remember	undertake

Sentences that illustrate the use of either a participle or infinitive complement with one of the above verbs are *Mary tried to cut her own hair* (infinitive complement) and *Mary tried cutting her own hair* (participle complement).

Another group of verbs can be immediately followed by participles, but not by infinitives as complements. This may cause difficulty and result in errors when a verb requiring a participle is similar in meaning to one that can be immediately followed by either an infinitive or participle, or only by an infinitive. An example would be *enjoy*, which is similar in meaning to *like*.

participle:	Bill enjoys swimming.	Bill likes swimming.
infinitive:	*Bill enjoys to swim.	Bill likes to swim.

Some verbs that can be immediately followed by participles as complements but not by infinitives are contained in the following list.

avoid	go on	postpone
consider	keep	practice
deny	keep on	prescribe
enjoy	mind	recommend
escape	miss	resume

Three of the verbs listed (*keep*, *keep on*, and *go on*) are idiomatic. These verbs express the meaning of *continue—The children kept talking, They will keep on playing until dark, He went on working*.

The verb *go* is used with a limited number of verbs in the *-ing* form (e.g., go hunting, go bowling, go sightseeing). *Go* carries the tense and aspect, and the participle carries the central meaning of the sentence. This form of complementation is more commonly used than the simpler form where the important verb is marked for tense and aspect.

Joe *goes hunting* every winter.	Joe *hunts* every winter.
We *went swimming* today.	We *swam* today.
We're *going fishing*.	We *shall* fish.

Complementation with participles is accomplished with the *Poss-ing* complementizer. When the subject of the embedded proposition (the participle phrase in the surface structure) is the same as the subject of the main verb, the *Poss* (a possessive determiner or noun) is not necessary. In the sentence *Mary stopped (Mary's) teasing the boys, Mary* is the subject of the main verb *stopped* and of *teasing* , the verb in the participle complement. Therefore, the sentence is *Mary stopped teasing the boys.* The possessive is present when it is necessary to identify a subject of the participle that is different from the subject of the main verb.

In the sentence *Mother hates Dad's getting up early, Mother* is the subject of the main verb *hates*, and *Dad* is the subject of *getting up*. In the sentence *His getting up early upsets Mother, his getting up early* is the subject of *upsets*, and *he* (Dad) is the subject of *getting up*. Without *Dad* or *his* in the sentences, the meaning would be different; the sentences would imply that Mother sometimes gets up early and she doesn't like it or is upset by it (e.g., Mother hates getting up early).

An alternative way of expressing the possessive is with an *of* phrase. This is another form of nominalization, and it may be used in place of the *Poss-ing* complementizer.

> The giggling of the girls annoyed the teacher.
> The girls' giggling annoyed the teacher.

As with sentences containing an infinitive, those sentences with a participle nominalization contain more than one proposition. For the examples in the preceding paragraphs, the propositions would be

> Mother hates (*something*), Dad gets up early
> (*something*) annoyed the teacher, the girls were giggling

The propositions in the last two sentences are the same for both types of nominalizations.

As previously stated, participle nominalizations occur as subjects, objects of a verb, predicate nominatives, or objects of prepositions. Participle nominalizations are more often used as subjects than infinitives; however, infinitive complements used as direct objects of the verb occur much more frequently than participle complements. Participle nominalizations also may function as objects of prepositions in adverbial phrases.

> Subject: *Walking around Haines Point* is good exercise.
> Direct Object: We enjoy *walking around Haines Point.*
> Pred Nomin: Our only exercise is *walking around Haines Point.*
> Obj of Prep: We get our exercise by *walking around Haines Point.*

The adverbial denoting manner in the fourth sentence is a prepositional phrase with a participle nominalization as the object of the preposition. An adverbial phrase of reason may also contain a participle nominalization—*The police should arrest that man for loitering.* Adverbials of reason with *for* also occur as complements of the copula.

The citation was *for rescuing a child from a fire.*
The reward was *for finding the Smith's dog.*

Adverbial phrases such as those just cited are also found as postnominal modifiers of nouns through relativization with deletion of the relative pronoun and *be.* In cases such as this, the phrases expand noun phrases but are not sentence constituents in the surface structure.

The reward (that was) for finding the Smiths' dog was $25.
Jack framed the citation (which was) for rescuing a child from a fire.

Participle nominalizations must be differentiated from participle modifiers resulting from relative clause reduction.

The people *standing on that corner* are waiting for the bus to the airport.
They don't like *standing on that corner in the cold.*

In the first sentence, *standing on that corner* is a participle phrase modifier, resulting from reduction of the relative clause *who are standing on that corner.* In the second sentence, the phrase is a participle nominalization, the object of the verb *like.* Note that *waiting* is a participle form, but is the main verb with a *be* auxiliary.

The prepositions *for* or *against* may also have participles as objects and may occur as a complement of the copula *be—Our class is against having a picnic, We're for going to the rodeo.*

Other forms of participle complementation occur with such verb phrases as *be aware of* and *be interested in—Jack was aware of Sara's flirting, Don is interested in becoming an engineer.*

Verbs such as *know, hear, learn,* etc., with the particle *about* may have complements consisting of a participle with or without a genitive specifying the subject of the participle.

Bill learned about building houses from his father.
Mother knows about James' staying out all night.

Participle nominalization and complementation occur relatively late in the pattern of language acquisition. Competence in some types of infinitive complementation occurs much earlier. As stated previously, children use the emerging infinitive complement in expressions such as *wanna see, gonna go,* and *lemme have it.* Lee (1974) gives the following as the pattern of development of infinitive and participle nominalizations and complements.

1. Wanna, gonna, gotta, lemme and let's + verb
2. infinitive of purpose, adjective plus infinitive
3. NP plus infinitive complement, accus pro + infinitive, infinitive with *wh*-complementizer (I know what to do.)
4. passive infinitives
5. participle nominalization

Lee found that children do not use infinitives as subjects or as predicate nominatives, and that participles used as subjects or in other positions were the latest in development.

Hearing-impaired children have been found to have more difficulty with complementation than with coordination or relativization. According to Quigley, Wilbur, and Montanelli (1974), deaf subjects spontaneously wrote, and accepted as correct, deviant forms of infinitive and participle complements. Although there was a decrease in error between the ages of 10 and 18, even at 18 years of age some of their deaf subjects were making both comprehension and production errors in complementation.

From an analysis of complements in reading materials, Russell, Quigley, and Power (1976) reported that complements occurred at a rate of about 4 per 100 sentences in the second primer and gradually increased to 62 per 100 sentences in a sixth-grade reader. The majority of complements were the *for . . . to* and *Poss-ing* infinitive and participle complements. They concluded that since hearing-impaired subjects also had difficulties with other syntactic structures, the subjects would experience difficulty in comprehending much of the language in reading materials such as the typical series that they analyzed. Other forms of complementation that were found to cause difficulty were *that* complements. These complements and others are discussed in the following chapters.

Turn to Exercise 41 for practice analyzing and using participle nominalization and complementation.

CHAPTER 20

Complementation with Direct and Indirect Discourse

There are syntactic forms for reporting discourse either verbatim (exactly, e.g., Mother said, "Dad will be late") or in an indirect way (e.g., Mother said that Dad would be late). These syntactic forms, **direct** and **indirect discourse**, involve forms of complementation. The reported spoken utterance is syntactically the object of the verb and therefore, a complement of the verb. Both direct and indirect discourse are commonly used in reading materials. They are syntactic forms that children must master to be able to comprehend what they read.

In indirect discourse, the complementizers *that, wh-words, if,* and *whether* as well as *wh + for . . . to* are used. Not all forms of complementation introduced by these words can be termed indirect discourse because they involve the use of verbs rarely used in direct discourse.

The syntactic complexities are the same, however, whether the complementation is an indirect reporting of discourse, or, complementation involving verbs like *know, wonder,* or *remember.* Both of these forms of complementation are included in this chapter.

Unit 1: Direct Discourse

Objectives
- Analyze sentences with direct discourse and other complexities
- List a minimum of ten action verbs that may be used in direct discourse
- Specify the order of constituents in direct discourse sentences with shifted constituents

Hargis (1973, 1977) stated that virtually all reading materials for children use the direct discourse form and that it is the single most frequently used of the syntactic forms in reading materials for the primary grades.

In direct discourse, a statement, question, or request expressed by a speaker is given verbatim. In print, direct discourse is enclosed in quotation marks. All sentences of direct discourse are syntactically of the pattern Subject–verb–direct object, $NP^1 + V + NP^2$. The speaker is the subject, and what is said is the object of the verb.

NP^1 V NP^2
Mary / said, / "I saw a good movie last night."
    NP^1 V NP^2
The boys / shouted, / "We beat the Panthers!"

The learning of direct discourse entails an understanding of the verbs in addition to *say* that are used to indicate a particular manner of utterance. If one looks over any kind of story, be it a child's story or an adult's novel, it can be seen that *say* is the most frequently used word in direct discourse. Other verbs that may be followed by direct discourse include *shout, whisper, cry, sing, murmur, exclaim, reply, answer, hint, retort, plead, beg, stutter,* and *gasp.*

Direct discourse has been found to cause comprehension problems for children with language difficulties. Hargis, Evans, and Masters (1973), reporting on a group of hearing-impaired subjects, found that reading passages consisting largely of direct discourse were significantly more difficult than passages not containing direct discourse selected from the same book.

There can be a number of factors responsible for difficulty with direct discourse. First, it is a syntactic form that children rarely hear in everyday conversations. Most children meet this form for the first time in being told stories or in being read to, and they see it in beginning reading materials. Secondly, the surface order, S–V–O, is often varied, so that the subject (the speaker) is not indicated first; it may follow the verb and direct object. Thirdly, a speaker often says more than one thing, so that the verb really has a series of objects, all of which may be indicated as complete sentences. In reading materials beyond the primary level, the speaker may not be indicated, and the change from speaker to speaker must be noted from the punctuation, paragraphing, or the context of the utterances. An example of this would be as follows:

Mary said to John, "You were late to school today."
"Yes, but all I missed was the homeroom period."
"We had some important announcements about the dance in homeroom."
"You can tell me about them."

In the example there are three changes of speaker with only one indication of who is speaking. The reader must use the content and the punctuation to see that the exchange of speakers is from Mary to John to Mary to John.

One of the major difficulties in primary reading materials is the variation in the components of direct discourse sentences. Variations from the S – V – O order that occur frequently in materials for the young reader are given below, with the simplest order first.

1. Sally said, "Look at those kittens. May I have one?"   (S – V – DO)
2. "You'll have to ask Daddy," Mother replied.   (DO – S – V)
3. "Can't we get one now?" pleaded Sally.   (DO – V – S)
4. "We'll go home," said Mother, "Daddy should be there, and you can ask him."   (DO – V – S – DO)
5. "You should come in now," Mother said to Jack.   (DO – S – V – IO)

Variations and complexities such as those given above plus the other complexities that may occur in either the complement or the other part of the sentence make direct discourse more difficult than one would expect. Both Hargis (1977) and Streng, Kretschmer, and Kretschmer (1978) recommended simplifying direct discourse in readers for the child's introduction to it. They suggested using pictures showing the discourse in a balloon with a line drawn to the speaker's mouth, as found in cartoons. In this way the speaker is more clearly indicated for the reader. Then the S-V-O pattern of direct discourse would be used, with variations in the pattern after the child has a good understanding of the direct discourse form. Those children to whom stories are often read or told could be expected to encounter less difficulty with direct discourse provided that the storyteller varies the direct discourse form in the same way as found in the basal readers.

It is recommended that the child with language difficulties demonstrate competence in comprehending direct discourse prior to being presented with the indirect form. This is apparently expected also in children with normal language development. Reading materials generally use direct discourse in the first readers and present indirect discourse later in the series.

Turn to Exercise 42 for practice analyzing direct discourse.

Unit 2: Indirect Discourse

Objectives
- Change given direct discourse to indirect discourse
- Analyze sentences with indirect discourse and other complexities

- Specify the changes in pronominalization necessary in given sentences when changing from direct to indirect discourse
- Specify the rule of attracted sequence of tense in indirect discourse
- Differentiate action verbs that may have noun clause complements from process verbs allowing this type complementation
- Identify the modality of given indirect discourse as a statement, yes-no or *wh*-question, or imperative
- State the propositions and semantic relationships expressed in sentences with direct or indirect discourse
- Identify the complementation in given sentences as a noun (*that*) clause complement of an action or process verb, an embedded *wh*- or yes-no question complement of an action or process verb, a *wh* + infinitive complement, or an adjective + noun (*that*) clause complement
- Identify various forms of complementation in given sentences, differentiating *that* clause complements from relative clauses, embedded *wh*-questions from adverbial clauses, embedded yes-no questions from conditional clauses
- Specify all the modality changes, conjoinings, elaborations, nominalizations, and transformations in given sentences

Indirect discourse involves a statement, question, or request related in a form that is not verbatim. Discourse indirectly stated is a form of complementation introduced by one of the complementizers: *that*, a *wh-word, if, whether,* or *for . . . to.* The particular complementizer is determined by the modality of the discourse that is being related: declarative, *wh-* or yes-no interrogative, or imperative.

The complementizer *that* introduces a noun clause that is the complement of the verb when the discourse is a statement. The following sets of sentences illustrate the direct and indirect discourse forms for sentences expressing the same underlying propositions. The *that* clause in the second sentence of each set is a noun clause complement functioning as the object of the verb *said.*

direct:	Mary said, "The bus was very late."
indirect:	Mary said that the bus was very late.
direct:	Mother said, "I feel tired today."
indirect:	Mother said that she feels (felt) tired today.

Embedded Declaratives

When a speaker relates a personal experience to another person in the form of a declarative statement, the speaker uses the indirect form shown in the second sentence in each of the sets. There are definite changes involving a number of syntactic rules that must be used in going from the form of the utterance one hears to that which is related to another. Since the modality of the utterance in the direct discourse examples is declarative, the complementizer *that* is used. This is the only change that had to be made in the first indirect discourse sentence. In the second, however, the personal pronouns *I* and *you* had to be changed to the third person, and the verb had to be changed to the third person present or past tense.

The use of the present tense in the noun clause in the second example (*feels*) would not always be correct. This is dependent, in part, upon the time of the communication exchanges. Assume that Tim's mother and father were in the bedroom one morning. Mother says to Father, "I *feel* tired today." Then, at the breakfast table Father says to Tim, "Mother said that she *feels* tired today." If, however, Father has gone to work and in the morning Mother was speaking to Tim, that evening Tim would say to Father, "Mother said that she *felt* tired today." The time in the first situation is early in the day, so *feels* is appropriate; in the second situation, most of the day is past, so *feels* would not be appropriate. Such nuances in the use of the appropriate verb tense make indirect discourse difficult, as do the pronominalization changes.

In the examples of indirect discourse presented thus far, the *that* complementizer has been included in the sentences. Often there is a deletion of *that—Mary said (that) the bus was very late, Sally told Tom she would go to the dance with him.* Sentences with indirect object preposing, as in the second example, have two noun phrases preceding the verb phrase *would go*, both of which could be construed as the subject of the verb in the noun cláuse by one who uses a surface order strategy. The retention of *that* separates the two noun phrases and more clearly indicates what the discourse is. In print, the utterance in direct discourse is clear because of the quotation marks. In indirect discourse there is no punctuation to indicate the discourse, and a reader can use the *that* as a clue.

As indirect discourse involves complementation, the sentences are complex and express more than one proposition.

Mother said that she was tired today.
Mother said (something)   Agent—action—complement
Mother was tired today   Entity—stative—condition—time

Embedded *Wh*-Questions

A question asked by one person may also be related by a listener to another person. When *wh*-questions are embedded as complements, the complementizer is one of the *wh*-words. The following sets of sentences contrast the direct and indirect discourse forms for the same underlying propositions.

direct:	Valerie asked, "Who is at the door?"
indirect:	Valerie asked who was at the door.
direct:	The girls asked, "When should we leave?"
indirect:	The girls asked when they should leave.
direct:	Judy asked Mother, "Where did Dad put the keys."
indirect:	Judy asked Mother where Dad put the keys.

Note that in the indirect discourse forms, the auxiliary inversion rule is not applied, and there is no need for *do*-support, as shown in the second and third examples. Syntactically, the question in the indirect discourse form could be considered less complex than in the direct discourse form. An embedded *wh*-question, however, cannot always be shown with a parallel direct discourse form, as will be discussed in a later section of this unit, so that on the whole, there is considerable complexity in this form of complementation.

Embedded Yes-No Questions

Yes-no questions are embedded as complements with the complementizers *if* or *whether*. The two complementizers are used interchangeably.

direct:	Jack asked, "Was the train on time?"
indirect:	Jack asked if the train were on time.
direct:	Sue asked, "Does Tom like school?"
indirect:	Sue asked whether Tom likes school.

In embedded yes-no questions, the auxiliary is not inverted and *do*-support is not required as it is in the direct discourse form with questions.

In the previous examples of indirect discourse forms, the tense of the verbs was varied in the noun clause complement; it was not always the same as the tense used in the main verb. Streng (1972) suggested that the rule of attracted sequence of tense should be followed in teaching. According to this rule, the tense of the main verb attracts the following verb to the same tense. Following this rule, the indirect discourse form of the second sentence would be *Sue asked whether Tom liked school.*

In both embedded *wh*- and yes-no questions, the underlying major proposition is the same as in embedded declaratives (Agent—action—complement) with the second proposition varying according to the question.

Embedded Imperatives

Requests, orders, and commands, when indirectly quoted to another, are embedded with infinitives after verbs such as *ask, tell, order,* and *command.* Some examples of indirect discourse with embedded imperatives are presented below with the corresponding direct discourse forms.

direct:	Mother said, "Put away your toys."
indirect:	Mother said to put away our toys.
	or
indirect:	Mother told us to put away our toys.
direct:	Jack asked Tom, "Help Sue with her homework."
indirect:	Jack asked Tom to help Sue with her homework.

In the indirect discourse form, the infinitive is used. In the sentence *Mother told us to put away our toys*, the semantic relationships are as follows:

Mother told something to someone	Agent—action—complement—recipient
someone put away toys	Agent—action—patient
someone have toys	Possessor—process—patient

Note the indirect object preposing with the verb *told*.

Other Complementation with *That, Wh-, If,* and *Whether*

The direct discourse form presented in the preceding unit of this chapter is a form primarily found in reading materials. In the examples given, the main verbs were action verbs referring to a manner of speech. The indirect discourse was also limited to complementation following the same kind of verbs. Much of what may be termed *indirect discourse* is complementation with verbs that indicate mental processes. Thus, one does not hear and report to another what has been told to him or her.

Verbs involved in indirect discourse include words like *know, think, imagine, wonder,* and *guess*. Verbs such as these are often used in communication, and they represent a fairly large group of words that have *that, wh-, if,* and *whether* complements. One does not ordinarily find a direct discourse parallel for these types of complements, although in reading materials a direct relating of what one is thinking or wondering (e.g., *Jack thought, "I'll save my money and get a bike"*) may occasionally be used. The complementation process is the same as presented previously.

Bob thought that Kim was coming.
Mother knew where the keys were.
The girls wondered if the party would be fun.

A large group of verbs may have *that* and *wh-* complements; the number of verbs that permit indirect yes-no question complements with *if* and *whether* is much smaller. The complementizer *that* is often deleted, so one must have an internalized knowledge of the type of verbs used in order to recognize this form of complementation.

In examining second-grade readers in Scott Foresman's *Reading Unlimited* series (1976), a variety of verbs in addition to *say, tell,* and *ask* were found with *wh-* or *that* complements with the complementizer present in some instances and deleted in others.

that *complementation*	**wh-** *complementation*
. . . see (that) . . .	. . . see what . . .
. . . decide (that) . . .	. . . notice how well (how many) . . .
. . . know (that) . . .	. . . know when (where, how) . . .
. . . make believe that . . .	. . . decide who . . .
. . . think (that) . . .	. . . guess what . . .
. . . guess that . . .	. . . understand what . . .
. . . bet (that) . . .	. . . remember what . . .
. . . hope that . . .	. . . believe what . . .
. . . forget (that) . . .	. . . wonder what + inf . . .
. . . wish that . . .	. . . learn how + inf . . .
. . . explain that . . .	

Only one instance of an indirect yes-no question was found with *wonder if*. The last two in the *wh-* column represent complementation with both *wh-* and *for . . . to*. Infinitive complements may occur after any of the *wh-*words so long as the subject of the infinitive is the same as the subject of the main verb.

> Jane decided where to go to college.
> Mother wondered how many pies to bake for Thanksgiving dinner.
> Bob learned how to swim.

The first two sentences may be expressed with only the *wh-*complementizer.

> Jane decided where she should go to college.
> Mother wondered how many pies she should bake for Thanksgiving dinner.

Another form of *that* clause complementation found in second-grade readers occurred with an adjective complement of a linking verb. The *that* clause in this case elaborates the adjective sentence constituent.

> NP   V$_L$ Adj
> Nancy / is / afraid that Mother will be angry.
> Mother was glad she had cleaned the house.
> Dave felt sure he had enough gas.
> The old man seemed happy that the children sang for him.

The relationship between the syntactic structure and the *that* clause complement of a process verb can be seen if we substitute *fear* for *is afraid* in the first sentence. Note in the second and third sentences the optional deletion of *that*.

Another form of complementation that occurs quite frequently in primary readers was referred to in the discussion of different ways in which cause and effect can be expressed (see pp. 140–141). The sentence *Mother was so upset that she went to bed* is an example of this type of *that* complement expressing effect. The adjective in a linking verb pattern is modified by the intensifier *so* and elaborated with a *that* clause complement.

All the types of complementation in this section are used frequently and appear often in primary-grade reading materials. Given sentence by sentence and without other complexities they do not appear too difficult. In actuality, this is not the case. Look at the following passage from a second-grade reader:

> Mrs. Wallace smiled as she looked at the table. "I'm glad I don't have to decide who has the best hobby," she said. "I can't say that cooking is a better hobby than growing things, or that a stamp collection is better than a penny collection. Every hobby is interesting enough to win first prize."
>
> (Lewis & Maxwell, 1974, p. 146)

At the beginning of the direct discourse in the passage, there is an adjective with a *that* complement. The complement clause is *(that) I don't have to decide who has the best hobby*. Within this noun clause is an infinitive complement: *to decide who has the best hobby*. The verb in the infinitive complement has an indirect question complement introduced by the complementizer *who*. The infinitive complement also contains a superlative adjective. The direct discourse form has an inversion of the NP[2] before the subject and verb. The *she* pronominalization is quite removed from its referent, *Mrs. Wallace*, and the direct discourse uses the personal pronoun *I*. The reader must be able to identify *Mrs. Wallace, she*, and *I* all as referring to the same person. Contractions, negation, and *do*-support are also used in the sentence.

The second sentence of the direct discourse is also complex. It contains the following complexities.

1. two instances of indirect discourse, or noun clause complements of *say* with alternation:
   a. *that cooking is a better hobby than growing things*
   b. *that a stamp collection is better than a penny collection*
2. participle nominalizations: *cooking* and *growing things*
3. comparative adjectives + than with deletion
4. noun phrases elaborated with noun adjuncts, *stamp* and *penny*

The last sentence contains an adjective + intensifier + infinitive complement, and the first sentence in the passage has a temporal adverbial clause with a personal pronominalization. Not one of the sentences is short; all are complex. However, the vocabulary is not at all difficult. The language-delayed child who could easily handle the concepts and vocabulary would have difficulty getting meaning from the passage, especially if the child is only at the level of comprehending and/or expressing S–V or S–V–O patterns of language.

It has been found that comprehension of complementation of the types presented in the previous chapter and in this one is more difficult for deaf students than is relativization (Quigley, Wilbur, & Montanelli, 1974). In comparing deaf students' writing with their performance on comprehension tasks, the same authors found *for . . . to* complements occured most frequently, *that* complements less frequently, and only rare use of *Poss-ing* complements. Action verbs were used most often with complements, process verbs occurred with less than one percent of the complements, and stative verbs with none. Subject complements, which are to be presented in the next chapter, were not found at all, but at least one object complement was found to be used by about one-fourth of the 10-year-old deaf subjects. This increased to over 90 percent in the 18-year-olds.

Because of their poor understanding and minimal use of complementation, one can expect that hearing-impaired children would have difficulty in reading materials with high frequency occurrence of infinitive and participle complements and complementation involving direct and indirect discourse.

Understanding and using direct and indirect discourse, even more importantly, requires that a child have participated in the give and take of discourse. Often the child is required by a teacher or clinician to answer a question or to make a statement about a picture or object. This does not enable the child to participate in discourse. Nor does emphasis on the interpretation of single sentences give the child the reading experiences needed for the discourse that is found in paragraphs. The structuring of communication situations between children, as suggested in the Kendall Demonstration Elementary School approach to language curriculum (1978), and the structuring of reading material containing discourse at the simplest levels presented in paragraphs will serve to help students more easily comprehend complexities such as referencing with pronouns and different forms of complementation, in addition to making them more aware of the ways in which the language functions.

Turn to Exercise 43 for practice analyzing indirect discourse.

CHAPTER 21

Complementation with *Wh*-Clauses, Factive Clauses, and Other Nominalizations

The last of the complexities to be presented in the text are also forms of nominalization and complementation. All of the possible complexities of English will not be presented; however, the author's intent has been to present the majority of the structures that the teacher or clinician needs to be aware of for evaluating, analyzing, and programming language. This chapter concentrates on other complementation and nominalization with *wh-* and *that* clauses, factive clauses, other nominalizations, and the extraposition and *it*-replacement transformations.

Unit 1: *Wh*-Clauses, *It*-Replacement, and Extraposition

Objectives
- Identify *wh*-clauses that are subjects, direct objects, predicate nominatives, indirect objects, and/or objects of prepositions
- Identify *that* clauses that are subjects or complements of verbs
- Apply the *it*-replacement and extraposition transformations to given sentences

Wh-Clauses

In the preceding chapter, complementation with the *wh*-complementizers was presented as embedded *wh*-questions after action verbs, indirect discourse, or *wh*-clause complements after verbs denoting mental processes.

Wh-clauses may also be nominalizations used as subjects of sentences, as direct or indirect objects, predicate nominatives, or objects of prepositions. Again, the clause introduced by a *wh*-question word serves as a noun phrase in a sentence, making the sentence more syntactically complex and adding another proposition. *Ever* may be added to most of the *wh*-words to form other *wh*-words that may introduce clauses—*whatever, whoever, wherever,* etc.

Some examples of *wh*-clauses as subjects are found in the following list.

What John did was wrong.
How you solve the puzzle makes no difference.
Whoever was here made a mess.
Whatever Tom does upsets the teacher.

A pronoun could be inserted in place of the italicized clauses showing that these clauses serve as nouns or nominals. For *What John did,* in the first sentence, we could insert *it* or *something.* As in the case of a number of the other complexities in the text, theories as to how these sentences are derived will not be presented. It is important, however, that you recognize the ways in which the *wh*-clauses function and the meaning underlying the surface structure. In each of the sentences two propositions are expressed. If we state the propositions in the first sentence, we have *(something) was wrong* and *John did (something).*

Note how *wh*-complements function as noun phrases in positions other than the subject in the following examples.

Direct Object:	The teacher saw *who put a frog in her desk.*
Indirect Object:	The company will send *whoever buys a coffee pot* a $5 refund.
Predicate Nominative:	That gift is *what you wanted.*
Object of Preposition:	The boys can arrive at *whatever time is convenient.*

These sentences and those presented in the previous chapter on embedded questions all contain *wh*-clause complements. In some instances, these complements are in indirect discourse. In all examples there are two propositions expressed. The propositions in the last sentence would be *the boys can arrive at (some) time* and *(some) time is convenient.*

That Clauses

The previous chapter dealt with *that* clauses in indirect discourse and as complements after process verbs such as *know, think,* etc. *That* clause nominalizations may also occur in subject positions.

That Greta gained weight is obvious.
That Bob received all As pleased Mother.
That rubella causes deafness is a fact.

The insertion of *that* makes possible the nominalization of a sentence or proposition so that it can function in the subject position. The word *that* in such sentences has no meaning. The sentences can be analyzed to show that the *that* clause is the subject or NP[1].

NP[1]   V_L NP[1]

That rubella causes deafness/is/a fact.

Extraposition and *It*-Replacement with *That* Clauses

The *that* clause in all of the above examples can be moved to what can be called a final position, away from the subject position. This is accomplished by means of the **extraposition** transformation. When this is done, the subject position is empty and the word *it* is used as a replacement. *It*, then, acts as a placeholder, occupying the position of the subject, which has been extraposed (moved) to a position at the end of the sentence. When applying the extraposition and *it*-replacement transformations, the previously cited sentences become

It is obvious that Greta gained weight.
It pleased Mother that Bob received all As.
It is a fact that rubella causes deafness.

Thus, all the sentences contain a *that* clause complement, *it*-replacement, and extraposition. The word *it* in this case is not a pronominalization.

The pattern of the sentences cannot be determined without removing the transformations.

NP[1]   V_L Adj

That Greta gained weight/is/obvious.

The propositions can be more easily determined also by using the above form (i.e., *something is obvious* and *Greta gained weight*).

***Turn to Exercise 44 for practice identifying* wh- *and* that *clauses and* it-replacement.**

Unit 2: Factive Clauses and Other Nominalizations

Objectives

• Identify noun phrases with factive clauses in given sentences

- Differentiate factive clauses from relative clauses and noun clause complements in given complex sentences
- Apply the passive and extraposition transformations to sentences containing factive clauses, when appropriate
- List the propositions and semantic relationship of given sentences with *wh-*, *that,* and factive clause complements
- Identify in sentences nominalizations with *of* phrases
- Identify the sentences (or propositions) from which given nominalizations are derived
- Identify in sentences the following complexities: nominalizations, *that* clause complements, and embedded questions in indirect discourse; relative clauses; *wh-*, *that,* and factive clause complements; and *it*-replacement, passive, and extraposition transformations
- Identify all the complexities in given sentences

Factive Clauses

Factive clauses are complements of noun phrases. Such clauses are introduced by the complementizer *that,* and they elaborate noun phrases. Nouns that may have *that* complements of this type include *fact, news, idea, report, theory, knowledge, opinion, belief, thought, feeling, suggestion, assertion,* and *conclusion.* Some examples follow.

The news *that Jim was in Thailand* was surprising.
The fact *that Bill made all As* pleased Mother.
Mother had the idea *that Bill would make all As.*
Many people do not accept the theory *that much deafness is genetic.*

In the first two sentences, the factive clauses elaborate the noun phrase that is the subject. In the last two sentences, the clauses elaborate the phrase that is the object.

Factive clauses superficially look like relative clauses with *that,* but you should be able to differentiate one from the other. In factive clauses, the clause actually spells out what the *news, fact,* etc., is. For example, in the first two sentences *the news = Jim was in Thailand* and *the fact = Bill made all As.* The complete subject noun phrases for these sentences are *The news that Jim was in Thailand* and *The fact that Bill made all As.*

Note that *which* cannot be substituted for *that* in the noun phrases just mentioned. This is a test that can be used to differentiate a factive clause from a relative clause. In the following sentences try this out to determine if the italicized noun phrases contain relative or factive clauses.

1. *The news that they reported about the hostages* has distressed many people.
2. *The news that Lucy is getting married* surprised everyone.
3. The jury reached *the verdict that the man was guilty.*
4. The jury reached *the verdict that the lawyers had expected.*

The italicized noun phrases in 2 and 3 contain factive clauses, while the phrases in 1 and 4 contain relative clauses.

When factive clauses are complements in noun phrases that are objects of the verb, as in 3, the passive and extraposition transformations may be applied.

The jury reached the verdict that the man was guilty.

Passive: The verdict that the man was guilty was reached by the jury.

Passive +

Extraposition: The verdict was reached by the jury that the man was guilty.

As you can see, the factive clause *that the man was guilty* has been moved away from the noun that it elaborates, *The verdict*, and is separated from the noun by the passive verb phrase *was reached by the jury.*

In sentences, such as 4, which contain relative clauses as elaborations in an object phrase, the passive but not the extraposition transformation may be applied.

The jury reached the verdict that the lawyers had expected.

The verdict that the lawyers had expected was reached by the jury.

*The verdict was reached by the jury that the lawyers had expected.

The relative clause appears to modify the NP, *the jury*, so that it should not be moved away from its referent (*the verdict*).

You have now learned about three types of clauses beginning with *that*. If you study the following examples, they may help you to more easily identify the different types of *that* clause elaborations.

The group accepted the idea *that Jack had for Mary's party.*	*relative clause*; can substitute *which* for *that*; *idea* is referent of relative pronoun (*that*)
The group heard *that Jack had an idea for Mary's party.*	*that clause complement*; object of verb *heard*
That Jack had the idea for Mary's party surprised the group.	*that clause complement*; subject of verb *surprised*
It surprised the group *that Jack had the idea for Mary's party.*	*that clause complement*; with *it*-replacement and extraposition of the clause to a position at the end of the sentence

The group accepted Jack's idea *that Mary's party should be a cookout on the beach.*	*factive clause* telling what the idea is; cannot substitute *which* for *that*
Jack's idea was accepted by the group *that Mary's party should be a cookout on the beach.*	*factive clause,* but extraposed from *idea*; a passive form of above sentence

Factive clauses and the other forms of complementation in this chapter occur only occasionally in basal reading materials at the third-grade level or below. Following are two examples from readers in the Scott Foresman *Reading Unlimited* Series (1976).

> He spoke of his hope that one day all people would live the words of the old slave song. . . .
> They want you to have the feeling that you will surely come back and that when you do, they will welcome you.

(Patterson, 1976, p. 72)

In the second example there are conjoined factive clauses (the feeling) *that you will surely come back* and (the feeling) *that when you do, they will welcome you.*

Nominalizations with *Of* Phrases

In determining the semantic depth of a sentence or passage one looks for the words denoting actions and processes: the verbs, verbals, nouns derived from verbs, and verbs functioning as nouns. Since actions, processes, and states are central to propositions, each verb denotes another proposition in the sentence. In the following sentence each of the italicized words is responsible for another proposition.

> The *ringing* of the bell *halted* the boys' *discussion* of the party they were *having* because of the principal's *retirement.*

Some nominalizations are expressed as a determiner plus a nominalized verb form and an *of* phrase. Examples of these would be *the crying of the baby, the crash of the helicopter, the refusal of the position,* and *the leader of the gang.* Each of the above is a noun phrase that represents a proposition. The first contains an *-ing* participle of an intransitive verb. It could also be expressed as *the baby's crying,* the *Poss-ing* nominalization presented in chapter 19.

In the phrase *the crash of the helicopter,* the base form of the verb takes on the characteristics of a noun and can be inflected for the plural. The noun phrase conveys the information *the helicopter crashed*. Other examples of this type of nominalization would be *the scream of the woman, the roar of the wind, the laugh of the witch,* and *the capture of the criminal.*

The last of this type of nominalization involves the derivation of a noun from a verb. The noun *refusal* is derived from the verb *refuse* by affixing the derivational suffix *-al*. Other derivational suffixes were presented in chapter 1; they include such nouns as *discussion* from *discuss, disappearance* from *disappear,* etc. A large number of nouns are derived with the agentive suffix, *-er*. These nouns carry the meaning of one who (or that which) does something. The phrase *a lover of music* is a nominalization expressing the proposition *someone loves music.*

Such nominalizations give us a variety of ways of expressing a particular proposition. The proposition *Rodney refuse position* can be expressed as

Rodney refused the position.
Rodney's refusing of the position
Rodney's refusal of the position
the refusal of the position by Rodney

The first example is a basic sentence. The others are all nominalizations. The last of the nominalizations in the list involves a passive, as we can see in the use of *by Rodney (the position was refused by Rodney)*. This type of nominalization is found in phrases like *the discovery of the vaccine by Salk, the assassination of the president by a madman,* and *the recovery of the jewels by the police.*

When noun phrases such as these occur, one unlocks the meaning by means of word attack skills (*recovery* = verb *recover* + *-y*) and by syntactic and semantic knowledge for recognition of the passive and interpretation of the meaning of the active form. For those of us who had no difficulty in acquiring our language, such phrases pose no problem; however, they are very difficult. Competence in dealing with these nominalizations occurs late in the pattern of normal language development (in the early elementary school years), and very late in children and youth with delayed language.

The syntactic complexities presented in this chapter were found to develop late in hearing children with normal language development. These complexities were extremely difficult for the hearing-impaired subjects in the research by Quigley and others at the University of Illinois. The Test of Syntactic Abilities (Quigley, Steinkamp, Power, & Jones, 1978), a battery designed primarily for the hearing impaired, contains one diagnostic test on nominalizations of the type presented in this chapter and two tests on the types of complementations presented in chapters 19, 20, and 21. These diagnostic tests are considered to include the most difficult of the syntactic structures for the hearing impaired, many of whom did not use or understand the structures when they were high-school age. An understanding of all of these structures, however, is necessary by the time children finish the third grade if they are to be able to handle the reading necessary in the program of the average fourth-grade student.

Quigley and King (1981, 1982, 1983, 1984a, 1984b, 1984c) have been developing a reading series with syntactic and vocabulary controls for deaf children, language-different, or dialectal children. Some of these children, although they may have a sophisticated knowledge of language, do not have the language of the materials they must read. The authors state that the process of learning to read becomes for such children a language-learning process, and thus there is a need for reading materials that focus on language development. They predict that a child completing all eight levels of their series, *Reading Milestones,* should be able to begin using and understanding most fourth-grade materials.

This chapter concludes the syntactic and semantic information presented in the text. You should now have sufficient background to be able to analyze the majority of the syntactic structures found in teaching materials. You should also have sufficient knowledge of both the syntactic and semantic relationships to undertake further study in language evaluation and language programming for children with delayed and/or deviant language. The following chapter is again a review providing further practice in language analysis.

Turn to Exercise 45 for practice identifying factive clauses and other nominalizations.

CHAPTER 22

Language Analysis IV and Review

Objectives

- Demonstrate the performance required in objectives for Language Analyses I, II, and III
- Identify in the syntactic description, the following complementation and nominalizations:
  - a. infinitive
  - b. participle
  - c. direct discourse
  - d. *that* cl complement
  - e. *wh*-clause complement
  - f. embedded yes-no question
  - g. *wh-* + inf complement
  - h. factive clause
  - i. nominalized verb + phrase
- Identify in the syntactic description the *it*-replacement, extraposition, passive, and deletion transformations in those of the above with which they are appropriate
- Determine the frequency of occurrence of the above elaborations and transformations in a given sample
- Identify the propositions and semantic relationships expressed in a sample of sentences with the above elaborations and transformations
- Analyze sentences containing complexities, including the above elaborations and transformations
- Differentiate between various elaborations and complementation
- Identify the subjects, direct objects, indirect objects, and predicate nominatives in given sentences
- Identify the modalities, conjoinings, elaborations, and transformations in given sentences
- Complete a syntactic and semantic description of a given sample
- Identify the complexities in a passage from a basal reader

The concluding chapter of the text is another review. It contains additional practice on a contrived sample of language that would be typical of a child who is developing language normally. There is also practice on locating complexities in language that would typically be found in reading materials at the elementary-school level.

The majority of people studying this text will in the future probably be working with children whose language is delayed or deviant. The majority of the references deal with the hearing impaired, a population in which there is a high incidence of language delay due to the necessary reliance on minimal cues from residual hearing and dependence upon visual cues, often through speechreading.

Children born to deaf parents who use American Sign Language, a small minority of the hearing-impaired population, may learn English as a second language. These children enter school with a language base. The vast majority of hearing-impaired children, unless they are detected early and are provided with sufficient language stimulation and the necessary social-emotional climate in which communication competence can develop, enter school with delayed language.

Earlier detection, improvements in amplification, earlier contact with hearing-impaired infants and their parents, the development of sign or cueing systems that closely parallel English, and the application of methods of teaching English as a second language are all making much more possible the development of English-language competence in hearing-impaired children at an age paralleling that of hearing children. We are, however, faced at the present time with large numbers of hearing-impaired children whose language, although following the normal pattern of development, is delayed. A smaller number of children exhibit language development that is deviant in addition to being delayed. There is evidence of an increase in the incidence of other handicaps in the hearing-impaired population. We can expect to find a relatively large percentage of multihandicapped hearing-impaired children with language problems stemming from causes other than their hearing impairment.

Other exceptional children, including the mentally retarded and the developmentally retarded with handicapping conditions such as cerebral palsy and other central nervous system dysfunction, also experience language delay. The aphasic child may display deviant patterns of development. In addition, there are large numbers of culturally deprived children in need of language development programs so that they can achieve the level of competence necessary for success in the language arts and reading tasks of elementary school.

Language assessment, language development programming, and the use of specially designed teaching materials may all be necessary. It has been the intent throughout the text to prepare you with the basic information necessary to use both the older and the newer approaches to language development. Traditional concepts and terminology have been presented so that you can make use of such materials as Fitzgerald's *Straight Language for the Deaf* (1926), Pugh's *Steps in Language Development* (1955), the Buell books (1953), etc., all of which are still in use.

Concepts and terminology from modern grammar have been presented so that you can more effectively evaluate and put to use curriculums such as *Appletree* (Anderson, Boren, Caniglia, Howard, & Krohn, 1980) and the Rhode Island Curriculum; teaching materials such as the Appletree storybooks (Cole, 1979); *Lessons in Syntax* (McCarr, 1973); The *TSA Syntax Programs* (Quigley & Power, 1979), which are designed to be used after a diagnosis has been made with the Test of Syntactic Abilities (Quigley, Steinkamp, Power, & Jones, 1978); and *Reading Milestones* (Quigley & King, 1981, 1982, 1983, 1984a, 1984b, 1984c). *Reading Milestones* is a new reading series that uses controlled syntax. The series includes student workbooks and a teacher's guide.

As was indicated earlier in the text, there are times when the teacher or clinician should control written language for children with language delay so that the language is at a level where the children can read it independently. Also, commercially available teaching materials must be matched to the reader's language capabilities.

The text does not afford practice in the recognition of deviant syntactic forms. However, you should have a sufficient grasp of standard syntactic forms and of the rules involved in their generation so as to determine how a rule the child is using deviates from the standard form.

Whether the syntax is delayed and/or deviant or not, the child's language carries meaning; i.e., the child can express varying semantic relationships. As the child's syntax becomes more complex, he or she is able to express more meanings in a single utterance. You should have a basic knowledge of how to determine the meaningful relationships in the child's utterances and of how to chart the child's cognitive development. This can be done by observing (a) the use of process and stative verbs after the early grasp of action verbs and (b) the increasing ability to assign attributes and to express various adverbial relationships.

Language assessment entails the use of a battery of tests plus observation and evaluation of the child's spontaneous utterances in varying communication situations. Up until the last few years, there have been no language tests standardized on a hearing-impaired population. As of now there are several new tests that bear promise of providing the teacher, clinician, and researcher with valuable and necessary information on the child's syntactic competence and performance. These tests include the Test of Syntactic Abilities (Quigley, Steinkamp, Power, & Jones, 1978), the Grammatical Analysis of Elicited Language-Presentence Level (GAEL-PS, Moog, Kozack, & Geers, 1983), the Grammatical Analysis of Elicited Language-Simple Sentence Level (GAEL-S, Moog & Geers, 1979), the Grammatical Analysis of Elicited Language-Complex Sentence Level (GAEL-C, Moog & Geers, 1980), and the Rhode Island Language Comprehension Test (Engen & Engen, 1983).

Kretschmer and Kretschmer's procedure (1978) for assessing language involves obtaining a language sample and then determining the child's communicative functioning and semantic and syntactic performance. Unfortunately, the emphasis in most of the aforementioned materials and tests has been on syntax. Kretschmer and Kretschmer's procedure, however, includes the pragmatic and semantic evaluations.

You should have the basic information to be able to follow Kretschmer and Kretschmer's procedure once you undertake study of the restrictions and deviances in language typical of the hearing impaired and/or other exceptional children. You also need to have a firm grasp of the semantic aspect of language as well as the communication devices and the varying intents of language use.

All the aspects of language are interrelated. Every child or adult has a particular intent in communicating. For example, one may want to get something done. Within the limits of the person's semantic and syntactic capability, different forms may be used to do this.

Tie shoe.
Tie my shoe.
Can you tie my shoe?
I want you to tie my shoe.
Would you like to tie this shoe for me?
With this bad hip I can't bend over and get this shoe tied.

These examples are all varying syntactic forms that might be used for the same result: one individual tying the shoe of another who cannot do it and who is directly or indirectly telling or asking another to do it. As mentioned before, we use various syntactic means to distinguish and make clear in communication new and old information and the topic that we are initiating or may want to discuss.

A thorough language evaluation includes assessment of all the aspects of language: pragmatic, semantic, and syntactic. Also one may evaluate specific language skills such as the students' control of the regular inflections of the language, vocabulary, etc. Programming for language development cannot and should not be undertaken until there has been assessment. Periodic reassessment is necessary to allow one to chart language growth and to chart the path the language programming should follow.

The following analysis of a language sample will provide you with further practice in determining a child's syntactic and semantic performance so that you may later apply this information in assessing delayed or deviant language in children and youth with whom you may work. The practice test is a review primarily of the last three chapters, but you are required to use knowledge and skills learned from all earlier chapters.

The short language sample that will be analyzed is a contrived sample. It has been constructed so as to include some of the complexities in the chapters in the last section of the book. At this level of language, one need no longer be looking for the noun and verb phrase modulations because the child would be expected to have good productive control of these when a sample contains standard English with no restrictions and deviations, as these sentences do.

With the hearing-impaired child, however, problems with determiners and other modulations may persist even beyond the high-school level. Hearing-impaired students at the high-school level may also omit auxiliaries in the verb phrase, the inflected form of the verb, and/or the copula. In addition, only relatively simple verb phrases without more than one auxiliary may be found. One may find a verb phrase such as *was worked in the house*. This type of restriction would be noted in the evaluation. In a case such as *was worked*, one would note the addition of the past auxiliary *be* with the past of an intransitive verb; the verb phrase should be *was working* or *worked*, depending upon whether or not the progressive aspect was necessary in the sentence.

The conceptual development of the hearing impaired or others who are experiencing language delay often parallels that of their peers with normal language development, although the syntactic complexity of their language does not. The semantic complexity of their utterances can be expected to increase, however. It is possible to determine the semantic complexity of language with restrictions and deviations. The semantic analysis often reveals that the individual is expressing multiple propositions in a single utterance, even though the utterance contains syntactic restrictions and/or deviations. One also can assess written language and can complete syntactic and semantic descriptions and summaries plus an analysis of the student's control of the discourse requirements of the different forms of written language.

In the following sample, we shall not note the noun and verb phrase modulations, but will look for the following in the syntactic description: the overall pattern of the sentence as (a) intransitive verb pattern, (b) transitive (S–V–O) pattern, or (c) linking verb pattern; the modalities; conjoinings; elaborations; and transformations. In the semantic description we shall note the noun, verb, and adverbial cases, and the attributes, as in the other samples.

Language Sample
Subject: Sue

1. I want Dad to show me how I should cut out the jack-o-lantern's eyes.
2. Some boys playing football on the playground hit Tom with a ball when we were walking home.
3. Tom thinks being a pilot would be fun, but he's never been on a plane.
4. Last night Dad said to me, "The meowing of that cat wakes me up every night, and so, put it in the shed before you go to bed."
5. It's good news that Mom's car wasn't smashed up by the driver of that milk truck that ran up into the driveway, or we would stay home this summer.

Syntactic Description

1. I want Dad to show me how to cut out the jack-o-lantern's eyes.
   - Sentence Pattern: transitive verb
   - Elaborations: infinitive complement, *wh*-clause + infinitive complement, possessive noun modifier
   - Transformations: personal pronominalization (2), indirect object preposing

2. Some boys playing football on the playground hit Tom with a ball when we were walking home.
   - Sentence Pattern: transitive verb
   - Conjoinings: subordination (adv cl of time)
   - Elaborations: participle phrase modifier
   - Transformations: personal pronominalization

3. Tom thinks being a pilot would be fun, but he's never been on a plane.
   - Sentence Pattern: transitive verb, linking verb
   - Modalities: negation
   - Conjoinings: coordination (disjunction)
   - Elaborations: *that* clause complement (that being . . .), participle nominalization
   - Transformations: deletion (that), personal pronominalization, contraction, adverbial preposing

4. Last night Dad said to me, "The meowing of that cat wakes me up every night, and so, put it in the shed before you go to bed."
   - Sentence Pattern: transitive verb, transitive verb
   - Modalities: imperative
   - Conjoinings: coordination (conjunction), subordination (adv cl time)
   - Elaborations: direct discourse, nominalization (participle nominalization + *of* phrase)
   - Transformations: adverbial preposing, personal pronominalization (4), particle movement.

5. It's good news that Mom's car wasn't smashed up by the driver of that milk truck that ran up into the driveway, or we would stay home this summer.
   - Sentence Pattern: linking verb, intransitive
   - Modalities: negation
   - Conjoinings: coordination (alternation)
   - Elaborations: adjective modifier, *that* clause complement, possessive noun modifier, nominalized verb + *of*, noun adjunct, relative clause
   - Transformations: *it*-replacement, contraction (2), extraposition, passive, personal pronominalization, relative pronoun

Syntactic Summary

Sentence patterns	Frequency of Occurrence	Comments
intransitive verb	1	
transitive verb	5	
linking verb	2	
Modalities		
imperative	1	
negation	2	
Conjoining		
coordination	3	conjunction, disjunction, and alternation
subordination	2	adv clauses of time
Elaborations		
possessive det or noun	2	poss nouns
adjective modifier	1	
noun adjunct modifier	1	
relative clause	1	
-ing participle phrase modifier	1	
infinitive compl/nominal	1	
participle compl/nominal	1 (1)	one in nominalization + *of* phrase
direct discourse	1	
that clause complement	2	one in extraposition
wh- + infinitive complement	1	complement of infinitive
nominalized verb + *of* phrase	2	participle + *of* phr and *-er* derivation of noun from verb
Transformations		
pronominalization	12	personal (11) relative (1)
adverbial preposing	2	prep phr
indirect object preposing	1	
contraction	3	contracted copula (2), *be* aux + neg
particle movement	1	
passive	1	irreversible nontruncated
deletion	1	*that* complementizer
it-replacement	1	⎰with *that* clause
extraposition	1	⎱complement

Semantic Description

1. I want Dad to show me how to cut out the jack-o-lantern's eyes.

a. Sue want (something)	Experiencer—process—complement
b. Dad show (something) to Sue	Agent—action—complement—beneficiary
c. Sue cut out eyes (somehow)	Agent—action—complement—manner
d. jack-o-lantern have eyes	Entity—stative—part

2. Some boys playing football on the playground hit Tom with a ball when we were walking home.

a. some boys hit Tom with ball (sometime)	Agent—action—patient—instrument—time
b. some boys were playing football on the playground	Agent—action—complement—location
c. someone walk home	Mover—action—location

3. Tom thinks being a pilot would be fun, but he's never been on a plane.

a. Tom thinks (something)	Experiencer—process—complement
b. Tom be a pilot	Entity—stative—equivalent
c. (something) would be fun	Entity—stative—equivalent
d. Tom has been on a plane never	Entity—stative—location—frequency

4. Last night Dad said to me, "The meowing of that cat wakes me up every night, and so, put it in the shed before you go to bed."

a. Dad said (something) to Sue last night	Agent—action—complement—recipient—time
b. (something) wakes up Dad every night	Agent—process—patient—frequency
c. that cat meow	Mover—action
d. Sue put the cat in the shed (sometime)	Agent—action—patient—location—time
e. Sue go to bed	Mover—action—location

5. It's good news that Mom's car wasn't smashed up by the driver of that milk truck that ran up into the driveway, or we would stay home this summer.

a. (something) is news	Entity—stative—equivalent
b. news is good	Entity—stative—quality
c. someone smashed up car	Agent—action—patient
d. (someone) drive that truck	Agent—action—patient
e. that truck was for milk	Entity—stative—reason
f. Mom has a car	Possessor—process—patient

g. that truck ran up into the drive-way (or)

(someone ran up into the driveway)

Patient—action—location (or)

Mover—action—location

h. someone stay home this summer   Entity—stative—location—time

Semantic Summary

Number of utterances:	5
Number of propositions:	24
Propositions per utterance:	4.8

Noun Cases	Frequency of Occurrence
Mover	3
Agent	9
Patient	6
Experiencer	2
Complement	6
Beneficiary (Recipient)	2
Possessor	1
Entity	8
Equivalent	2
Part	1
Verb Cases	
Action	12
Process	4
Stative	8
Adverbial Cases	
Location	6
Time	4
Frequency	2
Manner	1
Reason	1
Instrument	1
Attribute Cases	
Quality	1

Turn to Language Analysis IV Exercise for practice analyzing a language sample.

REFERENCES

All in free. (1976). Reading Unlimited. Glenview, IL: Scott Foresman & Co.

Allen, R. L. (1966). *The order of modifiers in noun clusters.* New York: Teachers College, Columbia University.

Anderson, M., Boren, N. J., Caniglia, J., Howard, W., & Krohn, E. (1980). *Appletree: A patterned program of linguistic expansion through reinforced experiences and evaluations.* Beaverton, OR: Dormac, Inc.

Blackwell, P. M., Engen, E., Fischgrund, J. E., & Zarcadoolas, C. (1978). *Sentences and other systems: A language and learning curriculum for hearing-impaired children.* Washington, DC: A. G. Bell Association for the Deaf.

Bloom, L. (1970). *Language development: Form and function in emerging grammars.* Cambridge, MA: MIT Press.

Bloom, L., & Lahey, M. (1978). *Language development and language disorders.* New York: John Wiley & Sons.

Buell, E. M. (1953). *Outline of language for deaf children* (Books 1 and 2). Washington, DC: The Volta Bureau.

Carrow, E. (1973). *Test of auditory comprehension of language.* Austin, TX: Urban Research Group.

Carrow, E. (1974). *Carrow elicited language inventory.* Austin, TX: Learning Concepts.

Chomsky, C. (1969). *The acquisition of syntax in children from 5 to 10* (Research Monograph 57). Cambridge, MA: MIT Press.

Chomsky, N. (1957). *Syntactic structures.* The Hague: Mouton.

Chomsky, N. (1965). *Aspects of the theory of syntax.* Cambridge, MA: MIT Press.

Cole, N. J. (1979). *Appletree story books.* Beaverton, OR: Dormac, Inc.

Dale, E., & Chall, J. (1948). A formula for predicting readability. *Educational Research Bulletin, 27,* 11-20, 37-54.

DeVilliers, J. G., & DeVilliers, P. A. (1978). *Language acquisition.* Cambridge, MA: Harvard University Press.

Engen, E., & Engen, T. (1983). *Rhode Island Test of Language Structure.* Baltimore: University Park Press.

Fitzgerald, E. (1926). *Straight language for the deaf.* Washington, DC: A. G. Bell Association for the Deaf.

Fry, E. (1968). A readability formula that saves time. *Journal of Reading, 11,* 513-516, 575-578.

Granowski, A., & Botel, M. (1974). Background for a new syntactic complexity formula. *Reading Teacher, 28,* 31-35.

Hader, B., & Hader, E. (1976). The story of Panelbo and the bull with the crooked tail. In *Taller than trees* (pp. 33-44). Reading Unlimited. Glenview, IL: Scott Foresman & Co.

Hamel, C. A. (1971). *The language curriculum*. Providence, RI: Rhode Island School for the Deaf.

Hargis, C. H. (1970). The relationship of available instructional materials to deficiency in reading achievement. *American Annals of the Deaf, 115*, 27–30.

Hargis, C. H. (1977). *English syntax: An outline for clinicians and teachers of language handicapped children*. Springfield, IL: Charles C. Thomas.

Hargis, C., Evans, C., & Masters, C. (1973). A criticism of the direct discourse form in primary level-basal readers. *Volta Review, 75*, 557–563.

Hirsh, M. (1976). How the world got its color. In *On your mark* (pp. 18–25). Reading Unlimited. Glenview, IL: Scott Foresman & Co.

Kendall Demonstration Elementary School. (1980). *A pragmatic approach to language for teachers of deaf children*. Washington, DC: Gallaudet College.

Kretschmer, R. R., & Kretschmer, L. W. (1978). *Language development and intervention with the hearing-impaired*. Baltimore: University Park Press.

Lee, L. (1974). *Developmental sentence analysis*. Evanston, IL: Northwestern University Press.

Lewis, M. J., & Maxwell, R. (1974). Sally Woo's hobby. In *You're it* (pp. 117–147). Reading Unlimited. Glenview, IL: Scott Foresman & Co.

Limber, J. (1973). The genesis of complex sentences. In T. Moore (Ed.), *Cognitive development and the acquisition of language* (pp. 169–185). New York: Academic Press.

McCarr, J. E. (1973). *Lessons in syntax*. Beaverton, OR: Dormac, Inc.

Moog, J. S., & Geers, A. E. (1979). *GAEL-S: Grammatical analysis of elicited language– Simple sentence level*. St. Louis: Central Institute for the Deaf.

Moog, J. S., & Geers, A. E. (1980). *GAEL-C: Grammatical analysis of elicited language– Complex sentence level*. St. Louis: Central Institute for the Deaf.

Moog, J. S., Kozack, V. J., & Geers, A. E. (1983). *GAEL-PS: Grammatical analysis of elicited language–Presentence level*. St. Louis: Central Institute for the Deaf.

Newcomer, P. L., & Hammill, D. D. (1977). *The test of language development*. Austin, TX: Empiric Press.

Patterson, L. (1976). Dr. Martin Luther King, Jr. In *A hundred eyes* (pp. 60–73). Reading Unlimited. Glenview, IL: Scott Foresman & Co.

Power, D. J. (1971). *Deaf children's acquisition of the passive voice*. Unpublished doctoral dissertation. University of Illinois, Urbana.

Power, D. J., & Quigley, S. P. (1973). Deaf children's acquisition of passive voice. *Journal of Speech and Hearing Research, 16*, 5–11.

Pugh, B. (1955). *Steps in language development*. Washington, DC: The Volta Bureau.

Quigley, S. P., & King, C. (1980). An invited article. Syntactic performances of hearing-impaired and normal hearing individuals. *Applied Psycholinguistics, 1*, 329–369.

Quigley, S. P., & King, C. M. (1981). *Reading milestones* (Levels 1, 2, 3). Beaverton, OR: Dormac, Inc.

Quigley, S. P., & King, C. M. (1982). *Reading milestones* (Level 4). Beaverton, OR: Dormac, Inc.

Quigley, S. P., & King, C. M. (1983). *Reading milestones* (Level 5). Beaverton, OR: Dormac, Inc.

Quigley, S. P., & King, C. M. (1984a). *Reading milestones* (Level 6). Beaverton, OR: Dormac, Inc.

Quigley, S. P., & King, C. M. (1984b). *Reading milestones* (Level 7). Beaverton, OR: Dormac, Inc.

Quigley, S. P., & King, C. M. (1984c). *Reading milestones* (Level 8). Beaverton, OR: Dormac, Inc.

Quigley, S. P., & Power, D. J. (Eds.). (1979). *TSA syntax program*. Beaverton, OR: Dormac, Inc.

Quigley, S. P., Smith, N., & Wilbur, R. B. (1974). Comprehension of relativized sentences by deaf students. *Journal of Speech and Hearing Research, 17,* 325–341.

Quigley, S. P., Steinkamp, M. W., Power, D. J., & Jones, B. W. (1978). *Test of syntactic abilities*. Beaverton, OR: Dormac, Inc.

Quigley, S. P., Wilbur, R. B., & Montanelli, D. S. (1974). Question formation in the language of deaf children. *Journal of Speech and Hearing Research, 17,* 699–713.

Reading unlimited. (1976). Glenview, IL: Scott Foresman & Co.

Roberts, P. (1968). *Modern grammar.* New York: Harcourt, Brace, & World, Inc.

Russell, W. K., Quigley, S. P., & Power, D. J. (1976). *Linguistics and deaf children.* Washington, DC: A. G. Bell Association for the Deaf.

Sheldon, A. (1977). On strategies for processing relative clauses: A comparison of children and adults. *Journal of Psycholinguistic Research, 6,* 305–318.

Spache, G. (1953). A new readability formula for primary grade reading materials. *Elementary School Journal, 53,* 410–413.

The story of Daedalus and Icarus. (1976). In *Catch a spoonful* (pp. 36–39). Glenview, IL: Scott Foresman & Co.

Streng, A. (1972). *Syntax, speech and hearing.* New York: Grune & Stratton.

Streng, A., Kretschmer, R. R., & Kretschmer, L. W. (1978). *Language, learning, and deafness.* New York: Grune & Stratton.

Turner, E. A., & Rommetveit, R. (1967). The acquisition of sentence voice and reversibility. *Child Development, 38,* 649–660.

Wiig, E. H., & Semel, E. M. (1980). *Language assessment and intervention for the learning disabled.* Columbus: Charles E. Merrill.

Wilbur, R. B., Quigley, S. P., & Montanelli, D. S. (1975). Conjoined structures in the language of deaf students. *Journal of Speech and Hearing Research, 12,* 319–335.

AUTHOR INDEX

SUBJECT INDEX